The Cou... W...

"While we were at breakfast this morning grandfather came and told us that Aunty had been ordered to leave her beautiful home to give place to a Yankee Colonel who had given her only half a day to move all her property ... Tongue cannot express her trouble in leaving, she has no home to go to elsewhere."

—*Mary Rawson, September 1864,*
Atlanta Georgia

"Cowering in the corner of our cave, holding my child to my heart—the only feeling I knew was the choking throb of my heart that rendered me almost breathless. As the shots fell short or beyond the cave, I was aroused by a feeling of thankfulness that was of short duration. Again and again the terrible fright came."

—*Mary Ann Loughborough, April 1863,*
Vicksburg, Mississippi

"Lead! Blood! Tears! Lead, blood and tears mingled and commingled. In vain did I try to dash the tears away. They would assert themselves upon lead stained with blood ... I cried like a baby, long and loud!"

—*Mary Ann Harris Gay, February, 1865,*
Decatur, Georgia

Also by Katharine M. Jones on the Mockingbird
Books List:

HEROINES OF DIXIE
Spring of High Hopes $4.95

MOCKINGBIRD BOOKS

Heroines Of Dixie

Volume II:

Winter of Desperation

Edited by Katharine M. Jones

MOCKINGBIRD BOOKS

To
The memory of my Grandmother
Mary Turner Garrison
Wife of
Lieutenant William David Garrison
16th South Carolina Regiment, C.S.A.

Copyright, 1955, by MACMILLAN PUBLISHING CO.

Library of Congress Catalog Card Number: 55:6825

ISBN 089176-033-4

By arrangement with Macmillan Publishing Co.
Cover design by Penstroke Graphics • Atlanta

First Printing: February 1975
Sixth Printing: September, 1990
Seventh Printing: June, 1993

Printed in the United States of America

R. Bemis Publishing
Mockingbird Books
P.O. Books 71088
Marietta, GA 30068

INTRODUCTION

In some of the more recent studies of the subject it has been strongly suggested that the prime reason for the defeat of the Confederacy was a decline in, or loss of, the will to fight. There is a certain merit in the point though the more remarkable fact, considering the course of the conflict, is that the will to fight remained so strong so long.

For that, the women of the Confederacy were in large measure responsible. Not every woman could be classed as a "heroine of Dixie," as the title of the present work puts it, but it was commonly observed at the time by foe and friend alike, and has been repeatedly noted since, that it was among the women of the South that the spirit of resistance flamed highest.

The harder part of war is the woman's part. True of all wars, this was particularly true of the war of the Sixties in the South. For a few women, some of whom left memoirs which have become famous, there were the excitement and sustaining sense of accomplishment to be derived from contact with stirring events and association with notable personalities. For the great majority, however, there was more of strain and anxiety, of fear and loneliness, and of hardship and privation than there was of glamour and excitement. To all these were added, in large sections of the South, the aggravation and frustration of invasion and occupation by Federal troops—or, even worse, the depredations of the lawless freebooters of either side, or neither, in those areas which were strongly held by neither army.

The story of the life of women in these years is scattered through diaries and letters written without thought of publication, as well as through the comparatively small number of published memoirs. Of the latter, even, not many are well known and readily available. Searching out the facts about the lives of Confederate women, therefore, calls for diligence and patience, while presentation of the

facts found requires judgment in selection and skill in
organization. Miss Jones has brought to her work the
qualities requisite for producing what is, in effect, a com-
posite autobiography of Confederate women.

In doing so, she lets the actors tell the story in their
own words, with a minimum of connective tissue to keep
events in focus. There is no attempt to round up views
from all sources on each phase of the story but the quo-
tations given are each of sufficient length to preserve their
flavor and effect.

The treatment is basically chronological, carrying the
story forward from the first secession conventions * to the
last meeting of the Confederate Cabinet at Washington,
Georgia, after which Miss Eliza Frances Andrews noted
that "this, I suppose, is the end of the Confederacy."

The familiar passages from well-known diarists dealing
with the Richmond scene are here but also are bits of
everyday life such as that on a remote farm in Texas where
saving the meat at hog-killing time was a problem and
where a hundred bales of cotton would "neither pay debts
or buy groceries"—with touches of all the range of living
in between.

To the author who has so patiently assembled and skillfully presented the story of the women of the Confederacy, the thanks of those interested in that story today
are eminently due.

ROBERT S. HENRY

Alexandria, Virginia.

* *Heroines of Dixie: Spring of High Hopes* Katharine M.
Jones, Ed., Ballantine Books, New York, 1974.

EDITOR'S FOREWORD

The military records and reports do not tell the story of the women of the Confederacy. They told it themselves —a few in magazine articles, pamphlets and books; many in letters and diaries. Only a part of it has been published; much survives in manuscripts cherished in family, historical society, public library and unversity collections. All manner of women told it—the rich and the poor, the educated and the ignorant.

A handful of these Confederate women saw active service as spies, hospital nurses, government clerks. The great majority were left back home, whether home was the big house or a cabin. They had vital work to do there. But almost from the outbreak of the struggle homes were broken up and women became exiles.

So their story is increasingly a story of refugees, of invaded and occupied cities, of burned and devastated dwellings, of hunger and want, of bitterness and human frailty. But it is also a story of love, of courage, of personal loyalty transcending heartbreak.

When the curtain rose, they expected the play to be over soon by a peaceful yielding of the North or a defeat of the Northern army. There were then some gleams of glamour about war—especially a war that might be over before it was well begun. With proud hearts these women watched the parade of their brave lads marching off to certain and easy victory, with the flags the women had made waving over them. Romances flowered quickly in those days. There was a gay, unquenchable humor in the ranks; anxiety and privation would leave little room for it behind the lines. There was the excitement of combat for soldiers; there was a little waltzing on happy, rare occasions but much more waiting, watching, work for the women.

Though their Southern patriotism was intense, for the women devotion to the family came first—always—and none of them would knowingly and willingly have chosen a course of war that reversed this order of devotion. At the very start—just after the Act of Secession was passed —a woman of South Carolina said, "What do I care for patriotism? My husband is my country. What is my country to me if he be killed?" As they faced the grim reality of a long and bitter struggle, this became more and more the secret or avowed question of their deeply troubled hearts.

From Virginia to Texas I have searched out and read every piece of their writing I could lay hands on. I have selected what I humbly hope may bring their varied story into focus and continuity—their autobiography of the war years.

TABLE OF CONTENTS

The Confederate Flag
"Requiescat in Pace"

The hands of our women made it!
  'Twas baptized in our mother's tears!
And drenched with blood of our kindred,
  While with hope for those four long years,
Across vale and plain we watched it,
  Where the red tide of battle rolled
And with tear-dimmed eyes we followed
  The wave of each silken fold.

As high o'er our hosts it floated,
  Through the dust and din of the fight,
We caught the glint of the spear-head
  And the flash of its crimson light!
While the blood of the men who bore it
  Flowed fast on the reddened plain,
Till our cry went up in anguish
  To God, for our martyred slain!

And we wept, and watched, and waited
  By our lonely household fire,
For the mother gave her first born,
  And the daughter gave her sire!
And the wife sent forth her husband,
  And the maiden her lover sweet;
And our hearts kept time in the silence
  To the rhythmic tread of their feet. . . .

LOUISE WIGFALL WRIGHT

HEROINES OF DIXIE:

The Winter of Desperation

I

HEARTBREAK

May 1863–April 1864

Independence Day 1863 marked the culmination of two great disasters to the Southern cause, and a third, not so great, followed hard upon them.

Having tried without success various ways of approaching and capturing Vicksburg, General Grant finally on April 30, 1863, managed to get an army across the river from the Louisiana side and land it down-river at Bruinsburg. He first marched northeast, placing his men between General Joe Johnston, at Jackson with a small force, and General John C. Pemberton's much larger force at Edward's Station on the railroad between Vicksburg and Jackson. Johnston, in general command of the whole southwest, wanted Pemberton, charged with the defense of the fortress city, to join him in fighting Grant in the open; Pemberton would attack the Union army from the rear while Johnston hit it in front. Pemberton wavered between doing what his immediate superior called for and what the commander in chief, President Davis, repeatedly ordered—to hold Vicksburg at all cost. He procrastinated, compromised—and was lost.

Grant, moving with fast determination, drove Johnston north out of Jackson and then turned toward the Mississippi to defeat three of Pemberton's divisions at Baker's Creek or Champion Hill on May 16. One of the Southern divisions—that of General William W. Loring ("Old Blizzards")—was cut off; the men from the other two poured across the Big Black River into Vicksburg, bedraggled but not in panic. Pemberton skillfully disposed them and the two divisions he had

1

kept in the city along the fifteen miles of trenches and rifle pits.

Grant tried to take the city by direct assault on May 22 but was beaten back with dreadful loss and settled down to siege operations. Reckoning from the eighteenth, the siege lasted forty-seven days. Grant's army, heavily reinforced, now numbered 70,000 before Vicksburg, while 30,000 held off Johnston. It was bountifully supplied. Pemberton's army of 28,000 was slowly reduced to a diet of horse, dog and rat. The people in the city lived in caves hurriedly dug into the sides of the steep hills. Finally on July 4 Pemberton surrendered. A Pennsylvanian by birth, he reckoned he could get better terms on the national holiday. He did: the garrison was paroled on the spot.

In late May and in June there had been three assaults on Port Hudson, the Confederacy's strong point on the Mississippi three hundred miles below Vicksburg. On July 8 General N. P. Banks ordered a fourth, but before this final attack got under way General Frank Gardner surrendered his starved and battered garrison after a six weeks' siege. The Mississippi was now open to Union shipping from St. Louis to New Orleans.

A thousand times the story of Gettysburg has been told, and it will be told as many more. A brief reference will be enough to recall the great current of events and to suggest what it must have meant to the Confederate women.

Lee in the early summer of 1863 decided to invade the North, partly for the military and political advantage of a decisive victory on Union soil, partly in the hope that it would bring recognition and material aid from Napoleon III. His army marched forth in three great corps, Ewell (who had succeeded Stonewall Jackson) in the lead, then Ambrose P. Hill, then Longstreet. Some of Heth's men of Ewell's corps came from the west into the town of Gettysburg in southern

Pennsylvania looking for shoes and stumbled into sol-diers of General Meade's Union army coming from the east—George Meade had succeeded Hooker—and so precipitated the greatest battle of the war on a field neither commander would have chosen.

The fortunes and failures of those first three days of July will never cease to be debated. The climax came on the third day of furious fighting—"Pickett's charge" of 15,000 down a slope, up a slope, two miles across open country, in full battle array, the men aligned, the ranking officers on horseback, winning a brief strug-gle among the massed guns on Cemetery Ridge, the "dread heights of destiny," then falling back under murderous direct and cross fire through those sloping fields again—so magnificent, so forlorn.

The afternoon of the fourth, General Lee started his wounded back toward the Potomac. And that night the army followed, over the mud, in the driving rain, through the passes of South Mountain. Meade thought his army too used up for any vigorous pursuit.

The Confederates suffered more than 15,000 casu-alties out of 60,000 engaged in the battle. The Union loss was 25,000 out of 90,000. The Union could re-place. The Confederacy could not.

On July 10 the Federals began a combined sea and land attack on Charleston—a bombardment that was to last with little respite through the summer and far into the autumn. Indeed, the port and city were in a state of virtual siege till near the end of the war when the Confederate troops were withdrawn for service else-where. A Union force was landed on Morris Island on the Southern side of the inlet to the harbor and on Folly Island farther south. Battery Wagner, guarding the harbor portal, was under constant shelling. Sumter was gradually reduced to a pile of ruins, but those ruins were still crowned with the Confederate flag and the heroic garrison resisted every attempt to land—a symbol of the South's will to survive.

General Bragg, who had evacuated Chattanooga, gave battle to General Rosecrans on September 19-20 at Chickamauga. Rosecrans and most of his men were driven in rout to Chattanooga, but General George H. Thomas hung on long after the rest had fled and won his sobriquet of the "Rock of Chickamauga." In this greatest battle of the West the Confederate casualties numbered 18,000. During the last week of November, in hard fighting around Chattanooga at Lookout Mountain, Orchard Knob and Missionary Ridge, Bragg was defeated by Grant who had replaced Rosecrans. This meant further loss to the Confederacy of about 6,500 men.

Active Union operations in the first third of 1864 were largely confined to the Mississippi Valley. General Banks undertook a grand expedition up through the Red River valley to Shreveport, headquarters of General Kirby Smith. As part of the strategy General Frederick Steele was to come down from Arkansas. Banks was badly mauled by General "Dick" Taylor at Mansfield, Louisiana, on April 8. Taylor struck again at Pleasant Hill the next day; his attack was repelled but Banks retreated to the Red. Meanwhile Steele had got below Camden, Arkansas. Kirby Smith went after him and, in a series of running fights which included one at Poison Springs on the eighteenth and a final Confederate victory at Jenkins' Ferry on the Saline River the thirtieth, drove Steele back to Little Rock. Then Kirby Smith turned round to join Dick Taylor, but their juncture was too late to destroy Banks's "grand" army which, bedraggled, reached the Mississippi.

Through the twelve months of conflict, disappointment, poignant sorrow, from May 1863 through April 1864, the women of the Confederacy noted in heart's blood what they heard and saw and did.

1. MARY ANN LOUGHBOROUGH—IN A CAVE
AT VICKSBURG

*Mrs. Loughborough gives us a graphic picture of
what the cave dwellers of Vicksburg endured.*

*An Arkansas girl, born Mary Ann Webster, she was
living with her husband and small daughter in Jackson
in 1861. On the eve of his departure with his regiment,
she decided, with his approval, to follow him. Mother
and child traveled to Memphis and other points in
Tennessee and in April 1863 visited Mr. Loughborough
in Vicksburg. When the Federals started shelling the
city, they hurried back to Jackson only to find Union
troops entering their home town. Back to Vicksburg
again at the beginning of May—and there, in spite of
Pemberton's order to evacuate all noncombatants, they
stayed throughout the siege.*

*The next year Mrs. Loughborough's journal was pub-
lished—oddly enough in New York—under the title*
My Cave Life in Vicksburg, *with letters of trial and
travel.*

Sunday, the 17th of May, 1863, as we were dressing for church, and had nearly completed the arrangement of shawls and gloves, we heard the loud booming of cannon. Frightened, for at this time we knew
not *what* "an hour would bring forth," seeing no one
who might account for the sudden alarm, we walked
down the street, hoping to find some friend that could
tell us if it were dangerous to remain away from home
at church. I feared leaving my little one for any length
of time, if there were any prospect of an engagement.
After walking a square or two, we met an officer, who
told us the report we heard proceeded from our own
guns, which were firing upon a party of soldiers, who
were burning some houses on the peninsula on the
Louisiana shore; he told us, also, it had been rumored

that General Pemberton had been repulsed—that many
citizens had gone out to attend to the wounded of yesterday's battle—all the ministers and surgeons that
could leave had also gone. Still, as the bells of the
Methodist church rang out clear and loud, my friend
and I decided to enter, and were glad that we did so,
for we heard words of cheer and comfort in this time
of trouble. The speaker was a traveller, who supplied
the pulpit this day, as the pastor was absent minister-
ing to the wounded and dying on the battle field.

As we returned home, we passed groups of anxious
men at the corners, with troubled faces; very few
soldiers were seen; some battery men and officers,
needed for the river defences, were passing hastily up
the street. Yet, in all the pleasant air and sunshine of
the day, an anxious gloom seemed to hang over the
faces of men: a sorrowful waiting for tidings, that all
knew now would tell of disaster. There seemed no life
in the city; sullen and expectant seemed the men—
tearful and hopeful the women—prayerful and hopeful, I might add; for many a mother, groaning in
spirit over the uncertainty of the welfare of those most
dear to her, knelt and laid her sorrows at the foot of
that Throne, where no earnest suppliant is ever re-
jected; where the sorrow of many a broken heart has
been turned in resignation to His will who afflicts not
willingly the children of men. And so, in all the dejected uncertainty, the stir of horsemen and wheels
began, and wagons came rattling down the street—
going rapidly one way, and then returning, seemingly,
without air or purpose: now and then a worn and
dusty soldier would be seen passing with his blanket
and canteen; soon, straggler after straggler came by,
then groups of soldiers worn and dusty with the long
march. "What can be the matter?" we all cried, as the
streets and pavements became full of these worn and
tired-looking men. We sent down to ask, and the reply
was: "We are whipped; and the Federals are after
us." We hastily seized veils and bonnets, and walked

down the avenue to the iron railing that separates the yard from the street.

"Where are you going?" we asked.

No one seemed disposed to answer the question. An embarrassed, pained look came over some of the faces that were raised to us; others seemed only to feel the weariness of the long march; again we asked:

"Where on earth are you going?"

At last one man looked up in a half-surly manner, and answered:

"We are running."

"From whom?" exclaimed one of the young girls of the house.

"The Feds, to be sure," said another, half laughing and half shamefaced.

"Oh! shame on you!" cried the ladies; "and you running!"

"It's all Pem's fault," said an awkward, long-limbed, weary-looking man.

"It's all your own fault. Why don't you stand your ground?" was the reply.

"Shame on you all!" cried some of the ladies across the street.

I could not but feel sorry for the poor worn fellows, who did seem heartily ashamed of themselves; some without arms, having probably lost them in the first break of the companies.

"We are disappointed in you!" cried some of the ladies. "Who shall we look to now for protection?"

"Oh!" said one of them, "it's the first time I ever ran. We are Georgians, and we never ran before; but we saw them all breaking and running, and we could not bear up alone."

We asked them if they did not want water; and some of them came in the yard to get it. The lady of the house offered them some supper; and while they were eating, we were so much interested, that we stood around questioning them about the result of the day. "It is all General Pemberton's fault," said a sergeant. "I'm a Missourian, and our boys stood it almost alone, not knowing what was wanted to be done; yet, fighting as long as possible, every one leaving us, and we were obliged to fall back. You know, madam, we Missourians always fight well, even if we have to retreat afterward."

"Oh!" spoke up an old man, "we would ha' fit well; but General Pemberton came up and said: 'Stand your ground, boys. Your General Pemberton is with you;' and then, bless you, lady! the next we see'd of him, he was sitting on his horse behind a house—close, too, at that; and when we see'd that, we thought 'tain't no use, if he's going to sit there."

We could not help laughing at the old man's tale and his anger. Afterward we were told that General Pemberton behaved with courage—that the fault lay in the arrangement of troops.

At dark the fresh troops from Warrenton marched by, going out to the intrenchments in the rear of the city about two miles; many of the officers were fearful that the fortifications, being so incomplete, would be taken, if the Federal troops pushed immediately on, following their advantage.

As the troops from Warrenton passed by, the ladies waved their handkerchiefs, cheering them, and crying:

"These are the troops that have not run. You'll stand by us, and protect us, won't you? You won't *retreat* and bring the Federals behind you."

And the men, who were fresh and lively, swung their hats, and promised to die for the ladies—never to retreat; while poor fellows on the pavement, sitting on their blankets—lying on the ground—leaning against trees, or anything to rest their wearied bodies, looked on silent and dejected. They were not to blame, these poor, weary fellows. If they were unsuccessful, it is what many a man has been before them; endurance of the long fasts in the rifle pits, and coolness amid the showers of ball and shell thrown at devoted Vicksburg afterward, show us that men, though unfortunate, can retrieve their character. . . .

What a sad evening we spent—continually hearing

of friends and acquaintances left dead on the field, or mortally wounded, and being brought in ambulances to the hospital! We almost feared to retire that night; no one seemed to know whether the Federal army was advancing or not; some told us that they were many miles away, and others that they were quite near. How did we know but in the night we might be awakened by the tumult of their arrival!

The streets were becoming quiet; the noise and bustle had died out with the excitement of the day, and, save now and then the rapid passing of some officer, or army wagon, they were almost deserted. . . .

The next morning all was quiet; we heard no startling rumors; the soldiers were being gathered together and taken out into the rifle pits; Vicksburg was regularly besieged, and we were to stay at our homes and watch the progress of the battle. The rifle pits and intrenchments were almost two miles from the city. We would be out of danger, so we thought; but we did not know what was in preparation for us around the bend of the river. The day wore on; still all was quiet. At night our hopes revived: the Federal troops had not yet come up—another calm night and morning. At three o'clock that evening, the artillery boomed from the intrenchments, roar after roar, followed by the rattle of musketry: the Federal forces were making their first attack. Looking out from the back veranda, we could plainly see the smoke before the report of the guns reached us.

The discharges of musketry were irregular. At every report our hearts beat quicker. The excitement was intense in the city. Groups of people stood on every available position where a view could be obtained of the distant hills, where the jets of white smoke constantly passed out from among the trees.

Some of our friends proposed going for a better view up on the balcony around the cupola of the court house. The view from there was most extensive and beautiful. Hill after hill arose in the distance, enclosing the city in the form of a crescent. Immediately in the

centre and east of the river, the firing seemed more
continuous, while to the left and running northly, the
rattle and roar would be sudden, sharp, and vigorous,
then ceasing for some time. The hills around near the
city, and indeed every place that seemed commanding
and secure, was covered with anxious spectators—many
of them ladies—fearing the result of the afternoon's
conflict.

It was amid the clump of trees on the far distant hill-
side, that the Federal batteries could be discerned by
the frequent puffings of smoke from the guns. Turning
to the river, we could see a gunboat that had the
temerity to come down as near the town as possible,
and lay just out of reach of the Confederate batteries,
with steam up.

Two more lay about half a mile above and nearer
the canal; two or three transports had gotten up steam,
and lay near the mouth of the canal. Below the city a
gunboat had come up and landed, out of reach, on the
Louisiana side, striving to engage the lower batteries of
the town—firing about every fifteen minutes. . . .

From gentlemen who called on the evening of the
attack in the rear of the town, we learned that it was
quite likely, judging from the movements on the river,
that the gunboats would make an attack that night. We
remained dressed during the night; once or twice we
sprang to our feet, startled by the report of a cannon;
but after waiting in the darkness of the veranda for
some time, the perfect quiet of the city convinced us
that our alarm was needless.

Next day, two or three shells were thrown from the
battlefield, exploding near the house. This was our first
shock, and a severe one. We did not dare to go in the
back part of the house all day.

In the evening we were terrified and much excited by
the loud rush and scream of mortar shells; we ran to
the small cave near the house, and were in it during the
night, by this time wearied and almost stupefied by the
loss of sleep.

The caves were plainly becoming a necessity, as

some persons had been killed on the street by fragments of shells. The room that I had so lately slept in had been struck by a fragment of a shell during the first night, and a large hole made in the ceiling. I shall never forget my extreme fear during the night, and my utter hopelessness of ever seeing the morning light. Terror stricken, we remained crouched in the cave, while shell after shell followed each other in quick succession. I endeavored by constant prayer to prepare myself for the sudden death I was almost certain awaited me. My heart stood still as we would hear the reports from the guns, and the rushing and fearful sound of the shell as it came toward us. As it neared, the noise became more deafening; the air was full of the rushing sound; pains darted through my temples; my ears were full of the confusing noise; and, as it exploded, the report flashed through my head like an electric shock, leaving me in a quiet state of terror the most painful that I can imagine—cowering in a corner, holding my child to my heart—the only feeling of my life being the choking throbs of my heart, that rendered me almost breathless. As singly they fell short, or beyond the cave, I was aroused by a feeling of thankfulness that was of short duration. Again and again the terrible fright came over in that night.

I saw one fall in the road without the mouth of the cave, like a flame of fire, making the earth tremble, and with a low, singing sound, the fragments sped on in their work of death.

Morning found us more dead than alive, with blanched faces and trembling lips. We were not reassured on hearing, from a man who took refuge in the cave, that a mortar shell in falling would not consider the thickness of earth above us a circumstance.

Some of the ladies, more courageous by daylight, asked him what he was in there for, if that was the case. He was silenced for an hour, when he left. As the day wore on, and we were still preserved, though the shells came as ever, we were somewhat encouraged.

The next morning we heard that Vicksburg would

not in all probability hold out more than a week or two, as the garrison was poorly provisioned; and one of General Pemberton's staff officers told us that the effective force of the garrison, upon being estimated, was found to be fifteen thousand men; General Loring having been cut off after the battle of Black River, with probably ten thousand.

The ladies all cried, "Oh, never surrender!" but after the experience of the night, I really could not tell what I wanted, or what my opinions were.

So constantly dropped the shells around the city, that the inhabitants all made preparations to live under the ground during the seige. M—— sent over and had a cave made in a hill near by. We seized the opportunity one evening, when the gunners were probably at their supper, for we had a few moments of quiet, to go over and take possession. We were under the care of a friend of M——, who was paymaster on the staff of the same General with whom M—— was Adjutant. We had neighbors on both sides of us; and it would have been an amusing sight to a spectator to witness the domestic scenes presented without by the number of servants preparing the meals under the high bank containing the caves.

Our dining, breakfast, and supper hours were quite irregular. When the shells were falling fast, the servants came in for safety, and our meals waited for completion some little time; again they would fall slowly, with the lapse of many minutes between, and out would start the cooks to their work.

Some families had light bread made in large quantities, and subsisted on it with milk (provided their cows were not killed from one milking time to another), without any more cooking, until called on to replenish. Though most of us lived on corn bread and bacon, served three times a day, the only luxury of the meal consisting in its warmth, I had some flour, and frequently had some hard, tough biscuit made from it, there being no soda or yeast to be procured. At this time we could, also, procure beef. A gentleman friend was kind enough to offer me his camp bed, a narrow spring mattress, which fitted within the contracted cave very comfortably; another had his tent fly stretched over the mouth of our residence to shield us from the sun; and thus I was the recipient of many favors, and under obligations to many gentlemen of the army for delicate and kind attentions. And so I went regularly to work, keeping house under ground. Our new habitation was an excavation made in the earth, and branching six feet from the entrance, forming a cave in the shape of a T. In one of the wings my bed fitted; the other I used as a kind of dressing room; in this the earth had been cut down a foot or two below the floor of the main cave; I could stand erect here; and when tired of sitting in other portions of my residence, I bowed myself into it, and stood impassively resting at full height—one of the variations in the still shell-expectant life. M——'s servant cooked for us under protection of the hill. Our quarters were close, indeed; yet I was more comfortable than I expected I could have been made under the earth in that fashion.

We were safe at least from fragments of shell—and they were flying in all directions; though no one seemed to think our cave any protection, should a mortar shell happen to fall directly on top of the ground above us. We had our roof arched and braced, the supports of the bracing taking up much room in our confined quarters. The earth was about five feet thick above, and seemed hard and compact; yet, poor M——, every time he came in, examined it, fearing, amid some of the shocks it sustained, that it might crack and fall upon us.

One afternoon, amid the rush and explosion of the shells, cries and screams arose—the screams of women amid the shrieks of the falling shells. The servant boy, George, after starting and coming back once or twice, his timidity overcoming his curiosity, at last gathered courage to go to the ravine near us, from whence the cries proceeded, and found that a negro man had been buried alive within a cave, he being alone at that time.

Workmen were instantly set to deliver him, if possible; but when found, the unfortunate man had evidently been dead some little time.

Another incident happened the same day: A gentleman, resident of Vicksburg, had a large cave made, and repeatedly urged his wife to leave the house and go into it. She steadily refused, and, being quite an invalid, was lying on the bed, when he took her by the hand and insisted upon her accompanying him so strongly, that she yielded; and they had scarcely left the house, when a mortar shell went crashing through, utterly demolishing the bed that had so lately been vacated, tearing up the floor, and almost completely destroying the room.

That night, after my little one had been laid in bed, I sat at the mouth of the cave, with the servants drawn around me, watching the brilliant display of fireworks the mortar boats were making—the passage of the shell, as it travelled through the heavens, looking like a swiftly moving star. As it fell, it approached the earth so rapidly, that it seemed to leave behind a track of fire.

This night we kept our seats, as they all passed rapidly over us, none falling near. The incendiary shells were still more beautiful in appearance. As they exploded in the air, the burning matter and balls fell like large, clear blue-and-amber stars, scattering hither and thither.

"Miss M——," said one of the more timid servants, "do they want to kill us all dead? Will they keep doing this until we all die?"

I said most heartily, "I hope not."

The servants we had with us seemed to possess more courage than is usually attributed to negroes. They seldom hesitated to cross the street for water at any time. The "boy" slept at the entrance of the cave, with a pistol I had given him, telling me I need not be "afeared—dat any one dat come dar would have to go over his body first."

He never refused to carry out any little article to M—— on the battle field. I laughed heartily at a dilemma he was placed in one day: The mule that he had mounted to ride out to the battle field took him to a dangerous locality, where the shells were flying thickly, and then, suddenly stopping, through fright, obstinately refused to stir. It was in vain that George kicked and beat him—go he would not; so, clenching his hand, he hit him severely in the head several times, jumped down, ran home, and left him. The mule stood a few minutes rigidly, then, looking around, and seeing George at some distance from him, turned and followed, quite demurely.

Days wore on, and the mortar shells had passed over continually without falling near us; so that I became quite at my ease, in view of our danger, when one of the Federal batteries opposite the intrenchments altered their range; so that, at about six o'clock every evening, Parrott shells came whirring into the city, frightening the inhabitants of caves wofully.

The cave we inhabited was about five squares from the levee. A great many had been made in a hill immediately beyond us; and near us; and near this hill we could see most of the shells fall. Caves were the fashion—the rage—over besieged Vicksburg. Negroes, who understood their business, hired themselves out to dig them, at from thirty to fifty dollars, according to the size. Many persons, considering different localities unsafe, would sell them to others, who had been less fortunate, or less provident; and so great was the demand for cave workmen, that a new branch of industry sprang up and became popular—particularly as the personal safety of the workmen was secured, and money withal.

Even the very animals seemed to share the general fear of a sudden and frightful death. The dogs would be seen in the midst of the noise to gallop up the street, and then to return, as if fear had maddened them. On hearing the descent of a shell, they would dart aside— then, as it exploded, sit down and howl in the most pitiful manner. There were many walking the street, apparently without homes. George carried on a con-

tinual warfare with them, as they came about the fire
where our meals were cooking.

The horses, belonging to the officers, and fastened
to the trees near the tents, would frequently strain the
halter to its full length, rearing high in the air, with a
loud snort of terror, as a shell would explode near. I
could hear them in the night cry out in the midst of the
uproar, ending in a low, plaintive whinny of fear.

The poor creatures subsisted entirely on cane tops
and mulberry leaves. Many of the mules and horses
had been driven outside of the lines, by order of General Pemberton, for subsistence. Only mules enough
were left, belonging to the Confederacy, to allow three
full teams to a regiment. Private property was not inter-
fered with.

The hill opposite our cave might be called "death's
point" from the number of animals that had been killed
in eating the grass on the sides and summit. In all
directions I can see the turf turned up, from the shells
that have gone ploughing into the earth. Horses or
mules that are tempted to mount the hill by the
promise of grass that grows profusely there, invariably
come limping down wounded, to die at the base, or are
brought down dead from the summit.

A certain number of mules are killed each day by
the commissaries, and are issued to the men, all of
whom prefer the fresh meat, though it be of mule, to
the bacon and salt rations that they have eaten so long
a time without change. There have already been some
cases of scurvy; the soldiers have a horror of the
disease; therefore, I suppose, the mule meat is all the
more welcome. Indeed, I petitioned M—— to have
some served on our table. He said: "No; wait a little
longer." He did not like to see me eating mule until
I was obliged to; that he trusted Providence would
send us some change shortly.

It was astonishing how the young officers kept up
their spirits, frequently singing quartets and glees amid
the pattering of Minié balls; and I often heard gay
peals of laughter from headquarters, as the officers

that had spent the day, and perhaps the night, previous in the rifle pits, would collect to make out reports. This evening a gentleman visited us, and, among other songs, sang words to the air of the "Mocking Bird," which I will write:

" 'Twas at the siege of Vicksburg,
  Of Vicksburg, of Vicksburg—
  'Twas at the siege of Vicksburg,
  When the Parrott shells were whistling through
      the air.

"Listen to the Parrot shells—
  Listen to the Parrot shells:
  The Parrot shells are whistling through the air.

"Oh! well will we remember—
  Remember—remember
  Tough mule meat, June *sans* November,
  And the Minié balls that whistled through
      the air.
  Listen to the Minié balls—
  Listen to the Minié balls:
  The Minié balls are singing in the air."

News came that one of the forts to the left of us had been undermined and blown up, killing sixty men; then of the death of the gallant Colonel Irwin, of Missouri; and again, the next day, of the death of the brave old General Green, of Missouri.

We were now swiftly nearing the end of our siege life: the rations had nearly all been given out. For the last, few days I had been sick; still I tried to overcome the languid feeling of utter prostration. My little one had swung in her hammock, reduced in strength, with a low fever flushing in her face. M—— was all anxiety, I could plainly see. A soldier brought up, one morning, a little jaybird, as a plaything for the child. After playing with it for a short time, she turned wearily away. "Miss Mary," said the servant, "she's hungry; let me

make her some soup from the bird." At first I refused:
the poor little plaything should not die; then, as I
thought of the child, I half consented. With the utmost
haste, Cinth disappeared; and the next time she appeared, it was with a cup of soup, and a little plate,
on which lay the white meat of the poor little bird.

On Saturday a painful calm prevailed: there had
been a truce proclaimed; and so long had the constant
firing been kept up, that the stillness now was absolutely oppressive.

At ten o'clock General Bowen passed by, dressed in
full uniform, accompanied by Colonel Montgomery,[1]
and preceded by a courier bearing a white flag. M——
came by, and asked me if I would like to walk out; so
I put on my bonnet and sallied forth beyond the terrace, for the first time since I entered. On the hill above
us, the earth was literally covered with fragments of
shell—Parrott, shrapnell, canister; besides lead in all
shapes and forms, and a long kind of solid shot, shaped
like a small Parrott shell. Minié balls lay in every direction, flattened, dented, and bent from the contact with
trees and pieces of wood in their flight. The grass
seemed deadened—the ground ploughed into furrows
in many places; while scattered over all, like giants'
pepper, in numberless quantity, were the shrapnell
balls.

I could now see how very near to the rifle pits my
cave lay: only a small ravine between the two hills
separated us. In about two hours, General Bowen returned. No one knew, or seemed to know, why a truce
had been made; but all believed that a treaty of surrender was pending. Nothing was talked about among
the officers but the all-engrossing theme. Many wished
to cut their way out and make the risk their own; but
I secretly hoped that no such bloody hazard would be
attempted.

The next morning, M—— came up, with a pale face,

[1] General John S. Bowen, division commander, and Colonel
L. M. Montgomery, aide-de-camp to General Pemberton.

saying: "It's all over! The white flag floats from our forts! Vicksburg has surrendered!"

He put on his uniform coat, silently buckled on his sword, and prepared to take out the men, to deliver up their arms in front of the fortification.

I felt a strange unrest, the quiet of the day was so unnatural. I walked up and down the cave until M—— returned. The day was extremely warm; and he came with a violent headache. He told me that the Federal troops had acted splendidly; they were stationed opposite the place where the Confederate troops marched up and stacked their arms; and they seemed to feel sorry for the poor fellows who had defended the place for so long a time. Far different from what he had expected, not a jeer or taunt came from any one of the Federal soldiers. Occasionally, a cheer would be heard; but the majority seemed to regard the poor unsuccessful soldiers with a generous sympathy.

After the surrender, the old gray-headed soldier, in passing on the hill near the cave, stopped, and touching his hat, said:

"It's a sad day this, madam; I little thought we'd come to it, when we first stopped in the intrenchments. I hope you'll yet be happy, madam, after all the trouble you've seen."

To which I mentally responded, "Amen."

The poor, hunchback soldier, who had been sick, and who, at home in Southern Missouri, is worth a million of dollars, I have been told, yet within Vicksburg has been nearly starved, walked out to-day in the pleasant air, for the first time for many days.

I stood in the doorway and caught my first sight of the Federal uniform since the surrender. That afternoon the road was filled with them, walking about, looking at the forts and the head-quarter horses: wagons also filled the road, drawn by the handsome United States horses. Poor M——, after keeping his horse upon mulberry leaves during the forty-eight days, saw him no more! After the surrender in the evening, George rode into the city on his mule: thinking to "shine," as the negroes say, he rode M——'s hand-some, silver-mounted dragoon-saddle. I could not help laughing when he returned, with a sorry face, reporting himself safe, but the saddle gone. M—— questioned and requestioned him, aghast at his loss; for a saddle was a valuable article in our little community; and George, who felt as badly as any one, said: "I met a Yankee, who told me: 'Get down off dat mule; I'm gwin' to hab dat saddle.' I said: 'No; I ain't gwin' to do no such thing.' He took out his pistol, and I jumped down."

So Mister George brought back to M—— a saddle that better befitted his mule than the one he rode off on—a much worn, common affair, made of wood. I felt sorry for M——. That evening George brought evil news again: another horse had been taken. His re-maining horse and his only saddle finished the news of the day.

The next morning, Monday, as I was passing through the cave, I saw something stirring at the base of one of the supports of the roof: taking a second look, I beheld a large snake curled between the earth and the upright post. I went out quickly and sent one of the servants for M——, who, coming up immediately, took up his sword and fastened one of the folds of the reptile to the post. It gave one quick dart toward him, with open jaws. Fortunately, the length of the sword was greater than the upper length of body; and the snake fell to the earth a few inches from M——, who set his heel firmly on it, and severed the head from the body with the sword. I have never seen so large a snake; it was fully as large round the body as the bowl of a good-sized glass tumbler, and over two yards long. . . .

The Confederate troops were being marched into Vicksburg to take the parole that the terms of the treaty of surrender demanded. In a few days they would leave the city they had held so long.

On Friday they began their march toward the South; and on Saturday poor George came to me, and said he had put on a pair of blue pants, and, thinking they would take him for a Federal soldier, had tried to slip through after M——, but he was turned back; so he came begging me to try to get him a pass: the effort was made; and to this day I do not know whether he ever reached M—— or not.

Saturday evening, Vicksburg, with her terraced hills —with her pleasant homes and sad memories, passed from my view in the gathering twilight—passed, but the river flowed on the same, and the stars shone out with the same calm light! . . .

2. ESTHER ALDEN—"WE DANCE AT FORT SUMTER"

Esther was sixteen when in June 1863 she returned home to cheerfulness and gaiety in resolute Charleston. The next month there was a new bombardment of the city, and of Fort Sumter, much more serious than the one in April. Women and children were advised to leave the city. Esther, her mother and sisters unwillingly departed for their plantation some miles away, and, when the safety of this region was threatened, they took refuge in western North Carolina.

Esther kept a war diary which ended abruptly on April 1, 1865. Few Southern women had the heart to record the fall of the Confederacy. Esther did not. But now, like Sally Pickett, she could dance as a crisis of life approached and so make the tragedy of life less dark.

Plantersville, S. C.

May 29, 1863.—Heigh ho! I am to leave school today never to return! I suppose I am grown up! The war is raging, but we, shut up here with our books, and our little school tragedies and comedies, have remained very ignorant of all that is going on outside. Now, I suppose I will know more of the exciting events taking place, as I am going to Charleston to-morrow and we will stay there as long as it is considered safe. We have had some hardships to endure this winter. Our fare has been very poor, but much better than that of poor C., who writes that at his school they have not had meat nor butter, tea nor coffee for a long time, but have lived entirely on squash and hominy! I do not think girls could stand that; they would rebel; but the boys all recognize that the master is doing his best for them. We have always had meat once a day; our supper consists of a huge tray of corn dodgers which is brought into the school-room and placed on the table, that we may help ourselves and the tray goes back empty. Most of us have been very quiet about it, but not long ago one of the girls left and it seems she had stowed away some dodgers in her trunk, which she displayed to sympathizing friends and relations when she got home, making a melancholy story of her sufferings. The dodgers, with age added to their actually adamantine character, were simply indestructible, and there was quite a stir made outside about our woes. We who remained at school, however, disapproved of her conduct as being very disloyal. In our own homes even there were many privations now, and we are rather proud to feel that we are sharing, at a very safe distance, some of the hardships borne by our brave soldiers.

Charleston, June 20.—It is too delightful to be at home! In spite of the war every one is so bright and cheerful, and the men are so charming and look so nice in their uniforms. We see a great many of them, and I have been to a most delightful dance in Fort Sumter. The night was lovely and we went down in rowing boats. It was a strange scene, cannon balls piled in every direction, sentinels pacing the ramparts, and within the casemates pretty, well-dressed women, and handsome well-bred men dancing, as though unconscious that we were actually under the guns of the blockading fleet. It was my first party, and the strange charm of the situation wove a spell around me; every man seemed to me a hero—not only a possible but an actual hero! One looks at a man so differently when you think he may be killed to-morrow! Men whom up to this time I have thought dull and commonplace that night seemed charming. I had a rude awakening as we rowed back to the city. When we came abreast of Fort Ripley, the sentinel halted us demanding the countersign, the oarsmen stopped, but Gen. R., who was steering the boat, ordered them to row on. Three times the sentinel spoke and then he fired. The ball passed over the boat and Gen. R. ordered his men to row up to the fort, called the officer of the day, and ordered the sentinel put under arrest! Of course I knew nothing about it, but it seemed to me frightfully unjust, and I was so indignant that I found it hard to keep quiet until we got home.

3. MRS. G. GRIFFIN WILCOX—YANKEES
PARADE IN NATCHEZ

A woman of Natchez left for posterity a glimpse of war in her day—the enemy occupation in the summer of 1863.

Natchez, Mississippi
July, 1863

Grand, exclusive, heroic Natchez, with her terraced hills and fragrant gardens, colonial mansions and prehistoric memories, was gorgeous in gala day attire.

The Stars and Stripes floated from the domes and windows of all public buildings, and were stretched over the street crossings.

General Tuttle,[1] mounted on his milk-white steed, and escorted by his staff, paraded the principal thoroughfares.

---

[1] General James M. Tuttle had been in the fight against Johnston in the Vicksburg campaign.

Handsomely-uniformed soldiers, arrayed in the paraphernalia and insignia of office, were moving hither and thither, reminding one of a vast assemblage of strange birds driven hence by terrific storms of foreign shores, but alas! the storm was in our own beautiful and loved Southland, and we were compelled, perforce, to look upon and admire the brilliant plumage of these strange, bright birds, who brought not the rich tidings of all glorious things, but sad disaster, on their starry wings.

When Natchez was first garrisoned by the Union troops it was deemed necessary by General Tuttle to erect fortifications on the site occupied by the Susette homestead, one of the most magnificent residences of the city. The mansion was situated in a famous grove of forest trees, among whch were grand old live oaks, elms and magnolias, planted more than half a century ago. The grounds were surrounded by one of the handsomest iron fences in the State.

The interior of the Susette home was furnished with exquisitely hand-carved Italian marble mantels. There were cut-glass window panes and a rosewood stairway. Most of the expensive furniture had come from Paris. Included in the dining-room appointments was silver plate of four generations back.

Federal soldiers had stripped the house of many of its costly furnishings. The edict had gone forth that the "Susette mansion must be blown up with gun-powder and other combustibles, to clear the way for the fort." Excavations were immediately made under and around the grand old edifice. These, together with the cellar, were filled with such immense quantities of powder that when the match was applied to the fuse the explosion was so terrific that half of the window panes in the town were shattered and broken.

Such is war.

4. LaSALLE CORBELL PICKETT—
"I MARRY MY GENERAL, THE HERO OF GETTYSBURG"

She was born at Chuckatuck in Nansemond County, southeastern Virginia, in 1843. When she was eight years old she met at Old Point Comfort a young lieutenant from Richmond, George E. Pickett, who was grieving over the recent death of his wife, Sally Minge Pickett. LaSalle found him fascinating and admitted that she loved him from the first day. After that their paths crossed at infrequent intervals. She went on to Lynchburg Academy and confidently prepared herself for the life of a soldier's wife. In the spring of 1863 General Pickett was encamped briefly near her home. She saw him daily, embroidered his cape, his slippers, the stars on his coat. She was being graduated in June when Lee's army was beginning the march to Pennsylvania that ended in Gettysburg.

Beautiful Sally Pickett was in Petersburg during the siege. Her baby was born there; she called him affectionately "the little general." When the Federals came into Richmond she was there, and that night fire destroyed the warehouse where all her wedding presents and other valuables were stored. The Picketts fled to Canada where they lived in one room in a boardinghouse under the assumed name of Edwards. A year later they came back to Virginia and occupied a cottage on the site of George Pickett's old home, which had been sacked and burned during the war.

After the war he declined a commission as brigadier-general in the Egyptian Army, and the marshalship of Virginia which Grant tendered him, accepted the Virginia agency of the Washington Life Insurance Company of New York. He died in 1875.

When she was a widow Sally wrote her reminiscences, Pickett and His Men.

The temperature of the summer of 1863 seemed to keep pace with the high tide of war. The heat was so excessive that the schools were closed early.

The first week in June I was graduated from my alma mater. I stopped in Richmond for a few days en route to my home within the Federal lines. The day after I arrived I received a letter dated at Culpeper Court-house, June 13, full of faith in a successful campaign, a short separation, and a "speedy termination of the difficulties." June 15 and 18 there came other letters, one written on the march to Winchester,[1] the other after reaching that place, breathing the same spirit of confidence and hope. Until the fatal third of July such letters came to me, expressing hope and trust —always hope and trust.

Then drifted to us rumors, faint and indefinite at first, of a great battle fought at Gettysburg. Gradually they grew stronger and brighter, and the mind of the South became imbued with the impression that a grand victory had been won. Thus the news first came to us, transmuted in the balmy air of the South from the appalling disaster it really was into the glorious triumph which our longing hearts hoped it might be. A few days of this glowing dream, and then—the heartbreaking truth.

I could hear nothing of the General except the vague rumor that he had been killed in the final charge. Our mail facilities were very meager, and our letters were smuggled through the lines by any trustworthy person who, having been given the privilege of going back and forth, happened to be at hand at the time. Many a mile I had ridden on mule-back, hoping to hear directly from the General, before I was rewarded.

"Reck," our old mule, had been a benefaction not only to us but to the whole country. Every other mule and every horse had been confiscated and taken by

---

[1] Longstreet's army corps, to which Pickett's division was attached, started for Pennsylvania on June 3 from Fredericksburg, crossed the Rapidan, proceeded to Culpeper Court House and then to and up the Valley.

the Federals. But for his wonderful memory, "Reck" would have changed owners, too, like all his half-brothers and sisters, for he was a fine-looking mule. When a colt his leg had been broken in crossing a bridge, and all the powers of coaxing and whipping and spurring after that accident could not make him step on a plank, much less cross a bridge, unless you pretended to mend the bridge, and first walked across it yourself in safety, and then came back and led him over. My last ride on "Reck" brought me as compensation a package of five or six letters. The first was the letter which the General, as he went into battle, had handed to General Longstreet, with its sad superscription—"If Old Peter's nod means death———." [1] The next was written on the second day after the great catastrophe.

Later there came to me the following:

> Williamsport, July 8, 1863.
> ... "I am crossing the river to-day, guarding some four thousand prisoners back to Winchester, where I shall take command and try to recruit my spirit-crushed, wearied, cut-up people. It is just two months this morning since I parted from you, and yet the disappointments and sorrows that have been crowded into the interval make the time seem years instead. My grand old division, which was so full of faith and courage then, is now almost extinguished. But one field-officer [2]

---

[1] It ended: "Now, I go; but remember always that I love you with all my heart and soul, with every fiber of my being; that now and forever I am yours—yours, my beloved. It is almost three o'clock. My soul reaches out to yours—my prayers. I'll keep up a skookum tumtum for Virginia and for you, my darling.

"YOUR SOLDIER.

"Gettysburg, July 3, 1863."

[2] Richard G. Garnett and Lewis Armistead, brigade commanders, and three of Pickett's five regimental commanders were killed, the others wounded. (The third field officer, who escaped, was James L. Kemper.) Of the supporting brigadiers, James J. Archer was severely wounded, Isaac R. Trimble wounded and captured, Alfred M. Scales wounded.

in the whole command escaped in that terrible third of July slaughter, and alas! alas! for the men who fearlessly followed their lead on to certain death.

"We were ordered to take a height. We *took* it, but under the most withering fire that I, even in my dreams, could ever have conceived of, and I have seen many battles. Alas! alas! no support came, and my poor fellows who had gotten in were overpowered. Your uncle, Colonel Phillips, behaved most gallantly—was wounded, but not seriously. Your cousins, Captain Cralle and C. C. Phillips, are among the missing. But for you, I should greatly have preferred to answer reveille on the fourth of July with the poor fellows over there, and how I escaped it is a miracle; how any of us survived is marvelous, unless it was by prayer.

"My heart is very, very sad, and it seems almost sacrilegious to think of happiness at such a time, but let my need of your sweet womanly sympathy and comfort in these sad hours plead extenuation, and be prepared, I beseech you, at a moment's notice to obey the summons that will make you my wife."

Two weeks later I received this letter:

Culpeper C. H. July, 1863

"The short but terrible campaign is over, and we are again on this side of the Blue Ridge. Would that we had never crossed the Potomac, or that the splendid army which we had on our arrival in Pennsylvania had not been fought in detail. If the charge made by my gallant Virginians on the fatal third of July had been supported,[1] or even if my other two brigades, Jenkins and Corse,[2] had been with me, we would now, I believe, have been in Washington, and the war practically over.

---

[1] Pickett was supported by Pettigrew's division—a Tennessee and Alabama brigade, a North Carolina brigade, Joe Davis's Mississippians, Brockenbrough's Virginians—and W. D. Pender's division of the two North Carolina brigades. But Pickett hoped for a great deal more support from the center and left.
[2] Generals Albert D. Jenkins and Montgomery D. Corse.

God in his wisdom has willed otherwise, and I fear there will be many more blood-drenched fields and broken hearts before the end does come. . . .

"I thank the great and good God that he has spared me to come back and claim your promise, and I pray your womanly assistance in helping me to its *immediate* fulfilment. This is no time for ceremonies. The future is all uncertain, and it is impossible for me to call a moment my own. Again, with all the graves I have left behind me, and with all the wretchedness and misery this fated campaign has made, we would not wish anything but a very silent, very quiet wedding, planning only the sacrament and blessing of the church, and, after that, back to my division and to the blessing of those few of them who, by God's miracle, were left.

"I gave Colonel Harrison [1] a gold luck-piece which was a parting gift to me from the officers of the Pacific, and told him to have it made into a wedding-ring at Tyler's. I asked him to have engraved within 'G. E. P. and S. C. Married ——,' and to leave sufficient space for date and motto, which you would direct. . . .''

Perhaps no girl just out of school ever had a more difficult problem sprung upon her than that which confronted me. Had we been living under the old regime nothing would have been easier than to prepare for a grand wedding in the stately old Southern style. Times had changed very greatly in the past few years, and how was a trousseau to be made away up in the frozen North, where all the pretty things seemed to have gone, and spirited through the lines to make a wedding brilliant enough to satisfy the girlish idea of propriety? And yet, how could a marriage take place without the accompaniments of white satin, misty laces, dainty slippers, and gloves, and all the other paraphernalia traditionally connected with that interesting event in a

---

[1] The reference seems to be to Colonel Burton N. Harrison, President Davis's secretary and later Constance Cary Harrison's husband.

young woman's life? However, if "Love laughs at lock-smiths," he has more serious methods of treating other obstacles in his way, and all the difficulties of millinery were finally overcome. But still there were lions in the path.

Longstreet lay under a tree at Culpeper Court-house, seeking repose from the burdens which would necessarily weigh upon the mind of a man in whose care was the destiny of the leading corps of the Army of Northern Virginia. As he leisurely reclined Pickett came up and sat on the grass beside him.

"General," he said, "I am going to be married, and want a furlough. This little girl"—handing my picture to General Longstreet—"says she is ready and willing to marry me at any minute, in spite of the risks of war, and will go with me to the furthest end of the earth, if need be."

The younger man had consulted the older about many things since the day when he had rushed forward into the place made vacant by the wounding of his superior officer and carried the flag to victory,[1] but he had never before confided to him an aspiration of so soulful and sacred a character. Longstreet considered the matter gravely for a time.

"I can't give it to you, Pickett. They are not granting any furloughs now. I might detail you for special duty, and of course you could stop off by the way and be married," said General Longstreet, with a twinkle in his eye.

It was not a time for insisting upon minor details, even in regard to very momentous subjects, and the General eagerly consented to be detailed for "special

---

[1] During the storming of Chapultepec in the War with Mexico, September 13, 1847, "Lieutenant James Longstreet . . . 'advancing, color in hand,' was shot down. The flag he carried was caught up and carried on by a very young lieutenant, George E. Pickett, hardly more than a year out of the Academy." *The Story of the Mexican War*, by Robert Selph Henry. Indianapolis: The Bobbs-Merrill Company, Inc., 1950, p. 361.

duty." Then there arose the problem of how to get the two necessary parties to the transaction within the essential proximity to each other. If the General attempted to cross the lines he might be arrested, and then not only would the wedding be indefinitely postponed, but one of the divisions of Longstreet's corps would lose its leader.

The General had purposed coming to meet me at the Blackwater River, which was the dividing line between the Federal and Confederate forces, but fortunately, through military exigencies, his plans were changed. As cautious as we had tried to be, the Federals, by some unknown power, caught a glimmering of what was expected, and some poor fellow en route to the Blackwater, as innocent of being the General as of committing matrimony, was ambushed and captured by a squad of cavalry sent out from Suffolk for the purpose, and, though he pleaded innocent to the charges against him, put into Suffolk jail, before he was recognized and released.

Thus, in the interests of the Confederacy, as well as of the marriage, it became necessary that I should be the one to cross the lines.

My uncle was a physician and because of his profesison was permitted to go where he wished, and I had often accompanied him on his professional visits.

On the 17th of September, my father and I set out to cross the lines under the protecting wing of this good uncle. Just before we were ferried over the Blackwater River, we came upon the Federal cavalry, who looked at us somewhat critically but, recognizing Dr. Phillips, evidently assumed that he was bent upon a mission of mercy—as, indeed, was he not?—and did not molest us.

We reached the railway station in safety. "Waverley," it was called, and the romantic associations clustering around the name filled my youthful fancy with pleasure. There we were met by my uncle, Colonel J. J. Phillips, and his wife, and by the General's brother and his aunt and uncle, Miss Olivia and Mr. Andrew Johnston.

Colonel Phillips was a warm personal friend of the
General and commanded a regiment in his division. He
had been wounded at Gettysburg and was just con-
valescing.

They accompanied us to Petersburg where, to my
great delight, the General awaited me at the station.
When we reached the hotel he and my father went out
for the purpose of procuring the license. They soon
returned with the sorrowful announcement that, owing
to some legal technicality, the license could not be
issued without a special decree of court, I not being
a resident of that jurisdiction. Court could not be convened until the next day, and the General must report
at headquarters that evening. He went away sorrowful,
and I fell into a flood of tears, thereby greatly shocking the prim, rigid maiden lady—a friend of my
mother—who had accompanied me as monitor and
bridesmaid, and who was intensely horrified by the ex-
pression of my impatience and the general impropriety
of my conduct in fretting over the delay.

As I sat in my room, drowned in grief, I heard the
newsboys crying the evening papers:

"All about the marriage of General Pickett, the hero
of Gettysburg, to the beautiful Miss Corbell, of Virginia!"

You know, a girl is always "beautiful" on her wedding-day, whatever she may have been the day before,
or will be the day after.

However, it was not my wedding-day, but only was
to have been, and I had serious doubts as to whether
my tear-washed eyes and disappointed, grief-stained
face would be likely to answer anybody's preconceived
convictions of the highest type of beauty. Again was
my mother's "prunes and prisms" friend unnecessarily
shocked, as I thought, because I had simply opened
the window to buy a paper containing the account of
my own marriage.

The next day the General returned to Petersburg,
and the court graciously convened. The license was

granted, and we were married [1] by the Rev. Dr. Platt in dear old St. Paul's Church before congregated thousands, for soldier and civilian, rich and poor, high and low, were all made welcome by my hero. We left for Richmond on the afternoon train amidst the salute of guns, hearty cheers, and chimes and bands and bugles.

It may not be supposed that, in those dark days of the Confederacy, we were likely to find a sumptuous banquet awaiting us in the capital, but we did. The river and the woods had given of their varied treasures to do honor to my General. It was in the sora season, and so plentifully was the game supplied that the banquet was afterward known as "the wedding-sora-supper." Had it required the expenditure of ammunition to provide this delicacy, it would probably have been lacking, for the South at that time could not afford to shoot at birds when there were so many more important targets to be found. They were killed at night with paddles, and many hundreds were sent as bridal presents by the plantation servants from Turkey Island. There were thousands of delicious beaten biscuit and gallons of terrapin stew made, and turkeys boned and made into salads, too, by the faithful old plantation servants under the supervision of Mrs. Mimms, the loyal old overseer's wife. Not having sugar, we had few sweets, but Mrs. Robert E. Lee had made for us with her own fair hands, a beautiful fruit-cake, the General's aunt-in-law, Mrs. Maria Dudley, the mother of the present Bishop, sent us as a bridal gift a black-cake that had been made and packed away for her own golden wedding, and some of our other friends had remembered us in similar ways. So we even had sweets at our wedding-supper.

It was a brilliant reception. The Army of Northern Virginia, then stationed around Richmond, came in uniform. Of the thousands present, only President Davis and his Cabinet, a few ministers, and a few *very* old men were in civilian clothes. The General and I

---

[1] September 15, 1863.

greeted and welcomed them all as they came; then they passed on to the banquet and the dance—dancing as only Richmond in the Confederacy could dance. With a step that never faltered she waltzed airily over the crater of a volcano. She threaded graceful mazes on the brink of the precipice. The rumbling of the coming earthquake struck no minor tones into her merry music. If people could not dance in the crises of life the tragedy of existence might be even darker than it is.

So they danced through the beautiful, bright September night, and when the last guests were going my General and I walked out upon the veranda with them and, as they closed the outer gates, watched the stars of night fade away before the coming dawn and the morning star rise and shine gloriously upon a new, happy day.

5. MARIE RAVENEL de la COSTE—
"SOMEBODY'S DARLING"

The author of what is perhaps the best-known Confederate poem spent her early days in Savannah where she was teaching French when hostilities began. Her father was Henri de la Coste and her mother Angèle Pérony d'Istria, natives of Frence. The inspiration of the poem came from the scenes she witnessed in Confederate hospitals. In 1910 she was living in Washington, D.C. "Somebody's Darling" was in every scrapbook and recited by many a school child in the Confederacy. It was published anonymously in 1864 by J. C. Schreiner & Son of Augusta, Georgia, as a song, with music by John Hill Hewitt. A later musical setting, by A. C. Matheson, was published by J. H. Snow of Mobile.[1]

[1] The version followed here is as printed in *The Home Book of Verse*, ed., Burton Egbert Stevenson. New York: Henry Holt & Company, 1912.

Into a ward of the whitewashed walls
  Where the dead and the dying lay—
Wounded by bayonets, shells, and balls—
  Somebody's darling was borne one day.
Somebody's darling! so young and so brave,
  Wearing still on his pale sweet face—
Soon to be hid by the dust of the grave—
  The lingering light of his boyhood's grace.

Matted and damp are the curls of gold
  Kissing the snow of that fair young brow,
Pale are the lips of delicate mould—
  Somebody's darling is dying now.
Back from the beautiful blue-veined brow
  Brush the wandering waves of gold;
Cross his hands on his bosom now—
  Somebody's darling is still and cold.

Kiss him once for Somebody's sake;
  Murmur a prayer, soft and low;
One bright curl from the cluster take—
  They were Somebody's pride, you know.
Somebody's hand hath rested there;
  Was it a mother's, soft and white?
And have the lips of a sister fair
  Been baptized in those waves of light?

God knows best. He has Somebody's love;
  Somebody's heart enshrined him there;
Somebody wafted his name above,
  Night and morn, on the wings of prayer.
Somebody wept when he marched away,
  Looking so handsome, brave, and grand;
Somebody's kiss on his forehead lay;
  Somebody clung to his parting hand;—

Somebody's watching and waiting for him,
  Yearning to hold him again to her heart;
There he lies—with the blue eyes dim
  And the smiling, child-like lips apart.

Tenderly bury the fair young dead,
  Pausing to drop on his grave a tear;
Carve on the wooden slab at his head,
  "Somebody's darling slumbers here!"

6. ROSE O'NEAL GREENHOW—
"CHARLESTON IS IN GREAT DANGER"

For six months Mrs. Greenhow and her youngest daughter, Rose, had seen degradation and misery in Old Capitol Prison in Washington. In June 1862 she was released and banished beyond the Federal lines. Richmond gave her a warm welcome. President Davis called to convey his thanks for her aid to the cause. "But for you," he said, "there would have been no battle of Bull Run."

Rose Greenhow continued as agent for the Confederacy, with her activities kept shrouded in secrecy. She arrived in Charleston in the summer of 1863 to look for a blockade-runner to take her to Europe as a sort of unofficial ambassador. Because of the bombardment Charleston was undergoing, she got ship from Wilmington, North Carolina, on August 5, carrying letters to John Slidell and James M. Mason, the Confederate Commissioners in Paris and London. She had been posted up to the minute on the economic situation. From Bermuda to England she sailed on a British man-of-war.

After placing young Rose in the Convent of the Sacred Heart in Paris she devoted herself to her special mission. She was cordially received by Napoleon III and by Queen Victoria. She did what she could to help the Commissioners and Commander Maury, who was trying to get ships. Her book My Imprisonment and the First Year of Abolition Rule in Washington *was published by Richard Bentley in London and greeted in rather agreeable fashion. She saw something of Robert Browning, who was friendly to Lincoln, and of*

Thomas Carlyle, who was not. She used all her accomplished arts of persuasion in government circles. She was feted. Lord Granville proposed and she was of a mind to accept him.

The recognition which all the Confederate agents sought was really further away than ever after the reverses in 1863 and 1864, but Rose was still confident and highly exhilarated when she sailed for home, August 10, '64, on the blockade-runner Condor. The morning of October 1 her fast ship was sighted by the Niphon, a Federal gunboat, off Cape Fear. Rose insisted, against the advice of the commander of the Condor, on being rowed to shore. A high wave overturned the boat, the men in it reached shore, but Rose, weighted down with sovereigns, was drowned. According to legend she carried her secret code with the money around her waist. Her body was washed ashore and buried in Wilmington with military honors. The grave bears a simple marble cross on which is carved: "Mrs. Rose O'N. Greenhow, a bearer of dispatches to the Confederate Government, Erected by the Ladies Memorial Association."

Carl Sandburg [1] *describes her as "a tall brunette with slumberous eyes . . . with gaunt beauty, education, manners and resourceful speech. . . . Her proud loyalty to the South and her will and courage set her apart as a woman who would welcome death from a firing squad if it would serve her cause."*

From Charleston Mrs. Greenhow writes to President Davis, and to her old friend Colonel Alexander Robinson Boteler, former aide to General Jackson and later to General J.E.B. Stuart.

---

[1] *Abraham Lincoln, The War Years,* I, 326. New York: Harcourt, Brace & Company, Inc., 1939. For a full biography see *Rebel Rose,* by Ishbel Ross. New York: Harper & Brothers, 1954.

Charleston July 16th 1863

To the President
My dear Sir

I arrived here yesterday (Wednesday) at noon after rather a fatiguing travel from Richmond, not stopping by the wayside long enough to wash my face.

The only thing to mark the journey was the excitement and anxiety manifested by all classes to hear the news from Richmond, and especially from Lee's army, and many a sigh of relief was uttered when I spoke of his calm confident tone. I endeavored also to impress upon every one your conviction as to the necessity of reinforcing the army by the most rigorous means.

Just as I left Richmond news of the fall of Fort Hudson had been received which was confirmed by the intelligence of the wayside.

On reaching Wilmington the situation of Charleston became the engrossing subject of conversation and of interest, which has not diminished by the accounts received from time to time by passengers who got on, the principal portion of whom were from Charleston or the vicinity. Doubt and anxiety as to the result was the general tone of the people, and occasionally severe animadversions upon the conduct of the military affairs, especially instancing the supineness in the construction of the defense. These I mention—nor do I attach importance to criticism of this nature but rather to show you the temper & spirit of the people.

Soon after getting upon the territory of S.C. handbills were distributed along the route setting forth the eminent peril of Charleston and calling upon the people for 3000 negroes to work on the defenses. On nearing the City the booming of the heavy guns was distinctly heard, and I learned that the attack had been going on with but little intermission for several days. I omitted to mention also that the cars coming out were laden with cotton and in many instances carriages & horses also being sent to the interior, & hence the sense of insecurity which very generally prevails. . . .

The impression here that Charleston is in great danger is sustained by the opinion of the Military Authorities. I saw Genrl Beauregard who came to call upon me, and had a long conversation with him, and he is deeply impressed with the gravity of the position. He says that three months since he called upon the planters to send him 2000 negroes to work upon the fortification at Morris Island and other points and that he could only get one hundred, and that they would not listen to his representations as to the threatened danger.—That he considered the late successes against the Yankee iron clads as a grave misfortune, as the people in despite of his protests to the contrary have been lulled with a fatal security.—That the Yankees are in force upon a portion of Morris Island from which it will be impossible to dislodge them, as they are protected by the sea and marsh on one side and by their iron clads on the other.—That we must eventually abandon the portion of the island which we now occupy, but that he is erecting works on James Island which will command those works—which he will destroy—and render it impossible for them to reconstruct. He says the fall of Charleston now depends upon his ability to carry out his plans. . . .

News reached here this morning that Johnston is still near Jackson [Mississippi] altho fighting was going on.[1] Vizitelli Frank of the London News [2] who has been down there has just left me and given me some very interesting details of that region. He says

[1] "When Vicksburg fell, General Johnston's inadequate relieving force was between Grant's lines and the city of Jackson. Immediately upon the fall of the fortress, and even before Port Hudson surrendered, the indefatigable Grant sent Sherman to drive Johnston off. By July 9, with some slight fighting, Sherman arrived in front of Jackson, to which Johnston had retired, and sat down for serious attack against the city. On the sixteenth, after a week of scattered skirmishing, the Confederates for the second time gave up the capital of Mississippi." *The Story of the Confederacy*, by Robert Selph Henry, p. 293. Indianapolis: The Bobbs-Merrill Company, Inc., 1931.

[2] Frank Vizetelly represented the *Illustrated London News* in America during the war.

that heavy responsibility rests some where for the fall of Vicksburg—and he gives me all that he gathers, altho under the seal of confidence as I told him that I should also tell you. He says the universal criticism is that had the Commissariat done his duty and properly provisioned the place that the greatest military move of modern times would have been accomplished.—But that instead of buying beef, bacon, corn &c. when offered at the most ridiculously low prices and urged upon him he had said he knew what was needed and refused. I then asked is any blame attached to Pemberton? No, not after the place was invested he did all that mortal man could do. That before the surrender his garrison had been five days on quarter rations and five days on mule meat which was then exhausted. He summoned his officers and men and put it to them whether they should cut their way out—he himself favored this—but it was found upon examination that not one out of a 100 of his garrison were able to march the eight miles even without equipments of any kind so exhausted were they from starvation—hence the surrender. He says had they been able to have held out twenty days that Grant's army would have been precisely in the position of Vicksburg—as Johnson, Smith and others were surrounding the avenues of his supplies. . . .

He thinks our people unduly depressed now by the events at Vicksburg & is writing a series of articles. . . . He says he is very glad that I am going to England as he knows I can be useful, and gives me some very good letters. . . .

The iron clads have been coming nearer all day, and now are firing at Sumter and Wagner and Moultrie which are returning the compliment. I have just returned from St. Stevens tower where I had a good view, and the shells are flying thick and fast and their gun boats are blackening the water—altho they have not yet got in reach of our torpedoes. All the vessels which come into the harbor are seized by Beauregard and torpedoes attached.

It is impossible to attempt to run the blockade from here—as there are no vessels. Mr. Trenholm [1] has just called upon me and told me of the impossibility of getting out from this Port and tells me that there are a number of Gov. vessels now at Wilmington and advised me to go there so I have once more, my kind friend, to trouble you. Will you cause the necessary directions to be sent me here so that I may be enabled to go from Wilmington and together with the permit to ship cotton for my expenses, and if it be not possible to ship the whole amount required by any one vessel can be distributed amongst the number so as to enable me to take the necessary amount. I shall remain here until Wednesday or Thursday and shall hope to get a letter from you which I can frame as an heirloom for my children. . . .

ROSE O'NEAL GREENHOW

Mills House
Charleston South Carolina
July 20 1863

To Alexander Robinson Boteler

Here am I, my friend, en route for the old world spell bound by fearful interest here. Perhaps at no time could I have visited this city under circumstances of deeper interest. The enemy have put forth every effort to capture it—and the skill and daring of our people will be taxed to the utmost to repell the brutal hoards who are now hovering around. For the last week the enemy has been attacking our batteries—having made a lodgment on Morris Island—one end of which we hold and upon which is planted Battery Wagner. This point commands the city, and it is here that all their energies have been put forth to get possession of the Battery. On Saturday they commenced a combined naval and land attack, and continued un-

---

[1] George A. Trenholm, head of the firm of Fraser, Trenholm & Company in Charleston, who operated a fleet of blockade-runners.

til dawn to shell this Battery. I witnessed the whole from St. Michael's tower and it was fearfully grand. At 6 o'clock they attempted to storm the Battery, the attack coming from the point we hold. Fort Sumter then opened upon them, in anticipation of which her guns had been ranged in the morning with fearful precision. The attacking party were driven on with heavy loss—but after dark it was renewed four times, and each time with fresh troops. At one time they succeeded in making a lodgment in the works and planted their banner upon one and also holding a gun for some little time. Talliaferro [1] here ordered the Charleston Battalion to bring down the flag and dislodge them —he leading. Not a man of the enemy got out alive— so they paid dearly for a momentary triumph—they were finally repulsed with great slaughter—their killed and wounded number 1500, eight hundred have already been buried. Our own one hundred in killed & wounded. Yesterday all day they were burying their dead whilst we were busy preparing further entertainment for them. It is possible that they may get possession of Battery Wagner—but it will be a dear bought and bootless triumph to them as Beauregard has prepared a better entertainment for them which will not aid their digestion.

General Beauregard is fully equal to his great reputation and still holds his place as the great captain of the age. He has just written me a note reminding me that the battle Saturday was fought on the anniversary of Bull Run, 18th July [2]—and has certainly added another leaf to the laurel which then bound his brow.

I will direct this to Richmond as I see by the papers that the Yankees have again paid their compliments to your region.

I shall go to Wilmington as it is possible that I may not be able to run the blockade from this port—in

---

[1] Brigadier-General William B. Taliaferro.

[2] The allusion seems to be to the Bull Run campaign which began on the eighteenth. First Manassas was fought on the twenty-first.

which case you shall hear from me. I have not had a line from you for a long time. Rose is here. Altho severely disturbed by the mosquitoes, the weather is delightful. I wish with all my heart that you were here. The day I left R. I had an opportunity of saying a kind thing for you. . . .

I am very unhappy. I have just got from Beauregard a permit to visit Sumter, although the enemies guns within the last half hour are again roaring. With best regards believe me always your friend,

ROSE O'N GREENHOW

7. BELLE BOYD—"AN ARROW STRUCK THE WALL OPPOSITE MY WINDOW"

While Belle was in Old Capitol Prison she had become engaged to a fellow prisoner, a Lieutenant Mc-Vay, but he was not exchanged when she was. Time and separation led to its being forgotten by both. On Stonewall Jackson's advice she left Virginia and traveled over the South. In June 1863 she came back home to Martinsburg, was again arrested, conveyed to Washington and confined in Carroll Prison, not far from Old Capitol, where the following incidents occurred.

The typhoid fever which she incurred led to her release again on December 1. Again she was bundled off to Richmond with a dire injunction to stay out of Union lines forever. Her father died. For her health's sake doctors advised a trip to Europe. Then developed the climaxing romance. The blockade-runner Grey-hound on which she embarked was captured by the U.S.S. Connecticut. Ensign Samuel Hardinge of Brooklyn was put in charge of the prize crew. He and Belle fell desperately in love. After landing Belle made her way to Canada and from there to England. Sam, who had been arrested, tried and dismissed from the Navy for neglect of duty, followed her and they were married

*at St. James's Church in Piccadilly August 25, 1864.
Converted to the Confederacy by his bride, Sam attempted to get to Richmond, was seized by Union
officials, imprisoned at various points, grew seriously
ill, was freed, rejoined Belle in England, in a short
time died, and left "la belle Rebelle" a widow at
twenty-one.*

*Belle had sold her jewels and trousseau in her ef-
forts to help Sam. Her book* Belle Boyd: In Camp
and Prison *was published in London in 1865, and the
next year she returned to America to continue the
theatrical career which had begun in England. In 1869
she married John Hammond, who had been a British
Army officer; she divorced him in 1885 and married
Nathaniel Rue High of Toledo, Ohio. With him she
toured the country giving dramatic recitals of her life
as a Confederate spy. She died suddenly from a heart
attack on June 9, 1900, at Wisconsin Dells, Wisconsin, where she was buried.*

Carroll Prison
Washington
August, 1863

When I arrived in Washington, tired and worn, I
was immediately taken, not to my former quarters
[Old Capitol Prison], but to Carroll Prison. This large,
unpretending brick building, situated near the Old
Capitol, was formerly used as a hotel, under the name
of Carroll Place. But, since my first taste of prison life,
it had been converted into a receptacle for rebels,
prisoners of state, hostages, blockade-runners, smug-
glers, desperadoes, spies, criminals under sentence of
death, and, lastly, a large number of Federal officers
convicted of defrauding the Government. Many of
these last were army contractors and quartermasters.

At the guarded gates of this Yankee Bastile, I bade
adieu to my father; and once more iron bars shut me
off from the outer world, and from all that is dear in
this life. I was conducted to what was termed the
"room for distinguished guests"—the best room which

this place boasts, except some offices attached to the building. In this apartment had been held, though not for a long period of time, Miss Antonia F., Nannie T., with her aged mother, and many other ladies belonging to our best families in the South. Again my monotonous prison routine began.

Friends who chanced to pass the Carroll would frequently stop and nod in kindly recognition of some familiar face at the windows; unconscious that in so doing, they violated prison regulations. When noticed by the sentries, these good Samaritans were immediately "halted"; and, if riding or driving, were often made to dismount by the officious and impudent corporal of the guard, and forced to enter the bureau of the prison—there to remain until such time as it should please their tormentors to let them depart.

A few days after my arrival at the prison, I heard the "old familiar sound" of a grating instrument against the wall, apparently coming from the room adjoining mine. Whilst engaged in watching to see the exact portion of the wall whence it came, I observed the plaster give way, and next instant the point of a knife-blade was perceptible. I immediately set to work on my side, and soon, to my unspeakable joy, had formed a hole large enough for the passing of tightly rolled notes.

Ascertaining my unfortunate neighbors to be, beyond a doubt, "sympathizers," I was greatly relieved; for our prison was not without its system of espionage to trap the incautious. These neighbors were Messrs. Brookes, Warren, Stuart, and Williams; and from them I learnt that they had been here for nine months, having been captured whilst attempting to get South and join the Southern army.

But soon, alas! the little paper correspondence, that enlivened, whilst it lasted, a portion of my heavy time, was put to a stop by Mr. Lockwood, the officer of the keys, whose duty it was to secure our rooms, and who was always prying about when not otherwise engaged. Although it was well concealed on both sides, our impromptu post-office could not escape his Yankee cunning; and he at once had the gentlemen removed into the room beyond, and the mural disturbance closed up with plaster.

Several days subsequently I learned that I was to have a companion in a Miss Ida P., arrested on the charge of being a rebel mail-carrier. She did not remain here long, for, having given her parole . . . she was released. . . .

One evening, about nine o'clock, while seated at my window, I was singing "Take me back to my own sunny South," when quite a crowd of people collected on the opposite side of the street, listening. After I had ceased they passed on; and I could not help heaving a sigh as I watched their retreating figures. What would I not have given for liberty!

I was soon startled from this reverie by hearing something whiz by my head into the room and strike the wall beyond. At the moment I was alarmed; for my first impression was that some hireling of the Yankee Government, following the plan of Spanish countries, had endeavored to put an end to my life. I almost screamed with terror; and it was some minutes before I regained sufficient self-command to turn on the gas, so that, if possible, I might discover what missile had entered the room.

Glancing curiously round, I saw, to my astonishment, that it was an arrow which had struck the wall opposite my window; and fastened to this arrow was a letter; I immediately tore it open, and found that it contained the following words:—

"Poor girl, you have the deepest sympathy of all the best community in Washington City, and there are many who would lay down their lives for you, but they are powerless to act or aid you at present. *You have many very warm friends;* and we daily watch the journals to see if there is any news of you. If you will listen attentively to the instructions that I give you, you will be able to correspond with and hear from your friends outside.

"On Thursday and Saturdays, in the evening, just after twilight, I will come into the square opposite the prison. When you hear some one whistling ' 'Twas within a mile of Edinbro' town,' if alone and all is safe, lower the gas as a signal and leave the window. I will then shoot an arrow into your room, as I have done this evening, with a letter attached. Do not be alarmed, as I am a good shot.

"The manner in which you will reply to these messages will be in this way: Procure a large india-rubber ball; open it, and place your communication within it, written on foreign paper; then sew it together. On Tuesdays I shall come, and you will know of my presence by the same signal. Then throw the ball, with as much force as you can exert, across the street into the square, and trust to me, I will get it.

"Do not be afraid. *I am really your friend.*

"C.H."

For a long time I was in doubt as to the propriety or safety of replying to this note; for I naturally reasoned that it was some Yankee who was seeking to gain evidence against me. But prudence at last yielded to my womanly delight at the really romantic way of corresponding with an unknown who vowed he was my friend; and I decided on replying.

It was an easy thing for me to procure an india-rubber ball without subjecting myself to the least suspicion; and by this means I commenced a correspondence which I had no reason to regret; for whoever the mysterious personage may have been, he was, without doubt, honorable and sincere in his profession of sympathy.

Through him I became possessed of much valuable information regarding the movements of the Federals; and in this unique style of correspondence I have again and again received small Confederate flags, made by the ladies of Washington City, with which I was only too proud and happy to adorn my chamber. . . .

On several occasions I fastened one of these ensigns to a broomstick, in lieu of a flag staff, after which I returned to the back part of the room, out of sight of

the sentinel. In a short time this would attract his attention—for, when on watch, the sentinels generally were
gazing heavenwards, the only time, I really believe,
that such was the case—and he would roar out at the
top of his voice some such command as—

"Take in that —— flag, or I'll blow your ——
brains out!"

Of course I paid no attention to this, for I was out
of danger, when the command would generally be followed up by the report of a musket; and I have often
heard the thud of the Minié-ball as it struck the ceiling
or wall of my room.

Just after this episode I was taken dangerously ill
with typhoid fever. . . .

8. SUSAN BRADFORD—"MANY THINGS ARE BECOMING SCARCE"

It has been more than two years since Susan Brad-
ford, now a young lady of seventeen, witnessed the
signing of the Ordinance of Secession in the capital of
Florida. The enemy's flag now waves over many points
in her state—Jacksonville, St. Augustine, Appalachi-
cola, Pensacola and Fort Pulaski. Her father has given
his time, his money and the products of his land to
the Confederacy; he has brought wounded soldiers to
his home to be nursed and cared for by Susan and her
mother. The blockade of Florida ports has caused a
scarcity of many things, including salt.

Pine Hill Plantation
Leon County, Florida

September 1, 1863.—We are busy spinning, weaving, sewing and knitting, trying to get together clothing to keep our dear soldiers warm this winter. Brother
Junius writes that he has worn all his under garments
to shreds and wants to know if it would be possible to
get some flannel, or some kind of wool goods to make

him some new ones? We have tried but none can be had, so I am spinning some wool into knitting yarn and with big wooden needles I have I am going to knit both drawers and shirts for him. I am so impatient to get to work on them and see if my plan is feasible, that I spend all the time I can at the spinning wheel. I know the shirts can be knit, for I made some for father last winter which he found quite comfortable but I am somewhat doubtful as to the drawers. After awhile we will learn how to supply most of our needs.

Cousin Rob did not have a hat when he was getting ready for school, which opens today, so I plaited palmetto and sewed it into shape and Aunt Robinson, who knows everything, pressed it on a block and then I sewed a ribbon around it and there it was, a sure enough hat and very becoming. He sat near and admired the braid all the time I was making it. I had no shoes except some terribly rough ones that old Mr. McDermid made and Cousin Rob tanned some squirrel skins and made me a pair of really beautiful shoes, nice enough to wear with my one and only silk dress. This dress, you must know, is "made of Mammy's old one" like Jim Crack Corn's coat—Little Diary, I am afraid you do not know very much of Mother Goose.

October 27, 1863.—We went to the salt works today and, though I am tired and dirty and have no good place to write, I am going to try to tell you about it.

A year ago salt began to get scarce but the people only had to economize in its use, but soon there was no salt and then Father got Cousin Joe Bradford to come down from Georgia and take charge of some salt works he was having installed on the coast. He had plenty of hands from the plantation but they had to have an intelligent head and then, too, it is a rather dangerous place to work, for the Yankee gunboats . . . may try shelling the works.

Though they have been in operation quite awhile this is my first visit. Father brought us with him and we will stay three days, so he can see just how they are getting on. We are to sleep in a tent, on a ticking filled with pine straw. It will be a novel experience.

I am so interested in seeing the salt made from the water. The great big sugar kettles are filled full of water and fires made beneath the kettles. They are a long time heating up and then they boil merrily. Ben and Tup and Sam keep the fires going, for they must not cool down the least little bit. A white foam comes at first and then the dirtiest scum you ever saw bubbles and dances over the surface, as the water boils away it seems to get thicker and thicker, at last only a wet mass of what looks like sand remains. This they spread on smooth oaken planks to dry. In bright weather the sun does the rest of the work of evaporation, but if the weather is bad fires are made just outside of a long, low shelter, where the planks are placed on blocks of wood. The shelter keeps off the rain and the fires give out heat enough to carry on the evaporation. The salt finished in fair weather is much whiter and nicer in every way than that dried in bad weather, but this dark salt is used to salt meat or to pickle pork. I think it is fine of Father to do all this. It is very troublesome and it takes nine men to do the work, besides Cousin Joe's time; and Father does not get any pay whatever for the salt he makes.

We expected to have a grand time swimming and fishing. We are both good swimmers, but Father and Cousin Joe will not allow us to go outside of this little cove. Yankee gun-boats have been sighted once lately and there is no knowing when the salt works may be attacked. . . .

9. PARTHENIA ANTOINETTE HAGUE—
DEPENDENT ON OUR OWN RESOURCES

Miss Hague, a native of Harris County, Georgia, was a teacher on a plantation near Eufaula in southern Alabama. Deprived of customary supplies and con-

veniences of daily life by the effectiveness of the Federal blockade, the plantation was forced to find all sorts of expedients and substitutes.

Most of the women of southern Alabama had small plots of ground for cultivating the indigo bush, for making "indigo blue," or "indigo mud," as it was sometimes called. The indigo weed also grew abundantly in the wild state in our vicinage. Those who did not care to bother with indigo cultivation used to gather, from the woods, the weed in the wild state when in season. Enough of the blue was always made either from the wild or cultivated indigo plant. We used to have our regular "indigo churnings," as they were called. When the weed had matured sufficiently for making the blue mud, which was about the time the plant began to flower, the plants were cut close to the ground, our steeping vats were closely packed with the weed, and water enough to cover the plant was poured in. The vat was then left eight or nine days undisturbed for fermentation, to extract the dye. Then the plant was rinsed out, so to speak, and the water in the vat was churned up and down with a basket for quite a while; weak lye was added as a precipitate, which caused the indigo particles held in solution to fall to the bottom of the vat; the water was poured off, and the "mud" was placed in a sack and hung up to drip and dry. It was just as clear and bright a blue as if it had passed through a more elaborate process.

. The woods, as well as being the great storehouse for all our dye-stuffs, were also our drug stores. The berries of the dogwood-tree were taken for quinine, as they contained the alkaloid properties of cinchona and Peruvian bark. A soothing and efficacious cordial for dysentery and similar ailments was made from blackberry roots; but ripe persimmons, when made into a cordial, were thought to be far superior to blackberry roots. An extract of the barks of the wild cherry, dogwood, poplar, and wahoo trees were used for chills and agues. For coughs and all lung diseases a syrup made with the leaves and roots of the mullein plant, globe flower, and wild-cherry tree bark was thought to be infallible. Of course the castor-bean plant was gathered in the wild state in the forest, for making castor oil.

Many also cultivated a few rows of poppies in their gardens to make opium, from which our laudanum was created; and this at times was very needful. The manner of extracting opium from poppies was of necessity crude. The heads or bulbs of the poppies were plucked when ripe, the capsules pierced with a large-sized sewing-needle, and the bulbs placed in some small vessel (a cup or saucer would answer) for the opium gum to exude and to become inspissated by evaporation. The soporific influence of this drug was not excelled by that of the imported articles.

Bicarbonate of soda, which had been in use for raising bread before the war, became "a thing of the past" soon after the blockade began; but it was not long ere some one found out that the ashes of corncobs possessed the alkaline property essential for raising dough. Whenever "soda" was needed, corn was shelled, care being taken to select all the red cobs, as they were thought to contain more carbonate of soda than white cobs. When the cobs were burned in a clean swept place, the ashes were gathered up and placed in a jar or jug, and so many measures of water were poured in, according to the quantity of ashes. When needed for bread-making, a teaspoonful or tablespoonful of the alkali was used to the measure of flour or meal required. . . .

All in our settlement learned to card, spin, and weave. Our days of novitiate were short. We soon became very apt at knitting and crocheting useful as well as ornamental woolen notions, such as capes, sacques, vandykes, shawls, gloves, socks, stockings, and men's suspenders. The clippings of lambs' wool were especially used by us for crocheting or knitting shawls, gloves, capes, sacques, and hoods. Our needles for such knitting were made of seasoned hickory or oakwood a foot long, or even longer. To have the hanks spotted or variegated, they were tightly braided or plaited, and so dyed; when the braids were unfolded a beautiful dappled color would result. Handsome mittens were knit or crocheted of the same lambs' wool dyed jet black, gray, garnet, or whatever color was preferred; a bordering of vines, with green leaves and rosebuds of bright colors, was deftly knitted in on the edge and top of the gloves. . . .

Our shoes, particularly those of women and children, were made of cloth, or knit. Some one had learned to knit slippers, and it was not long before most of the women of our settlement had a pair of slippers on the knitting needles. They were knit of our homespun thread, either cotton or wool, which was, for slippers, generally dyed a dark brown, gray, or black. When taken off the needles, the slippers or shoes were lined with cloth of suitable texture. The upper edges were bound with strips of cloth, of color to blend with the hue of the knit work. . . .

Sometimes we put on the soles ourselves by taking wornout shoes, whose soles were thought sufficiently strong to carry another pair of uppers, ripping the soles off, placing them in warm water to make them more pliable and to make it easier to pick out all the old stitches, and then in the same perforations stitching our knit slippers or cloth-made shoes. We also had to cut out soles for shoes from our hometanned leather, with the soles of an old shoe as our pattern, and with an awl perforate the sole for sewing on the upper. . . . We used to hold our selfmade shoes at arm's length and say, as they were inspected: "What is the blockade to us, so far as shoes are concerned, when we can not only knit the uppers but cut the soles and stitch them on? Each woman and girl her own shoemaker; away with bought shoes; we want none of them!" But alas, we really knew not how fickle a few months would prove that we were. . . .

We became quite skilled in making designs of palmetto and straw braiding and plaiting for hats. Fans, baskets, and mats we made of the braided palmetto and straw also. Then there was the "bonnet squash," known also as the "Spanish dish-rag," that was cultivated by some for making bonnets and hats for women and children. Such hats presented a fine appearance, but they were rather heavy. Many would make the frame for their bonnets or hats, then cover it with the small white feathers and down of the goose, color bright red with the juice of poke berries, or blue with indigo mud, some of the larger feathers, and on a small wire form a wreath or plume with bright-colored and white feathers blended together; or, if wire was convenient, a fold or two of heavy cloth, or paper doubled, was used to sew the combination of feathers for wreath, plume, or rosette. . . .

One of our most difficult tasks was to find a good substitute for coffee. This palatable drink, if not a real necessary of life, is almost indispensable to the enjoyment of a good meal, and some Southerners took it three times a day. Coffee soon rose to thirty dollars per pound; from that it went to sixty and seventy dollars per pound. Good workmen received thirty dollars per day; so it took two days' hard labor to buy one pound of coffee, and scarcely any could be had even at that fabulous price. Some imagined themselves much better in health for the absence of coffee, and wondered why they had ever used it at all, and declared it good for nothing any way; but "Sour grapes" would be the reply for such as they. Others saved a few handfuls of coffee, and used it on very important occasions, and then only as an extract, so to speak, for flavoring substitutes for coffee.

There were those who planted long rows of the okra plant on the borders of their cotton or corn fields, and cultivated this with the corn and cotton. The seeds of this, when mature, and nicely browned, came nearer in flavor to the real coffee than any other substitute I now remember. Yam potatoes used to be peeled, sliced thin, cut into small squares, dried, and then parched brown; they were thought to be next best to okra for coffee. Browned wheat, meal, and burnt corn made passable beverages; even meal-bran was browned and used for coffee if other substitutes were not obtainable.

We had several substitutes for tea. Prominent among these substitutes were raspberry leaves. Many during the blockade planted and cultivated the raspberry-vine all around their garden palings, as much for tea as the berries for jams or pies; these leaves were considered the best substitute for tea. The leaves of the blackberry bush, huckleberry leaves, and the leaves of the holly-tree when dried in the shade, also made a palatable tea. /

Persimmons dried served for dates. . . .

In place of kerosene for lights, the oil of cotton seed and ground peas, together with the oil of compressed lard, was used, and served well the need of the times. For lights we had also to fall back on moulding candles, which had long years lain obsolete. When beeswax was plentiful it was mixed with tallow for moulding candles. Long rows of candles so moulded would be hung on the lower limbs of wide-spreading oaks, where, sheltered by the dense foliage from the direct rays of the sun, they would remain suspended day and night until they were bleached as white as the sperm candles we had been wont to buy, and almost as transparent as wax candles. When there was no oil for the lamps or tallow for moulding candles, which at times befell our households, mother-wit would suggest some expedient by which the intricate problem of light could be solved.

One evening at a neighbor's, where we had gone to tea, when we took our seats at the supper-table we were diverted by the lights we were to eat by, the like of which, up to that time, we had not seen, nor even thought of.

In the absence of any of the ordinary materials for lighting, the good woman of the house had gone to the woods and gathered a basketful of round globes

of the sweet-gum tree. She had taken two shallow
bowls and put some lard, melted, into them, then
placed two or three of the sweet-gum balls in each of
the vessels, which, soon becoming thoroughly satu-
rated with the melted lard, gave a fairylike light, floating round in the shallow vessels of oil like stars.

At other times rude lamps or candles were impro-
vised, anything but attractive in appearance, though
the light was fairly bright. Medium-sized bottles were
taken, and several strands of spun thread twisted together to form a wick two or three yards long were
well steeped in beeswax and tallow, and coiled around
the bottle from base to neck closely and evenly. When
ready for lighting, one or more of the coils of thread
would be loosed from the bottle, raised above the
mouth an inch or so, and pressed with the thumb to
the neck of the bottle. When the wick had burned to
the bottle's mouth, the same process of uncoiling and
pressing the wick to the bottle would be repeated.
This gave a steady flame. When beeswax could not be
had, tallow was used for steeping the strands.

Sewing societies were formed in every hamlet, as well
as in our cities, to keep the soldiers of the Confederacy clothed as best we could. They met once every
week, at some lady's house, if it was in the country.
To such societies all the cloth that could be spared
from each household was given and made into soldiers' garments. . . .

In many settlements there were spinning "bees."
Wheels, cards, and cotton were all hauled in a wagon
to the place appointed. On the way, as often as not, a
long flexible twig would be cut from the woods, and
attached to one of the spinning wheels; from the top of
such flagstaff would play loosely to the wind, and jolts
of the wagon, a large bunch of lint cotton, as our ensign. Sometimes as many as six or eight wheels would
be whirring at the same time in one house. . . . We
were drawn together in a closer union, a tenderer feeling of humanity linking us all together, both rich and

poor; from the princely planter, who could scarce get off his wide domains in a day's ride, and who could count his slaves by the thousand, down to the humble tenants of the log-cabin on rented or leased land.

10. SARA RICE PRYOR—CHRISTMAS IN PETERSBURG

"Agnes's" friend Sara Pryor was the daughter of the Reverend Samuel Blair Rice of Halifax County, Virginia, who became a chaplain in the Confederate Army. At eighteen she married Roger A. Pryor, who came from the vicinity of Petersburg. In 1851 they moved to Washington, where Mr. Pryor was successively on the staff of the Union, the South and the States. In 1855 he went to Greece as a special commissioner. He was elected to Congress in 1859, reelected in 1860, resigned March 3, 1861, to join the Confederacy.

He stood beside the gun at Charleston that fired the first shot of the war, enlisted and became colonel of the 3rd Virginia. After First Manassas Sara determined to follow the regiment. She was in Richmond during the Seven Days' battles, working as a volunteer nurse in the hospitals. She was with Roger at Culpeper, and in the winter of 1862 lived near his camp on the Blackwater. General Joe Johnston had made Roger a brigadier-general for bravery on the battlefield of Williamsburg, but feeling that he was a brigadier without a brigade he gave up his rank on August 18, 1863, and served as a special courier with Fitzhugh Lee's cavalry. From the fall of 1863 on, Sara was in Petersburg.

Having no longer a home of my own, it was decided that I should go to my people in Charlotte County, Virginia. One of my sons, Theo, and two of my little daughters were already there, and there I expected to remain until the end of the war.

But repeated attempts to reach my country home resulted in failure. Marauding parties and guerillas were flying all over the country. There had been alarm at a bridge over the Staunton near the Oaks, and the old men and boys had driven away the enemy. I positively *could* not venture alone.

So it was decided that I should return to my husband's old district, to Petersburg, and there find board in some private family.

I reached Petersburg in the autumn [1863] and wandered about for days seeking refuge in some household. Many of my old friends had left town. Strangers and refugees had rented the houses of some of these, while others were filled with the homeless among their own kindred. There was no room anywhere for me, and my small purse was growing so slender that I became anxious. Finally my brother-in-law offered me an overseer's house on one of his "quarters." The small dwelling he placed at my disposal was to be considered temporary only; some one of his town houses would soon be vacant. When I drove out to the little house, I found it hardly better than a hovel. We entered a rude, unplastered kitchen, the planks of the floor loose and wide apart, the earth beneath plainly visible. There were no windows in this smoke-blackened kitchen. A door opened into a tiny room with a fireplace, window, and out-door of its own; and a short flight of stairs led to an unplastered attic, so that the little apartment was entered by two doors and a staircase. It was already cold, but we had to beat a hasty retreat and sit outside while a colored boy made a "smudge" in the house to dislodge the wasps that had tenanted it for many months. My brother had lent me bedding for the overseer's pine bedstead and the low trundle-bed underneath. The latter, when drawn out at night, left no room for us to stand. When that was done, we had to go to bed. For furniture we had only two or three wooden chairs and a small table. There were no curtains, neither carpet nor rugs, no china. There was wood at the woodpile, and a little store of meal and rice, with a small bit of bacon in the overseer's grimy closet. This was to be my winter home.

Petersburg was already virtually in a state of siege. Not a tithe of the food needed for its army of refugees could be brought to the city. Our highway, the river, was filled, except for a short distance, with Federal gunboats. The markets had long been closed. The stores of provisions had been exhausted, so that a grocery could offer little except a barrel or two of molasses made from the domestic sorghum sugar-cane—an acrid and unwholesome sweet used instead of sugar for drink with water or milk, and for eating with bread. The little boys at once began to keep house. They valiantly attacked the woodpile, and found favor in the eyes of Mary and the man, whom I never knew as other than "Mary's husband." He and Mary were left in charge of the quarter and had a cabin near us.

I had no books, no newspapers, no means of communicating with the outside world; but I had one neighbor, Mrs. Laighton, a daughter of Winston Henry, granddaughter of Patrick Henry. She lived near me with her husband—a Northern man. Both were very cultivated, very poor, very kind. Mrs. Laighton, as Lucy Henry,—a brilliant young girl,—had been one of the habitués of the Oaks. We had much in common, and her kind heart went out in love and pity for me.

She taught me many expedients: that to float tea on the top of a cup of hot water would make it "go farther" than steeped in the usual way; also that the herb, "life everlasting," which grew in the fields, would make excellent yeast, having somewhat the property of hops; and that the best substitute for coffee was not the dried cubes of sweet potato, but parched corn or parched meal, making a nourishing drink. And Mrs. Laighton kept me a "living soul" in other and higher ways. She reckoned intellectual ability the greatest of God's gifts, raising us so far above the petty need of

material things that we could live in spite of their loss.
Her talk was a tonic to me. It stimulated me to play
my part with courage, seeing I had been deemed
worthy, by the God who made me, to suffer in this
sublime struggle for liberty.

I had not my good Eliza Page this winter. She had
fallen ill. I had a stout little black girl, Julia, as my
only servant; but Mary had a friend, a "corn-field
hand," "Anarchy," who managed to help me at odd
hours. Mrs. Laighton sent me every morning a print
of butter as large as a silver dollar, with two or three
perfect biscuits, and sometimes a bowl of persimmons
or stewed dried peaches. She had a cow, and churned
every day, making her biscuits of the buttermilk, which
was much too precious to drink.

A great snow-storm overtook us a day or two before Christmas. My little boys kindled a roaring fire
in the cold, open kitchen, roasted chestnuts, and set
traps for the rabbits and "snowbirds" which never entered them. They made no murmur at the bare Christmas; they were loyal little fellows to their mother. My
day had been spent in mending their garments,—making them was a privilege denied me, for I had no materials. I was not "all unhappy!" The rosy cheeks at
my fireside consoled me for my privations, and something within me proudly rebelled against weakness or
complaining.

The flakes were falling thickly at midnight, when I
suddenly became very ill. I sent out for Mary's husband and bade him gallop in to Petersburg, three miles
distant, and fetch me Dr. Withers. I was dreadfully ill
when he arrived—and as he stood at the foot of my
bed I said to him: "It doesn't matter much for me,
Doctor! But my husband will be grateful if you keep
me alive."

When I awoke from a long sleep, he was still standing at the foot of my bed where I had left him—it
seemed to me ages ago! I put out my hand and it
touched a little warm bundle beside me. God had given
me a dear child!

The doctor spoke to me gravely and most kindly. "I must leave you now," he said, "and alas! I cannot come again. There are so many, so many sick. Call all your courage to your aid. Remember the pioneer women, and all they were able to survive. This woman," indicating Anarchy, "is a field-hand, but she is a mother, and she has agreed to help you during the Christmas holidays—her own time. And now, God bless you, and goodby!"

I soon slept again—and when I awoke the very Angel of Strength and Peace had descended and abode with me. I resolved to prove to myself that if I was called to be a great woman, I *could* be a great woman. Looking at me from my bedside were my two little boys. They had been taken the night before across the snow-laden fields to my brother's house, but had risen at daybreak and had "come home to take care" of me!

My little maid Julia left me Christmas morning. She said it was too lonesome, and her "mistis" always let her choose her own places. I engaged "Anarchy" at twenty-five dollars a week for all her nights. But her hands, knotted by work in the fields, were too rough to touch my babe. I was propped upon pillows and dressed her myself, sometimes fainting when the exertion was over.

I was still in my bed three weeks afterwards, when one of my boys ran in, exclaiming in a frightened voice, "Oh, mamma, an old gray soldier is coming in!"

He stood—this old gray soldier—and looked at me, leaning on his sabre.

"Is this the reward my country gives me?" he said; and not until he spoke did I recognize my husband. Turning on his heel, he went out, and I heard him call:—

"John! John! Take those horses into town and sell them! Do not return until you do—sell them for anything! Get a cart and bring butter, eggs, and everything you can find for Mrs. Pryor's comfort."

He had been with Fitz Lee on that dreadful tramp

through the snow after Averill.[1] He had suffered cold
and hunger, had slept on the ground without shelter,
sharing his blanket with John. He had used his own
horses, and now if the government needed him the
government might mount him. He had no furlough, and
soon reported for duty; but not before he had moved
us, early in January, into town—one of my brother-
in-law's houses having been vacated at the beginning
of the year. John knew his master too well to construe
him literally, and had reserved the fine gray, Jubal
Early, for his use. That I might not again fall into the
sad plight in which he had found me, he purchased
three hundred dollars in gold, and instructed me to
prepare a girdle to be worn all the time around my
waist, concealed by my gown. The coins were quilted
in; each had a separate section to itself, so that with
scissors I might extract one at a time without disturbing the rest. . . .

11. BELLE EDMONDSON—SMUGGLING FROM MEMPHIS

*At eighteen Belle Edmondson was living with her
family at their plantation house near Nonconnah in
Shelby County, Tennessee, where her father had large
holdings of land and slaves. A war romance ended
sadly when her Confederate soldier boy was transferred
to Mobile and transferred his affections. Perhaps because of this unhappy love affair, Belle, according to*

---

[1] General W. W. Averell on December 8, 1863, started a
long raid through the Allegheny Mountains and, striking the
supply line of the Virginia & Tennessee Railroad at Salem,
Virginia, on the sixteenth, destroyed a store of cereals and
wrecked bridges and track. General Robert E. Lee was so
disturbed that he gave up the idea of spending Christmas with
his family. General Jubal Early sent General Fitzhugh Lee in
pursuit of Averell, but bad weather prevented his scotching
the foe. See D. S. Freeman, *R. E. Lee*, III, 215; *Lee's Lieutenants*, III, 325.

*family tradition, volunteered as a secret agent for the
Confederacy. After near-by Memphis was occupied
by Federal troops in June 1862, she engaged in the
dangerous business of smuggling contraband between
the lines. Her father served as a volunteer scout and
her two brothers were with General Forrest.*

*During the war years Belle kept a diary which is a
lively account of life on the plantation and her activities in occupied Memphis, the center of drug and cotton smuggling.*

near Nonconnah

March   Sunday 13   1864

Today is the first anniversary of the happiest day
in my life—just one short year ago, twas then on Friday morning, he came for me to walk on the hill to
listen to the echoes of our triumph at Fort Pemberton
(Greenwood) [1]—I rushed on to meet my fate, oh!
God that it had never overtaken me—yet tis the
brightest spot in my sad life—his love. . . . Oh! who
in the course of his life has not felt some joy without
a security, and without the certainty of a morrow!
Time hath power over hours, none over the soul. Time
had power over his heart, yet none over my true and
holy love. Today he woos the daughter of a more sunny clime—Miss Sallie Anderson of Mobile, may she
never know the pangs of a deceived heart. . . .

March   Monday 14   1864

. . . We have been delighted by the visit of a Rebel
Major, Maj. Allen, who spent the day with us. . . .
Maj. A. went down to Col. Perkins to stay until Thursday, when I will have returned from Memphis—having
attended to his wants. . . . we have a pleasant evening—music, conversation, &c. Anna Nelson and I have
made our arrangements to go into Memphis tomorrow
and not return till next day. Oh! Lord, deliver me from

[1] On March 11, 1863, this small work at the head of the
Yazoo River beat off a Federal attack.

getting in any trouble with the Yanks, this will be a
hard trip, I have a great risk to run. . . .

March Tuesday 15 1864

Anna Nelson and I started to Memphis about 9
o'clock, suffered very much with the cold, stopped at
Mr. Roberts to warm—from here we passed through
the Pickets to the Pigeon Roost Road—found Mr. Harbut's after much searching—did not reach Memphis
until 10 o'clock, left our horse & buggy at Mr. Barbier's, went up town—and not one thing would the
Merchants sell us, because we did not live in their
lines. I consoled myself with a wheel that could not
turn—could not spin—went to see my friend Mrs.
Facklen, she went up town and bought the things for
me—poor deluded fools, I would like to see them
thwart a Southerner in such an undertaking as I had.
Spent a very pleasant evening with Mrs. Facklen's
family—all Rebels, and we talked just as we please!

Mrs. F. and I did not go to sleep until 2 o'c, this being the first time I had seen her since she returned
from Dixie, I have finished all my provisions, and will
have nothing to do tomorrow except fixing my things
for smuggling.

March Wednesday 16 1864

Went up Street directly after Breakfast to finish a
little job I forgot on yesterday. At one o'clock Mrs.
Facklen, Mrs. Kirk and I began to fix my articles for
smuggling, we made a balmoral of the Grey cloth for
uniform, pin'd the Hats to the inside of my hoops—
tied the boots with a strong list, letting them fall directly in front, the cloth having monopolized the back
& the Hats the side—All my letters, brass buttons,
money, &c in my bosom—left at 2 o'clock to meet
Anna at Mr. Barbier's—started to walk, impossible
that—hailed a hack—rather suspicious of it, afraid of
small-pox, weight of contrabands ruled—jumped in,
with orders for a hurried drive to Cor Main & Vance
—arrived, found Anna not ready, had to wait for her

until 5 o'clock, very impatient—started at last—arrived at Pickets, no trouble at all, although I suffered horribly in anticipation of trouble. Arrived at home at dusk, found Mr. Wilson & Harbut, gave them late papers and all news. Mrs. Harbut here to meet her Bro. Bro't Mr. Wilson a letter from Home in Ky. Worn out. 8 yds. Long cloth, 2 Hats, 1 pr Boots, 1 doz. Buttons, letters, &c. 2 Cords, 8 tassels. . . .

March   Wednesday 23   1864

Tate & I went to Memphis this morning bright and early. Stopped at Mrs. Apperson's first—from there to Cousin Frazer. Tate met me at Mrs. Worsham's room. We then went up street, walked until three o'clock, attended to all affairs entrusted to our care, ready to leave at half past three. All of the Yankee Cavalry moving, destination not known—could hear no particulars. Think they are going after Forrest, who we think is on his way to Kentucky.[1] . . . We came through white Picketts. I think we will not try them again—the Negroes are ten times more lenient. We came by Wash Taylor's, got two hats for soldiers—came through Yankee Camp. If the Lord forgives me I will never do it again. Yankee soldier drove our horse in Nonconnah for us—seemed to be a gentleman, for which we were very grateful. Found Mr. Harbut awaiting our report. Mr. John & Henry Nelson & Mr. Harbut took Tea with us. Jim & Mr. Pugh completed the list for a nice Rebel meeting. Brought a great deal through lines this eve—Yankee pickets took our papers.

March   Wednesday 30   1864

It seems I can never go to Memphis without some disagreeable arrangements and sayings. I was greatly disappointed in my trip. Tate and I went together. I stopped at Mrs. Facklen's on Union St. She went on up to Cousin Frazer's in the buggy. Mrs. Facklen and

---

[1] Forrest was indeed making for Paducah, Kentucky.

Mrs. Kirk in great distress, old Hurlbut [1] gave her ten days to abandon her house. She took an old Yankee Officer, his Wife & two children to board with her, hoping he would recall the heartless order to make her and her little children homeless. I did not smuggle a thing through the lines except some letters. Mr. Tommery gave me a permit to bring 2 Gals Whiskey and 5 bbs Tobacco—which I got home safely.

March   Thursday 31   1864

Jim & Mr. Pugh are trying to find a way to join Forrest. They had not been gone more than five minutes when four Yankees, belonging to 6th. Ill. Cavalry came riding in, asked if we had seen any Confederates. Of course we said no. I think they came to steal, but we were polite to them, and they left—only wanted some milk, which they got. Tate & Nannie went to town today. Mr. Perryman got them a pass—they got home safe, but saw Anna Nelson and Sallie Hilderbrand arrested and carried back with a Negro guard, for smuggling a pair of boots.

April   Tuesday 5   1864

I was awakened at daylight by a servant with a note from Miss Hudson who has succeeded in getting all she wants out of Memphis, and promised to take the things I had for Mrs. Hudson to her. I regreted not having all the things through the lines, but sent what I had.

April   Thursday 7   1864

Tate and Nannie went to the Picketts this morning, were turned back, the lines closed. Capt. Barber & Mr. Kirk cannot get their things. I had not the heart to see them disappointed, so rob'd old Mr. McMahon of 2d. Mo. Mr. Kirk took his Boots, Capt. Barber his uniform. I will get him more through the lines before he comes for them. Nannie &c very busy sewing all

[1] The Union general Stephen A. Hurlbut, in command at Memphis.

day. Nannie & I made two shirts for a Kentucky'n who is so far from home, and no one to take an interest in his need. I sent him a pair of Pants too.

April   Monday 11   1864

Helen, Father, the children and myself spent the day alone, the rest all in Memphis. Joanna came home, succeeded in getting Father's permit for supplies, brought no news. Miss Perdue & Noble banished, leave tomorrow. I expect I will be next. I was so happy to hear Miss Em is expected today, my future plans depend upon her advice. Mr. McMahon, 2d. Mo. Cavalry came this eve. I was so disappointed about letting his things go—though he seemed perfectly satisfied, as he had replenished his wardrobe from Yankee Prison in Grierson's raid.[1] He has been quite sick, is now on his way to Camp at Jackson, Tennessee. He has his fine horse again. God grant him a safe journey, for he is a splendid Soldier.

April   Wednesday 13   1864

This has indeed been an exciting day, heavy firing all last night & this morning. Forrest has captured Fort Pillow.[2] The firing we heard was between the Fort and Gun Boats. The Yanks in Memphis are frightened to death.

April   Thursday 14   1864

Father heard a rumor [3] this evening that our Virginia

[1] At the beginning of the Vicksburg campaign a raid by Grierson's Federal cavalry played havoc with railroads and supply depots in Mississippi.

[2] On April 12, 1864, General N. B. Forrest and his swift-moving troops stormed and captured Fort Pillow, on the river forty miles north of Memphis. It was a bloody affair, and Forrest was accused of having committed an atrocity, but no clear case was ever made against him and the "massacre" seems rather to have been due to an overstubborn defense, unskillfully conducted.

[3] A false report.

General (Robert Lee) had ruined the left wing of
Grant's Army. God grant it may be so. Grant is a fool
to think he can whip Gen. Lee. Gen. Forrest still at
Fort Pillow last account we had.

April   Saturday 16   1864
Another day of excitement—about 30 Yanks passed
early this morning, only six came in for their breakfast. They did not feed their horses—they behaved very
well, and seemed to be gentlemen, in fact we so seldom
see gentlemen among the Yankees that we can appreciate them when they are met with.

April   Tuesday 19   1864
No Yanks today. No news from Forrest. We have
not seen any one today, or heard a word of news.
Joanna and Bettie went to Memphis today. Sallie went
with them—got a Permit. I am going to try my luck in
the city tomorrow. Father is not willing I should go.

April   Wednesday 20   1864
Tate and I arrived in Memphis quite early, put the
horse up, then walked up street together. Met Nannie
and Anna Perkins. Nannie gave me two letters, one
from St. Lewis to Mr. Welch, an exile in La Grange,
Georgia, one from New York from a stranger, asking
assistance through me to communicate with Mrs. Van
Hook at Selma, Alabama. I received a letter from Maj.
Price at Selma, by Mrs. Flaherty. I dined with Mrs.
Jones, and Mrs. Kirk—went round for Hat after dinner,
she went with me to see Capt. Woodward, to know
what I must do in regard to an order which I heard was
issued for my arrest. He advised me to keep very quiet
until he could see the Provost Marshall and learn something in regard to it.

April   Thursday 21   1864
I went round according to appointment, met Capt.
Woodward at 11 o'clock. Col. Patterson went with me.
Capt. W. had not seen the Provost Marshall. He went

as soon as I left, came round to Mrs. Facklen's after dinner, and brought bad news—though having approached Capt. Williams as aid for a heroine of Jericho, he could not treat me as the order read—it was issued from old Hurlbut. I was to be arrested and carried to Alton on first Boat that passed—for carrying letters through the lines, and smuggling, and aiding the Rebellion in every way in my power—he sent me word I must not think of attending Jennie Eave's wedding, or go out of doors at all, he would be compelled to arrest me if it came to him Officially, but as my Father was a Royal Arch Mason, and I a Mason, he would take no steps, if I would be quiet. . . .

12. MARY BYSON—"SISTER SUSAN HAS LOST THREE SONS"

Mary Byson of Red River, Texas, and her family, though far from the scene of battles, have not been spared their tragic consequences. Her correspondence with her friend Margaret Butler of Louisiana continued through the war years.

Red River Texas March 21/64

My dear Margaret

The Federals have not come to this part of the country though we have been expecting them all last fall. Our army may be able to keep them out this spring, at least I hope so. Horse-stealing and murder are going on in this part of the country—supposed to be done by some Missouri Bushwhackers who came here last fall but it is thought some of the people in the country are concerned in it.

Times are hard but I do not think we ought to complain. We have plenty of meat and bread and flour and sugar for the next year. I have been wearing homespun dresses this winter to save my calico and knit my stockings keeping my bought ones for summer. I am in hopes the war will end this year. Sister Susan has lost three sons since the war commenced. . . .

We hear of news but do not know when to believe any as so much is only rumor. . . .

Ever yours affectionately
M. BYSON

13. SUSAN BRADFORD—"TODAY I HAVE NO SHOES"

To find a substitute for shoe leather taxed the ingenuity of many a Southern woman. Some made shoes from old felt hats; some knit them. Sometimes ladies appeared with their feet wrapped in lint. Mrs. Pryor, in Petersburg, made shoes from an old carpet, and Judith McGuire, in Richmond, made them from parts of a canvas sail rescued from a vessel wrecked on the James River. Parthenia Hague has told what she did. Her cousin Rob had tanned some squirrel skins for Susan Bradford. Now Susan has another bright idea.

After the war she married Nicholas Ware Epps, a young Confederate soldier. They lived in Tallahassee and enjoyed a long, happy life together. In her late years she produced two books, The Negro of the Old South *and* Verses from Florida. *In 1926 her war diary,* Through Some Eventful Years, *was published. She died on July 2, 1942, in her ninety-sixth year, survived by three daughters, Susan, Alice and Martha.*

Pine Hill Plantation
Leon County, Florida

April 7th, 1864.—Today I have no shoes to put on. All my life I have never wanted to go bare-footed, as most Southern children do. The very touch of my naked foot to the bare ground made me shiver. Lula my Mammy scolds me about this—even yet she claims the privilege of taking me to task when she thinks I need it.

"Look here, chile," she says, "don't you know you
is made outen the dus' er de earth? Don't you onder-
stand dat when you is dead you is gwine back ter dat
dus'?"

"Yes, Lula," I answer meekly.

"Well, den, what is you so foolish fur? Better folks
dan you is gone bare-footed."

I listen to all she has to say but a thought has come
to me and I have no time to argue the point. Until
the shoes for the army are finished, Mr. McDearnmid
will not have time to make any shoes for anyone else,
this is right, for our dear soldiers must come first in
everything, but I will stop writing now and get to work.

April 9th, 1864.—Today I have on railroad stockings and slippers. Guess what these slippers are made
of? Whenever I go to uncle Richard's I see an old
black uncle, hard at work plaiting shucks and weaving
the plaits together into door mats. It seemed to me a
lighter braid might be sewed into something resembling shoes, so I picked out the softest shucks and soon
had enough to make one slipper. So pleased was I that
I soon had a pair of shoes ready to wear. They are a
little rough so I have pasted inside a lining of velvet.
Everybody laughed, but I feel quite proud.

14. VIRGINIA McCOLLUM STINSON—
YANKEES IN CAMDEN, ARKANSAS

*Virginia was the wife of George H. Stinson, who
had lost an eye at Shiloh and come home to Camden to
work in the quartermaster department. She had three
small children, the youngest a baby. Her brother-in-
law John M. Daly had been killed at the Battle of
Corinth. After the war Mrs. Stinson wrote her recollections of the occupation of Camden by enemy troops
under General Frederick Steele. She seems to have
accepted the responsibility for her household—the chil-*

dren, Aunt Sallie a trusted old cook, and three other
servants. The younger sister Kate, that "saucy little
rebel," apparently divided her time between Mrs. Stin-
son's and Mrs. Daly's.

On the morning of April 15th, 1864 all the women
on West Washington Street and other streets in Camden who could were busy cooking rations for our dear
men in grey. Everybody was excited for the news all
day long was "the Yankees are nearing town." Women
were flying about in the town to pay their last calls.
They were not dressed in silk or fine hats or bonnets.
There had been no "Spring Opening" for three years.
They wore sunbonnets or maybe nothing at all on their
heads. I could not go out visiting on account of my
feeble health, so my good neighbors came to see me.

When the cry came "the Yankees are in sight," all
the visitors rushed home and said good-bye. We did not
know when we would meet again, for we women had
resolved we would stay in our homes and save our
household goods and stores.

Kate, my young lady sister, ran in the house and
said, "Sis the Yankees are almost here." Such a noise
they did make, shooting guns and pistols, and the
tramp of feet and yelling of voices—it was distressing
indeed. I gathered my household together and closed
my doors and blinds. No glad welcome was extended
them, our hearts were lifted to God in prayer for protection. We peeped through the blinds and saw them
rush in our vacant lot, then in a short time our grounds
were covered with blue coats. They were as thick as
blackbirds in springtime and chattering in louder voices.
They began to take a look at our house, then came to
the back door. Aunt Sallie went to the door to see what
was wanted. I had given her all the keys to the smoke
house and store room and told her to claim everything
on the place. The Yankees demanded the keys from
her. She said: "You can't have them." They replied,
"We must have them because we need meat, flour and
meal." Sister Kate went out to help Aunt Sallie. She

would not let the doors be broken open, but unlocked them and let them take whatever they wished, but when they were taking nearly all of the meat from the smoke house, Kate said, "You surely don't mean to rob my sister of all the meat she has?" They then decided to leave some. They only left two of the smallest hams in the lot, but we had some stored away that they could not find.

Their robbery was begun about 6 P.M. and lasted until midnight. What a night of terror it was. Next morning they began to rob us again; this time I went to the store-room door myself. As Aunt Sallie opened it fifteen Yankees were there to grab whatever they could lay their hands on. I spoke to them in this pathetic manner: "Haven't you men mothers, wives or sisters in your northern homes? If so, how would you like for our Southern soldiers to rob them as you are robbing me?" One or two looked ashamed, while the others were defiant and kept taking. Sister Kate had gone for a guard over at Gen. Steele's headquarters, which was at my neighbors, Mrs. Maj. Graham's home. While the Yankees were still taking rice and flour their commanding officers rode right up to my back door with a guard and robbing ceased. Kate told what a time she had to get a guard.

Before the Yankees occupied Camden a Confederate officer's wife, a Mrs. Maj. Sneed, who boarded with our sister Mrs. Daly, told us in case the Yankees came that she was well acquainted with Col. Mantor, one of Gen. Steele's staff officers, and if we needed help to go to him for he was a gentleman. So Kate applied to him for a guard for her sisters, but Col. Mantor did not treat her as a perfect gentleman should a lady. At last Kate told him, "I would not have asked you at all, but a lady of your acquaintance, Mrs. Maj. Sneed, told me that you were a gentleman and would aid helpless women and children." He then flew around and said: "Why didn't you tell me that at first?" "I did not think it necessary for I thought you were a perfect gentleman." He ordered guards to be sent in haste. The same day the guard came, Mrs. Graham advised me to take a Federal officer to board. A very nice one applied for board that day. This officer's regiment camped on a vacant lot east of my home. After the guard came and the Federal officer, I had no more serious trouble. The Federal officer also took interest in saving things for me. My husband had given me a bale of cotton that he took for debt, so the Federal officer had his men roll it in the barn for safe keeping.

Next morning after the Yankees came, Mr. Dan Fellows and Mr. Skelton came to see if I needed anything. Each one of these men had a water bucket with meal and salt, they feared the Yankees had left me little to eat. Mr. Skelton, who was always full of fun, said to me "Why Mrs. Stinson, you were strongly reinforced last night." At the same time pointing to the thousand Yankees on my left I replied, 'that is true, but I prefer men in gray instead of blue." Things began to be a little easier for us. The Federal officer was a perfect gentleman and so thoughtful of our comfort, but the guard was just the opposite, not at all refined and would eavesdrop every time any of my friends called to see me. I never thought of his doing such a mean thing as that until Aunt Sallie caught him one day with his ear at the key hole of my room and she warned us to be careful what we had to say. After that all of our conversation was in a whisper.

Aunt Sallie and I felt that we had our hands full, a boarder and that guard to lodge and feed and seven of our own household to care for and our larder quite low. We did the best we could for them, gave them rye-coffee, bread, rice, and meat. Sister Kate dined with us several times, but she and the guard were not on good terms. The Federal officer seemed to enjoy the hot discussions Kate and the guard had. They soon found her to be a saucy little rebel, she cared not what she said, I constantly reminded her that silence was golden, for I feared the guard would capture her on account of her freedom of speech.

The Yankees took possession of all the cows, sheep and hogs they could drive into the vacant lots to slaughter them. One afternoon Kate saw them driving a lot of cows in my pasture, she spied one of my cows in the drove—she rushed out with a big stick and told the men not to drive her sister's cow to slaughter. The cow was trying to get to my barn-yard, so it was easy for Kate to drive her in. I did not know she was going to do it until I saw her running after the cow. I trembled for her safety among all those rough men, but she saved the cow. . . . After the battle of Poison Springs,[1] only thirteen miles from Camden, one of her friends, a young Confederate officer who was taken prisoner and brought to Camden, asked to visit Kate and he was allowed to do so under guard. At first he went to see our sister, Mrs. Daly, but as he did not find Kate there, he came to my house. I did not see him at all, but he made Kate quite a long visit. Yet he was between two fires, for my mean guard stood at the parlor door and the guard that came with him near by. So the soldier and Kate were watched real closely, that he did not know how to convey a letter to Kate that he had written some time before he came. This letter told of the whereabouts of our men and also of our brother Hugh, who was a warm friend of the officer. At last he picked up a book off the table, turned the leaves and tried to attract Kate's attention and watched the guards, when a good chance came he slipped the letter in the book, still kept it in his hands, finally Kate understood what the book contained. As soon as he took his leave she watched our guard and took the book and concealed the letter—never told me anything about it, but slipped off to our sisters and had a chance to read it without our guard watching her.

These were trying times to us, we were almost like prisoners in our own homes, but our faith in God was strong. Only one thing stirred my Southern blood to heat, was when a negro regiment passed my home going to fight our own dear men at Poison Springs. How

[1] April 18, 1864.

fierce they did look, it was then that I gave vent to my feelings, but I must say our good old family servants were loyal to us. . . .

As the days moved slowly on we got through some how, each day we prayed that the Yankees would leave, but we saw no signs. Not a word could we hear from our dear men and not a word could they hear from us. After the Yankees had been here a week, rumors came that a battle was to be fought right here in town. In fact they made preparations for it. Placed cannon at Ft. Southerland and made ready at Ft. Simmons, even fired off guns, so that our windows rattled and the earth trembled beneath our feet, props fell from transoms on our floors. The women and children were ordered to leave town. What a strain on our nerves. To run to the river bottom and leave our homes to the mercy of the Yankees and then what! Oh! where could we go? Not a horse nor a mule in town belonging to us. My sister Mrs. Daly was one of the impulsive ones, so she decided to pack up all her silver and valuables and a few clothes for herself and little son Richard and go down to the Dan Fellows home and get in his cellar until after the battle. She had only gone as far as Mr. Ben Johnson's house, when she met her neighbor Mr. John Silliman.

"Why Mollie where are you going?" Then she explained to him. "But give me the basket you are carrying, your fingers are bleeding, it is too heavy for your delicate hands. Don't be alarmed, I do not think we will have a battle today."

Her mind was soon quieted, and he saw that she got safely home. After she had been there a while a gentleman called, whom she had met at Clarksville, Tenn., an acquaintance of the Daly's—a Southern man, he told her he had been captured by the Yankees and was with them. She was glad to see him and asked his advice about the battle that was sure to come off early next morning. He told her he would help her to get out of town, that he had a mule that could be driven before our large buggy. How surprised I was

that night when he and she came over to make arrange-
for me, Aunt Sallie and the three children to pack up
and go to the river bottom that night. I just told them
I could not do it. Just think of me driving a strange
mule and a buggy full of children and one a wee baby.
She, Kate, the friend and the servants were to walk.
Aunt Sallie said "Miss Mary Ann, Miss Virginia is not
able to go." I then said I am going to stay at home
and we can all die together.

While we were discussing that mule ride, some one
knocked at the front door. My sister flew to the door
and in a short time returned and said there was a
Federal officer and two ladies who wanted to stay all
night. She invited them in the parlor, but said to them,
my sister has no more room vacant, then they asked
to just let them stay in the parlor and with a fire and
a quilt or two they could rest on the sofas and rocking
chairs. They informed Kate there would be no battle
the next morning, so our minds were at ease. I felt so
distracted that I did not see the people. I consented
for them to stay without seeing them, for my children
needed my attention.

My sister went on home with her Tennessee friend,
who afterwards proved to be a spy against his Southland. Then Aunt Sallie went in to see what manner of
women we were giving lodging to that night. She came
and whispered to me after she had returned from the
room, that she didn't like their looks, they wasn't my
style of ladies. And said, all your silk dresses and best
clothes are in the parlor closet and the door is not
locked, "I am going to lock it for no telling what kind
of people they are."

I told her to go get something out of the closet and
then lock the door, it would look bad to just go in and
lock the door. Then she filled the key hole with paper,
so not a sound could be heard from either room. The
next morning the two women said they would like to
have breakfast, and so we gave them a good one. After
it was over they came to my room and offered me for
lodging and breakfast a few pins, just a few rolls of

pins, not even a paper. It made me angry because they said "they thought pins might be scarce down South," I thanked them and told them I had several papers of pins and had never been without. The officer that came with them the night before came for them and then I learned that he was Col. of the negro regiment that I saw pass my house a few days before. Then I had no use for him. He came in my room and spoke about what a cross baby I had, I told him she had colic and children suffering with such could not keep from crying. Indeed I was glad when he and his women left for I did not feel honored to have such people in my home.

My boarder, Capt. Rohadaback, the Federal officer, said he was glad I had gotten rid of those women for he had known them to go to peoples houses and almost take possession of the house, that I was fortunate to get them out of my house. It then flashed across my mind what kind of women they were. Oh, how thankful I was they had gone. We were kept in such a strain of excitement that we didn't know what would be next. If we could only hear from our dear ones in the army, to know that all were alive. And our father and mother who were seven miles from Camden on their plantation with fifty or sixty of their negroes, we feared to hear from them. After the Yankees had been here ten days, the morning of the last day, Capt. Rohadaback came hurriedly in and said, "Mrs. Stinson, I have orders to go away and may not return, I want to pay my board bill for the time I have been with you." So he paid me six dollars ($6.00) in green back, the first I had ever seen, but I was so distressed when he bid me good-bye, for I felt I would be at the mercy of his regiment. Woman like I burst into tears and said "Oh! Capt. Rohadaback what will become of me and my little children, when you are gone." He tried to comfort me and said "I don't think my men will molest you at all."

I was not wise enough to know that Gen. Steele's whole army was going that very night, our guard went

away too, at least I did not see him after Capt. Rohadaback left. The Yankee soldiers kept Aunt Sallie busy
cooking rations for them all day. We could see from
their movements they were up to something. At last
they said they had orders to leave, but where they were
going nobody knew. They threatened to burn the town
before they left. How terrified we helpless women and
children and faithful servants were. When night came
on our nerves were completely unstrung. Just about
dark the Yankees began shooting my chickens and
they kept it up until they had killed every chicken
except an old setting hen they did not find. What a
night of terror it was. Aunt Sallie and I gathered our
household together save the sixteen year old negro boy
who was persuaded by the Yankees to go with them,
lots of silly negroes followed the Yankees off. The
regiment east of me did not get off until morning. Aunt
Sallie tried to get a guard but could not. My good
friend, Mrs. Richmond, who was with Mrs. Graham,
sent her only son Nat, who was only fourteen years old
to stay with me. He was a brave boy and laughed at
Aunt Sallie's terrors. But that night was a hard one for
us for we sat up nearly all night.

What alarmed us most was the different squads of
men around my house talking in low tones and once
in a while a pistol shot off quite near my house. Then
we feared they would fire our house, as one or two
houses had been set on fire the first of the night.

No one but the children could sleep that night, our
hearts were lifted to God in prayer for protection.
Mother Elliott told me of her terror that night. She
said her friend, Mrs. Norton, was with her, but she
could not sleep and about midnight the mocking birds
in the trees around her home began to sing so sweetly,
both of them thought it was a good omen for they had
not heard the birds sing so since the Yankees came and
sure enough when morning came, not a blue coat was
in our town. They silently folded their tents, wrapped
the wheels of their wagons with cotton and left town

without noise, and it was daylight when the last wagon left.

Camden looked like a deserted town, no noise or Yankees in town, Oh! what relief it was to be free of them. We did not know what joy was in store for us that day—didn't know that our boys in grey were so near us, Oh! what joy when our dear men came marching in town—what waving of hands and handkerchiefs, women and children greeting their loved ones. My husband came that night, my brother Hugh McCollum and Col. Grinstead came with their regiment at noon and so many of my dear soldier friends in grey came. All that day and night and the next day too they were coming. We did not have much to give them to eat, for the Yankees had almost robbed us of all we had of some things, but for all that we divided cheerfully with them, but they were hurrying on in pursuit of the Yankees, so their stay with us was brief.

The Choctaw and Cherokee Indians who were Confederate soldiers came the second day. We gave them something to eat, they only asked for bread and sat on the ground to eat it. They were riding their Indian ponies and had their hats ornamented with gray peafowl's feathers, but they were very quiet, yet, the negroes were afraid of them.

Gen. Kirby Smith and staff officers came after the Yankees left, and asked permission to camp in our front yard. My husband and I were delighted to have them for our lawn is so large and is covered with giant oaks. The general and all his staff were perfect gentlemen and treated us so nicely. They would even ask permission to get water from our well and also for the use of the cooking stove to bake bread etc. They had a splendid cook, one that the General brought from his old home. Every morning a nice breakfast of hot rolls, beefsteak and genuine coffee was sent me with the compliments of Gen. Smith and staff. How neighborly they were. I tried to do all I could for them while they were here. When we got news that my brother Hugh was wounded at the battle of Jenkins ferry,[1] my husband started with my father and sister Kate to the battle field, but they met a courier the first night and he said that "Hugh had passed over the river" and his body would be sent home next day. Maj. Gen. Boggs one of Gen. Smith's staff came right away to see me and offer aid and Major Feris another of the staff officers was so kind to me in my sorrow. They offered me conveyances or horses.

Maj. Feris was such a lover of home and his sweet wife and little girl, who he said he had not seen for a long time. He asked, as a favor from me, that I would let my little Lizzie, who was just the age of his little daughter come and sit on his knees so when I put on her fresh dress in the morning the nurse would take her to his tent which was in sight of my room door. He said seeing her reminded him of home, of his child that he had not seen in so long, and might never see again.

Gen. Kirby Smith and staff remained but a short time with us. They moved on to other fields of duty. I shall never forget him and his staff officers for their kindness to me and mine. . . .

15. VARINA HOWELL DAVIS—"THEY LEFT US ALONE WITH OUR DEAD"

Mrs. Davis had long since sold her horses and the fine carriage in which she and the children had ridden about the streets of Richmond. The grounds of the White House were neglected and inside the house spies were believed to have entered at will. It was from the high north piazza that the little son, Joseph Emory Davis, fell. Mrs. Chestnut, waiting in the drawing room after the accident, said she could hear through the live-long night the tramp of Jefferson Davis's feet above, as he paced up and down in grief.

In remembrance of her own grief, Mrs. Davis, in

[1] April 30, 1864.

an article she wrote for the Montgomery Advertiser *in 1893, quoted with sympathy this letter from an un-named Confederate woman to her husband:*

"Twenty grains of quinine would have saved our two children; they were too nauseated to drink the bitter willow tea and they are now at rest, and I have no one to work for but you. I am well and strong and am not dismayed. I think day and night of your sorrow. I have their little graves near me."

On April 30th, 1864, when we were threatened on every side, and encompassed so perfectly that we could only hope by a miracle to overcome our foes, Mr. Davis's health declined from loss of sleep so that he forgot to eat, and I resumed the practice of carrying him something at one o'clock. I left my children quite well, playing in my room, and had just uncovered my basket in his office, when a servant came for me. The most beautiful and brightest of my children, Joseph Emory, had, in play, climbed over the connecting angle of a bannister and fallen to the brick pavement below. He died a few minutes after we reached his side. This child was Mr. Davis's hope, and greatest joy in life. At intervals, he ejaculated, "Not mine, oh, Lord, but thine."

A courier came with a despatch. He took it, held it open for some moments, and looked at me fixedly, saying, "Did you tell me what was in it?" I saw his mind was momentarily paralyzed by the blow, but at last he tried to write an answer, and then called out, in a heartbroken tone, "I must have this day with my little child." Somebody took the despatch to General Cooper and left us alone with our dead. . . .

II

BLOWS OF THE HAMMER

May–October, 1864

On March 9, 1864, President Lincoln appointed Ulysses S. Grant lieutenant-general in supreme command of all the Union armies. According to Grant's plans of general strategy:

The Army of the Potomac, under General Meade but with Grant's personal direction, would attack General Lee's Army of Northern Virginia;

Ben Butler was to advance on Richmond up the south bank of the James River from Fortress Monroe;

Sigel would sweep through the Shenandoah Valley;

Sherman would move from Chattanooga for Atlanta against Joe Johnston's army;

Banks would go against Mobile.

As things developed the brilliant Beauregard promptly disposed of the egregious Butler on May 16 and bottled him up in the neck of land between the James and Appomattox rivers. Breckinridge and Imboden, with boys from the V.M.I., sent Sigel flying down the Valley after the Battle of New Market on May 15. When old David Hunter replaced Sigel he tried a little of the fire-and-destruction campaign that the Germans called "thoroughness" in World War I. He had some initial success, but General Jubal A. Early took good care of him. By June 22 "Old Jube" was well north in the Valley. In July he rode on, defeating Lew Wallace's little force at the Monocacy River on the ninth, getting within the suburbs of Washington, scaring the Federal government into conniptions and diverting a whole army corps from Grant. Then he drew back into the Shenandoah, where Sheridan succeeded Hunter.

*In September Sheridan, now in general command of
the Union cavalry, with fifty thousand men defeated
Early's twenty thousand at Fisher's Hill near the north
end of Massanutten Mountain and drove them back
to New Market. Then all the way from Staunton to
Winchester Sheridan put the fair Valley into utter
desolation, with the real "thoroughness" at which
Hunter was a novice. It was said if a crow tried to fly
across, it would have to carry its own rations. Early
followed behind and while Sheridan was in Washington for a conference hit the Union army at Cedar Creek
on October 19—hit it hard on front, flank and rear,
and might have won a decisive victory, but Sheridan,
riding "from Winchester twenty miles away," rallied
his troops and put the Confederates to flight. Hence-
forth the Valley could not be used to subsist the army
or to threaten Washington.*

*These were diversions. The great hammer blows,
the main attacks of Grant and Sherman, were different matters.*

*Grant, with 118,000 in the four corps of Hancock,
Warren, Sedgwick and Burnside, crossed the Rapidan,
and was promptly engaged by Lee in the desperate
struggles of the Wilderness. It was a case of Grant's
bludgeon against Lee's rapier, of Grant's determined
resolution against Lee's mobility and skill. In the same
jungle of ravines, copses and undergrowth close to
suffocation where Hooker had been trapped and en-
tangled the year before, Grant tried to slug it out, ever
attempting movements by the left flank around Lee's
right. There were the Battle of the Wilderness (May
5-7), of Spottsylvania Court House (May 8-18), of the
North Anna and Totopotomoy Creek (May 23-28) and
Cold Harbor (June 1-3). Cold Harbor was Grant's
worst battle: he lost 5,000 men in the ten minutes of
direct assault. By then, since the campaign had started,
his casualties amounted to 55,000. That was too much
for the North even with its vast resources. A storm of
protest arose behind him.*

Grant had been aiming straight for Richmond. He

*could not make it. Lee was ever in the way. Grant
thought then he might shift around suddenly to the
south and take Petersburg, the nexus of the roads to
the Confederate capital. He nearly did it. But the advance was sluggish. Beauregard with a mere handful
held it off till Lee in utmost urgency could bring in re-
inforcements on June 18.*

*Then began the siege of Petersburg, which was to
last till the first of April, 1865. Grant had not destroyed Lee's army, but he had pinned it down. As
part of the siege operations the Federals by tunneling
placed a mine under a salient in the Confederate defense line. It was exploded on July thirtieth and a
fierce combat resulted—all to Confederate advantage.
Four Union divisions were trapped in the Crater—
hoist with their own petard—and 4,000 Federals were
lost there. Lee made the Petersburg lines as solid as
human skill and ingenuity could make them.*

*Starting his campaign on the same day as Grant,
Sherman, with 100,000 men in three armies under
Thomas, McPherson and Schofield, advanced directly
south on Atlanta, important communications center,
focal point of the railroads between Richmond and
the Deep South. Opposed to him was Joe Johnston,
the South's redoubtable Fabian general, master of the
strategic retreat. Never feeling himself able to commit
his force to an all-out engagement against superior
numbers, Johnston could attempt a blow only when
things looked peculiarly propitious. He sparred like a
practiced boxer. He would take a position behind
breastworks, resist, and when Sherman, marching first
by the right and then by the left, would endanger
Johnston's flank, General Joe would slip out to a new
stand farther south. There were incessant cavalry
clashes. There were notable battles at Dalton, Resaca,
Allatoona and New Hope Church in May, at and all
about Kennesaw Mountain in June, and at Smyrna
Station and the crossing of the Chattahoochee early
in July.*

Bragg came down to look things over for President

Davis and reported that the morale of the soldiers required a new commander who would go on the offensive. Governor Brown of Georgia supported Bragg; the military were interfering with commercial traffic. On July 17 Johnston was relieved and the command of the Army of Tennessee given to lionhearted John B. Hood. Nothing was more congenial to Hood than a stand-up fight. But at Peach Tree Creek on July 20, the Battle of Atlanta on the twenty-second and Ezra Church on the twenty-eighth he was unsuccessful and his losses were great. The siege of the city began. On August 31 the last open railroad connection—the one to Macon—was broken in a fight at Jonesboro. On September 1 Atlanta was evacuated by Hood and the next day occupied by Sherman.

On August 23 the last but one of the open ports was closed to blockade-runners when Admiral Farragut captured Mobile. The Confederate women have told with what ingenuity they countered the blockade, but such resourcefulness could not hold out forever.

On June 10 the Confederate Congress had authorized the use of boys of seventeen and eighteen, of men between forty-five and fifty, for military service.

How the Southern women felt as these great blows of the Northern hammer rang in their ears is eloquently voiced by Louly Wigfall, the daughter of Louis T. Wigfall, in the poem that is printed on the last page of this collection.

1. LORETA JANETA VELAZQUEZ—
SPECIAL AGENT

Loreta was born in the West Indies in 1838, married a New Orleans planter named Roach and was living in St. James Parish, Louisiana, in 1861. After her husband's enlistment and early death in the Confederate cause, she raised a company of cavalry in Arkansas and equipped it at her own expense. Dis-

guised as a man, she proceeded to Virginia where she took part in First Manassas and served for many months under Colonel Dreaux before her sex was discovered. She was ordered home, but instead, resuming her disguise, went to Columbus, Kentucky, and fought under General Polk in Kentucky and in Tennessee, where she was twice wounded. She was in New Orleans when Federals occupied the city in the spring of 1862. She married a Captain De Caulp who was soon killed in action.

Loreta was now engaged by the Confederate government as a spy and special agent. She passed freely between the lines. As a counter spy in Washington she managed without suspicion to become a member of the operating staff of Colonel Lafayette C. Baker, chief of the U.S. secret service. Her contemporaries described her as "the beautiful Confederate spy whose black eyes bewitched passes from Union generals."

Madame Velasquez was ordered to Canada in the spring of 1864, where Confederate commissioners were planning the "Northwest Conspiracy." This involved freeing the Confederate officers imprisoned on Johnson's Island in Sandusky Bay—10,000 were there at one time or another, though 3,000 filled capacity at any one time—at Camp Douglas, Chicago; Camp Morton, Indianapolis; and Camp Chase, Columbus; a total of about 26,000 men. The attempt on Johnson's Island was made unsuccessfully in September 1864.

On my arrival in Richmond, I immediately communicated with the authorities, delivered the messages and despatches submitted to me, sent letters to merchants in Wilmington and Savannah, as I had been directed to do, and gave all the information I could about the condition of things at the North, the proposed raid, and other matters.

Within a few days I heard, by special messenger, from the parties in Wilmington and Savannah. This man delivered to me a package which was to be taken through to Canada, and also orders and sailing directions for certain blockade-runners, and drafts which were to be cashed, and the money disposed of in certain ways for the benefit of the Confederate cause. I also received directions from parties in Richmond to confer with the Confederate agents, and if agreeable on all sides, to visit the prisons; it being thought that, as a woman, I would be able to obtain admission, and to be permitted to speak to the prisoners, where a man would be denied.

Then, freighted with my small, but precious package, several important despatches and other papers, and a number of letters for Confederates in Canada, I started to return. I would have been a rich prize for the Federals, if they should capture me; and, while on my way back, I wondered what Colonel Baker would think and say, in case some of his emissaries should chance to lay hands upon me, and conduct me into his presence, laden with all this contraband of war.

In consideration of the value of the baggage I was carrying, it was thought to be too great a risk for me to attempt to reach the North by any of the more direct routes, and I was consequently compelled to make a long detour by way of Parkersburg, in West Virginia. This involved a long and very tiresome journey, but it was undoubtedly the best course for me to pursue.

The wisdom in choosing this route was demonstrated by the result, and I succeeded in reaching Parkersburg without being suspected in the least by any one. At that place I found General Kelley [1] in command, and from him procured transportation to Baltimore, on the strength of my being an attaché of Colonel Baker's corps, which was a very satisfactory stroke of business for me, as it saved both trouble and expense.

The instructions under which I was moving required me to go to Baltimore, and from there inform the different parties interested of my arrival, and wait to hear from them as to whether they were ready to meet me at the appointed places, before proceeding farther.

---

[1] General Benjamin F. Kelley, U.S.A.

I was also to wait there for some drafts for large sums, which were to be cashed in New York, and the money taken to Canada. This involved considerable delay, which was particularly unpleasant just then, as I was getting very short of funds, and was, moreover, quite sick, the excitement I had gone through with—for this was a more exciting life even than soldiering—and the fatigue of a very long and tedious journey having quite used me up.

On arriving in Baltimore, fearing that I would not have enough money to see me through until I could obtain a remittance, I went to a store kept by a lady to whom I was told to appeal in event of being detained on account of lack of funds, and explaining who I was, and the business I was on, asked her if she would not assist me. She looked very hard at me, asked me a great many questions, and requested me to show her my papers. I said that this was impossible, as not only my honor and life were at stake, but that interests of great moment were involved in the preservation of the secrets I had in possession.

This, I thought, ought to have satisfied her; but it apparently did not, for she evidently regarded me with extreme suspicion. Her indisposition to trust me might have been caused by my rather dilapidated appearance, although my soiled travelling dress ought to have been proof of the fact that I had just been making a long, and very rough journey. Finally, another lady coming in, she walked back in the store with her, and I, supposing that she did not intend to take any more notice to me, arose to go out. She, however, seeing this movement, called for me to wait a moment. Shortly after she returned, and, handling me a sum of money, said, "I am a Union woman; but as you seem to be in distress, I will have to aid you. This is as much as I can afford to give."

I, of course, understood that this speech was intended for any other ears than mine that might be listening, and, merely giving her a meaning glance, walked out of the store, without saying anything further.

Having obtained this money, I went back to Barnum's Hotel, where I was stopping, feeling considerably relieved, so far as the exigencies of the moment were concerned, but not knowing to what poverty I might yet be reduced before I received my expected remittances. At first I was very much vexed at the behavior of the lady in the store, as I thought that the statement I made her, and the names of persons I mentioned as having referred me to her ought to have gained me her confidence at once. On reflection, however, I came to the conclusion that she might not be so much to blame after all, as she was obliged to be careful, on the one hand, not to be imposed upon, and, on the other not to be caught having secret dealings with the Confederates.

That night I was so sick that I had to send for a doctor. I offered him my watch for his services, stating that I was out of funds, and was detained in Baltimore through the non-arrival of money which I was expecting. He, however, refused to take it, and said that I might pay him if I ever was able, but that it would not matter a great deal one way or the other. The next day I was considerably better, and was able to go about a little, and I continued to improve with rest and quiet.

While stopping at Barnum's Hotel, I became acquainted with a young captain in the Federal army, and, as I made a practice of doing with all Federal officers—I did not know when they might be useful to me—I courted his friendship, and told him a story about myself similar to that I had told on several other occasions—that I had lost everything through the rebellion—that my husband was a U.S. army officer and had died about the outbreak of the war—had been so badly treated by rebels had been forced to come North. . . . I was especially bitter in my denunciations of the rebels. The captain was so affected by my pitiful narrative, that he introduced me to General E.

B. Tyler, who was very affable and courteous, and who, learning that I was anxious to travel northward, and was short of money, kindly procured for me a pass to New York.

Finally, I received notice that one of the blockade-runners, with whom I was to communicate, was at Lewes, Delaware, and, on proceeding to that place, found an English brig, the Captain of which was anxiously waiting to receive instructions as what port he was to sail for. The cargo was principally powder, clothing, and drugs, and the Captain was exceedingly glad to see me, as he wanted to get away as fast as he could, there being a liability that the Federal authorities might pounce upon him at any moment. I accordingly gave him his sailing papers, which contained directions for him to proceed to Wadling's Island, on the North of Cuba, where he was to transfer his cargo to another vessel, which was to run for any port it could make in the Confederacy. The Captain handed me the cards of several houses in Liverpool and Havre, which were extensively engaged in blockade-running, and I bade him adieu, wishing him a safe and pleasant trip.

This errand having been satisfactorily despatched, I went to Philadelphia, where I took a room at the Continental Hotel, and telegraphed for my papers, money package, etc., to be forwarded to me from New York by express. The next morning I received, in reply to this, my expected drafts, and also the following characteristic letter:

"Quebec, Canada.

"Mrs. Sue Battle: You will find enclosed a card of your government agent here, B——. Any orders you have for your government, if forwarded, we will execute and despatch quickly, according to your instructions. Messrs. B. & T. have several clippers, which they will put in the trade, if desired. I will drink your ladyship's good health in a bottle of good old Scotch ale. Let us hear from you at your earliest convenience. I will await your answer to return to Europe.

"With great respect, and hopes of success,
  "I am, Madam, yours truly,
                              "R. W. L."

I now proceeded, without further delay, to New
York, where I was met, at the Desbrosses Street ferry,
by my associate in that city, who conducted me to
Taylor's Hotel, where he had engaged a room for me.
He said that he had been getting somewhat anxious for
my safety, the more especially as he was informed that
the detectives had received some information of my
doings, and were on the watch for me. This made me
a trifle uneasy, as I did not know but my friend,
Colonel Baker, had discovered some facts about me
which had served to convince him that I was not likely
to be as valuable a member of his corps as he had supposed I would when he started me on my Richmond
trip. Since my return to the North I had been endeavoring to keep myself concealed from Baker and all his
people, as I did not wish to renew my acquaintance
with the Colonel until I had visited Canada. That accomplished, I proposed to see him again, and to make
use of his good offices for the purpose of putting into
execution a still more daring scheme.

My New York accomplice said that he did not think
I was in any immediate danger, although I would have
to take care of myself. He himself had seen one of
the detectives who were on my track, and, while I was
evidently the person he was after, the description he
had of me was a very imperfect one; so that, by the
exercise of a little skill, I ought to be able to evade
him. To put him on the wrong track, my accomplice
had told this detective that he thought he knew the
person he was searching for, and had procured a photograph of a very different looking woman, and given it
to him.

Having cashed my drafts, and gotten everything
ready, I started for Canada, carrying, in addition to
valuable letters, orders, and packages, the large sum
of eighty-two thousand dollars in my satchel. Mr. L.,

the correspondent whose letter has been quoted, was requested, by a telegraphic despatch, to meet me on my arrival in Canada.

Under ordinary circumstances, the great value of the baggage I was carrying would not have disturbed my peace of mind; but I knew that, in addition to the money I had with me, my capture would involve the officers of the Federal government obtaining possession of papers of the utmost importance, from which they would scarcely fail to gain quite sufficient information concerning the proposed raid to put them on their guard, and enable them to adopt measures for preventing the execution of the great scheme. It was not comfortable, therefore, for me to feel that the detectives were after me, and to be under the apprehension that one of them might tap me on the shoulder at any moment, and say, in that bland tone detectives use on such occasions, "Come, my good woman, you are wanted."

I was absolutely startled when, on approaching the depot, my companion, pointing to a man in the crowd, said, "There, that is the fellow to whom I gave the photograph. He is looking for you; so beware of him." Then, thinking it best that we should not be seen together by Mr. Detective, he wished me good luck, and said goodbye, leaving me to procure my ticket, and to carry my heavy satchel to the cars myself.

I watched the detective as well as I could without looking at him so hard as to attract his attention, and saw that he was rather anxiously surveying the people as they passed into the depot. . . .

After getting into the cars I lost sight of the detective until the arrival of the train in Rochester, and was congratulating myself that, not seeing the original of the photograph, he had remained in New York. At Rochester, however, to my infinite horror, he entered the car where I was, and took a seat near me.

When the conductor came through, after the train had started, the detective said something to him in a low tone, and showed him a photograph. The con-

ductor shook his head on looking at it, and made a
remark that I could not hear. I did, however, hear the
detective say, "I'll catch her yet."

This whispered conference reassured me a little, as
it showed that the officer was keeping his eye open
for the original of the photograph which he had in
his pocket. I concluded that I would try and strike up
an acquaintance with this gentleman, in order to find
out what he had to say for himself. . . .

I picked up my shawl and satchel and removed to
the seat immediately back of him. The window was up,
and I made a pretence of not being able to put it
down, so that after a bit the detective's attention was
attracted, and he very gallantly came to my assistance.
When he had closed the window, I thanked him, with
a rather effusive politeness, and he, probably feeling
a trifle lonesome, seated himself beside me, and opened
a conversation.

After passing the compliments of the day we
launched into a general conversation, I attempting to
speak with a touch of the Irish brogue, thinking that
it would induce him to believe me to be a foreigner.

"You are going to Canada, are you not?" inquired
my new-made friend.

"Yes, sir."

"Do you live there?"

"O, no, sir, I live in England. I am only going to
Canada to visit some friends."

"Have you been in America long?"

"Only about eight months."

"How do you like this country?"

"O, I like living in England much better than I do
here, and expect to go back as soon as I get through
with my Canada visit. There is too much fighting going on here to suit me."

"O, you need not mind that; besides, the war will
soon be over now."

"Do you think so? I will be glad when the fighting
is over. It is terrible to hear every day of so many men
being killed."

"O, that is nothing; we get used to it."

The detective now took out of his pocket the photograph which my associate in New York had given him, and which I was anxious to see, and handing it to me, said, "Did you ever see anybody resembling this? I am after the lady, and would like very much to find her."

"She is very handsome," I replied. "Is she your wife?"

"Wife! no," said he, apparently disgusted at the suggestion that he was in pursuit of a faithless spouse. "She is a rebel spy, and I am trying to catch her."

"Why, what has she been doing?"

"Well, she has been doing a good deal that our government would like to pay her off for. She is one of the smartest of the whole gang." This I thought was rather complimentary than otherwise. "I am on her track now, however, sure."

"But perhaps this lady is not a spy, after all. She looks too pretty and nice for anything of that kind. How do you know about her?"

"O, some of our force have been on the track of her for a long time. She has been working for these Copperheads and rebel agents here at the North, and has been running through the lines with despatches and goods. She came through from Richmond only a short time ago, and she is now on her way to Canada, with a lot of despatches and a big sum of money, which I would like to capture."

"I wonder how you can find out so much, when there must be a great many people coming and going all the time. Supposing that this lady is a spy, as you say, how do you know that she has not already reached Canada?"

"Maybe she has," he replied, "but I don't think so. I have got her down pretty fine, and feel tolerably certain of taking her before she gets over the line."

As he seemed inclined to change the subject, I was afraid to seem too inquisitive, and we dropped into a general conversation.

The detective seemed determined to be as polite to me as he could; and on leaving the cars he carried my satchel, containing eighty-two thousand dollars belonging to the Confederate government, and a variety of other matters which he would have taken possession of with the utmost pleasure, could he have known what they were. When we passed on board the boat I took the satchel from him, and thanking him for his attention proceeded to get out of his sight as expeditiously as I could.

When the custom-house officer examined my luggage, I gave him a wink, and whispered the pass-word I had been instructed to use, and he merely turned up the shawl which was on my arm, and went through the form of looking into my satchel.

On reaching the Canada shore I was met by Mr. L., who gave me a very hearty greeting; but I cautioned him to say as little as possible just then, as we might be watched. Glancing back, I saw my friend the detective, anxiously surveying the passing crowd. . . .

On my arrival in Canada I was welcomed with great cordiality by the Confederates there, who were eager to know all about my trip, how things were looking at Richmond, whether I had letters for so and so, and anything else that I was able to tell them. I distributed my letters and despatches according to instructions; mailed packages for the commanders of the cruisers Shenandoah and Florida, which I had received with especial injunctions to be particularly careful of, as they were very important; and then proceeded to the transaction of such other business, commercial as well as political, as I had on hand.

There were a good many matters of more importance than trade and finance, however, which demanded my immediate consideration, and many and long were the conferences held with regard to the proposed grand movement on the enemy's rear. There were a number of points about this grand scheme that I would have liked to have been informed of; but those who were making the arrangements for the raid were so fearful of their plans in some way getting to the ears of the Federal authorities, that they were unwilling to tell me, and other special agents, more than was absolutely necessary for the fulfillment of the duties intrusted to us. . . .

I was merely furnished with a general idea of the contemplated attack, and was assigned to special duties in connection with it. These duties were to visit Johnson's Island, in Lake Erie, and, if possible, other military prisons, for the purpose of informing the Confederates confined in them of what was being done towards effecting their release, and what was expected of them when they were released. I was then to telegraph to certain agents that the prisoners were warned, and such other information as I might deem it important for them to be possessed of, in accordance with an arranged system of signals. This being done, I was to proceed to the execution of other tasks, the exact details of which, however, were made dependent upon circumstances, and upon directions I might receive from the agents in the States, under whose orders I was to act.

This plan for a grand raid by way of the lakes excited my enthusiasm greatly, and I had very strong hopes of its success. . . .

2. SARAH ALEXANDER LAWTON—
"HOW ALONE GENERAL LEE SEEMS!"

The daughter of A. L. Alexander of Washington, Georgia, Sarah Gilbert Alexander married Alexander Robert Lawton, member of the Savannah bar. He became a brigadier-general at the outbreak of hostilities, was in the Seven Days' battles, Second Manassas and Antietam—"Lawton's Georgians" were famous fighters —was wounded at Sharpsburg in September 1862, and on August 7, 1863, appointed quartermaster-general. Mrs. Lawton and the four children came from Georgia to be with him in Richmond.

In lieu of letters Mrs. Lawton sent extracts from her diary to members of her family back home. This report of dark days went to her sister, Mrs. George Gilmer Hull.

Richmond—May 9 [1864] Monday. Mr. Lawton came upstairs after dinner and said to me "I have made arrangements for all of you to leave, day-after-tomorrow." It came like a thunder-clap upon me. Our arms had seemed so successful that we were beginning to breathe freely and to think the enemy were foiled. At least *I* cannot go away.

May 10. Tired and sick tonight—after a sad and busy day—preparing the children to go—they are all ready now. Corinne was bitterly opposed to going—but her father talked to her a long time and she now seems cheerful and reconciled.

May 11. They are gone. I feel sad and desolate enough—but have not time to indulge it. I must pack my trunks, so as to be ready for anything. . . .

Thursday—12th. Rain—but I went visiting. I had been at home for several days and knew little of the state of feeling in town. We heard last night that the children had safely reached the end of their railroad journey, so I felt relieved about them. Mr. Lawton was kept up late last night and waked up early this morning by business connected with getting a train of corn thro' to Gen. Lee's Army. Well, I went visiting. I went first to Mrs. S's—found her tete a tete with Mr. T.—made the acquaintance of that silver tongued Frenchman and learned from his magnetic eyes the secret of his power over the bewitching and bewitched lady.

I learned that on Tuesday there was great alarm in the city. Many ladies sat up all night, dressed in all their best clothes with their jewelry on. Congressmen besieged the war department all night—so that Gen.

Bragg [1] was called out of bed to go down to them after midnight. We knew nothing of all the excitement—absorbed in the grief of our expected family parting. We slept as we best could each in our quiet chamber. . . .

Friday—13th. Early this morning we were waked by the tidings that the Danville road was cut. We next learned that Gen. Stuart was dead—sad news. After breakfast I had a trunk or two to pack—while thus engaged, Mrs. Stanard sent for me to sit the morning with her. . . .

I had a very pleasant morning with Mrs. Stanard and returned home just before Mr. Lawton and the Doctor came to dinner. Mr. L. hurried off soon to be pall-bearer at Gen. Stuart's funeral. Not long after, the Doctor returned to his office—rain set in—I had a dreary afternoon—we are all alone this evening—a rare occurrence. The gentlemen are talking about how terrified the Congressmen are—how anxious to get horses. We are now hemmed in on all sides.

Sunday 15th. . . . The excitements yesterday were the cannonading at Drury's Bluff [2]—and the impressment of negroes to work on the fortifications. Jake was caught. Paul and Lysander took flight and hid—and all day Paul did not dare go out.

There is much feeling against Gen. Bragg and about Pemberton's being put in command of the artillery around the city. Members of Congress are much ex-

[1] After General Bragg's unsuccessful Chattanooga campaign, General Joseph E. Johnston had been put in command of the Army of Tennessee and Bragg called to Richmond to be President Davis's chief-of-staff.

[2] About May 11 General Ben Butler advanced slowly until he reached Drewry's Bluff, halfway between Bermuda Hundred and Richmond. Beauregard had been gathering reinforcements. On the sixteenth he attacked Butler with vigor and with such success as to limit materially the usefulness of the Army of the James as a factor in the campaign.

cited and there is indignation against the President on his account.

Today we had some cannonading at Drury's again— Beauregard is preparing to give the enemy battle. We expect a heavy fight in a day or two. A train went off on the Central Road today. Several families left on it, en route for the South.

Wednesday 25. For a week we have been more quiet. Business begins to receive attention. Letters are once more delivered. We are expecting, however, daily to hear of a terrible battle between Lee and Grant. We have all been much excited by the tidings that Gen. Johnston has retreated below Marietta and abandoned upper Georgia.

May 30—Sunday. 9½ P.M. Gen. Lawton has just returned from a long ride. He has been out to Gen. Lee's headquarters at Atlee Station, 10 miles from town. He reports the Gen. very unwell and looking worn down. No wonder—the wonder is that he has kept up so long, with so intense a strain upon his mental powers. Gen. Lee seems to expect that the enemy will attack him tomorrow. He telegraphed for Beauregard who went up to him this afternoon. Butler is said to have been heavily reinforced—and I suppose Beauregard will not venture to stay long away from his command. We are all discussing the probability that Grant will not attack, but will cross the Chickahominy, thus forcing Gen. Lee to the city. A siege is far more to be dreaded by us than a battle.

Mr. Lawton was saying how alone Gen. Lee seems to be in his responsibilities. Ewell is out of the field— broken down,[1] Jackson gone, Longstreet wounded [2]—

[1] Ewell, who had been in the thick of the fighting since the Wilderness campaign began, was "in danger of collapse under his burdens."—D. S. Freeman, *Lee's Lieutenants*, III, 433.

[2] Near the Plank Road in the Wilderness fighting on May 6 Longstreet had been seriously wounded by a ball mistakenly fired by one of his own men. It passed through his throat into his shoulder.

So few of whom he can rely for counsel.

June 19. Sunday. The enemy have been beleaguring Petersburg and shelling it. Refugees from there have been coming here and there are uncertain tidings of great battles—but nothing authentic is known. We here feel still very calm and cheerful and never think on the ifs of Grant's success. Household matters still fill up my daily life, as in peace times, and the struggle to live comfortably requires considerable effort and forethought. We continue to have all our wants supplied. I send to market every morning and get fresh vegetables. We have fresh meat in small quantities, some two or three times a week—the rest of the time, ham. I will append my market bills for a week.
Wednesday, 5½ lbs. of veal, $33.00. 1 peck green peas $12.
Thursday. Lettuce $1.50. Cherries, 2 qts for $3.00.
Friday, Squash. 1 doz. for $6. Asparagus, $3.00.
Saturday, Snap beans, $4. gooseberries $2.00. Butter, 4 lbs. for $48.00.
Sunday and Monday—nothing.
Tuesday, Lettuce $1.50. Beans, $4, Raspberries $20.

We have been to church this morning and tonight. I think all the sermons we hear now show want of thought. Our ministers have no time for study—they are so engaged with visits to the afflicted, to hospitals, to the wounded and with funerals.

Tuesday 21. The air is full of sorrowful tales. Last week we walked to the Armory to see Mrs. Gorgas.[1] She has just heard that her brother-in-law was severely wounded. . . .

Friday—June 24. All our railroads cut [2]—Enemy fortifying on the Weldon road. The Gen'l. getting very

[1] Brigadier-General Josiah Gorgas was chief of the Ordnance Department.
[2] This was only a rumor. Trains continued to roll into Richmond.

anxious about the supplies of corn for the Army. The
Doctor working hard with the sick and wounded at
Jackson Hospital. 2300 patients there—thermometer
at 92—Daily prayer meetings. . .

3. JUDITH BROCKENBROUGH McGUIRE—
"GENERAL STUART DIED LAST NIGHT"

*After Chantilly in the spring of 1861 the McGuires
found refuge in Danville, Lynchburg, Charlottesville
and other Virginia cities and towns. In November 1863
they went to Richmond, where Mrs. McGuire got a position in the Commissary Department and, as always,
helped in the hospitals.*

*General Stuart, the Bayard of the Confederacy, was
only thirty-one when he was mortally wounded by a
pistol shot in a skirmish with Sheridan at Yellow
Tavern, six miles from Richmond, on May 11. When
he was a young lieutenant at Fort Leavenworth, Kansas, and she a girl in her teens, he had fallen in love
with Flora, daughter of Colonel Philip St. George
Cooke, the most capable cavalry officer in the United
States Army. They were married in 1855. During the
crucial days of battle they had been able to snatch only
fleeting moments of happiness together. Mrs. Stuart
was at Colonel Edmund Fontaine's plantation at Beaver
Dam when she heard the general was wounded. She
started at once for his bedside but Union raiders had
cut the communications and she did not reach Richmond till four hours after he had died. The hymn for
which he asked was "Rock of Ages."*

Richmond, Virginia
May 13, 1864

General Stuart died of his wounds last night, twenty-
four hours after he was shot. He was a member of the
Episcopal Church, and expressed to the Rev. Dr. Peter-
kin his resignation to the will of God. After much

conversation with his friends and Dr. P., and joining them in a hymn which he requested should be sung, he calmly resigned his redeemed spirit to the God who gave it. Thus passed away our great cavalry general, just one year after the Immortal Jackson. This seems darkly mysterious to us, but God's will be done. The funeral took place this evening, from St. James's Church. My duty to the living prevented my attending it, for which I am very sorry; but I was in the hospital from three o'clock until eight, soothing the sufferers in the only way I could by fanning them, bathing their wounds, and giving them a word of comfort.

May 23.—Our young relative, Lieutenant G., a member of General Stuart's staff, has just been giving us a most gratifying account of General Stuart's habits. He says, that although he considered him one of the most sprightly men he has ever seen, devoted to society, particularly to that of the ladies, always social and cheerful, yet he has never seen him do any thing, even under the strongest excitement, unbecoming his Christian profession or his high position as a soldier; he never saw him drink, or heard an oath escape his lips; his sentiments were always high-minded, pure, and honorable, and his actions entirely coincided with them. In short, he considered him, whether on the field or in the private circle, the model of a Christian gentleman and soldier.

When speaking of his gallantry as an officer, Lieutenant G.'s admiration knows no bounds. He speaks of the devotion of the soldiers to him as enthusiastic in the extreme. The evening before his fatal wound, he sent his troops on in pursuit of Sheridan, under the command of General Fitz Lee,[1] as he was unavoidably detained for some three or four hours. General Lee overtook the enemy, and a sharp skirmish ensued, in which Sheridan's rear suffered very much. In the meantime, General Stuart determined to overtake General Lee, and, with his staff, rode very rapidly

[1] Major-General Fitzhugh Lee, eldest son of Sydney Smith Lee, who was an elder brother of Robert E. Lee.

sixteen miles, and reached him about nightfall. They
were halting for a few moments, as General Stuart
rode up quietly, no one suspecting he was there, until
a plain-looking soldier crossed the road, stopped, peered
through the darkness into his face, and shouted out,
"Old Jeb has come!" In a instant the air was rent with
huzzas. General Stuart waved his cap in recognition;
but called out in rather a sad voice, "My friends, we
won't halloo until we get out of the woods!" intimating
that there was serious work before them. . . .

4. CORNELIA PEAKE McDONALD—
HUNTER BURNS THE V.M.I.

*Mrs. McDonald stayed in Winchester till the sum-
mer of 1863. Then she and the children became refugees in various parts of Virginia. The winter found
them in Lexington, where, some months later, they
were joined by Colonel McDonald, who had been seriously ill in Richmond.*

*In early June 1864 news came that General David
Hunter was advancing toward Lexington with little
Confederate opposition. He had defeated a small force
of the Valley reserves, men and boys under General
William E. Jones, at the Battle of Piedmont on the
fourth. At Staunton he was reinforced by General
George Crook and General W. W. Averell with cavalry
from the Kanawha Valley. Hunter decided to move up
the Shenandoah Valley to Lexington. Mrs. McDonald
tells what happened. When Jubal Early came into the
Shenandoah on June 18, things took a different turn.*

*Colonel McDonald died in December 1864. After
Appomattox Mrs. McDonald went to Louisville, where
three of her sons lived. She died there on March 11,
1909, but her body was taken to Richmond to lie beside her husband's in Hollywood Cemetery.*

*Meanwhile in 1875 she had filled out her wartime
diary with a narrative. Then in 1934 Hunter McDon-*

*ald, the "very cute" boy of the '60s, annotated and
supplemented them. Dr. D. S. Freeman calls* A Diary
with Reminiscences of the War and Refugee Life in the
Shenandoah Valley, 1860–1865, *"one of the most thrilling of the war books."*

June 11th [1864] the approach of the enemy was
announced. Everybody connected with the army prepared to fly. Gen. Smith[1] departed with the corps of
cadets, and Gen. McCausland,[2] after burning the bridge
that led to the town, made good his retreat, leaving the
terror-stricken people to their fears, and to the tender
mercies of the enemy. My husband determined to go
a few miles into the country, and remain till they had
passed on their way. So he prepared to leave with
Harry in an ambulance.

As he stood on the porch giving orders for his journey, he looked so little able to undertake even a short
journey, that it filled me with misgivings. He spoke
cheerfully of coming back, but in the morning he had
told me that if he never saw me again, I must bring
up the children as he would like to have them brought
up, his boys to be true and brave, and his little girl
modest and gentle. He also said that if his property
should be confiscated, as he was sure it would be, I had
a right to one-third which could not be taken from
me; that if I could struggle on till the close of the war,
I would have abundance. I scarcely heard what he
said, for I felt that the future was nothing if only the
terrible present was not here, portentous and dreadful, and I thought only of his going, and that he might
not ever come back.

Will had gone off in another direction, on horseback,
and when the ambulance had driven off with my husband and Harry we all felt lonely enough, and filled
with apprehension.

[1] General Francis H. Smith, commandant of the Virginia
Military Institute, who brought about 300 cadets into the con-
centration against Hunter.

[2] Brigadier-General John McCausland.

Early the next morning the enemy began the bombardment of the town, imagining McCausland still there. Some shells went through the houses, frightening the inhabitants terribly. They were posted on the opposite bank of the river, and bombarded quite vigorously. Our house was struck in several places but no harm done. Indeed I was past being frightened by shot and shell. Nevertheless, I, the children and Flora retreated to the basement and waited there till the storm should be over. After a while there was a lull, and Flora, wishing to see what was going on, raised the window and put her head out.

Just as she did so, a piece of shell struck the window sill, knocking off a large piece.

No one looked out any more. At high noon the bombardment ceased, and soon through the deserted streets of the little town poured the enemy, coming in at every point. A troop rode by our house, Averill's cavalry. Two negro women rode at the head of the column by the side of the officers. We had shut all the doors and pulled down every blind, but peeped, to see without being seen. Looking down, Flora espied Hunter sitting on the front steps earnestly gazing at the passing soldiers. She immediately raised the window and called to him, "Hunter, are you not ashamed to be looking at those Yankees? Go under that porch, and dont you look at them again." Poor little fellow, perhaps he thought they were old friends. He retired under the porch, and did not emerge till they were all gone by.

We had been engaged all the morning in hiding the things we thought might be taken from us, among the rest a few hens and chickens that I had been trying to raise. The children quickly caught and transported them to a garret where we also put a few other things that might tempt them, the silver, etc. I was passing by the stairs and saw Hunter sitting on the lowest step crying bitterly. I stopped to kiss and comfort my poor little three year old baby and asked him what the matter was, when amid his sobs, he said "The Yankees are coming to our house and they will take all our breakfast, and will capture me and Fanny." Fanny was Nelly's doll which was nearly as large as he was, and who he had been taught by her to consider quite as important a member of the household. We remained as quiet as possible all the afternoon while the town was alive with soldiers plundering and robbing the inhabitants. Some came into our yard, robbed the milk house of its contents and passed on their way, picking up everything they could use or destroy. About four o'clock I heard a knock at the front door, and cautiously looking out before opening it I saw Maj. Quinn.[1] He came in, and I must plead guilty to having been glad to see at least one Yankee. He offered to remain at the house to prevent any annoyance to us or injury to property, and seated himself in the porch. Of course no marauding parties came near while he was there. I declined his offer to stay during the night, as I thought the sight they had had of him in the porch would serve to warn them off. The next morning a squad of men with an officer came to search for provisions and arms. They laughed when on examining the pantry they found only a half barrel of flour and a little tea, all the supplies we had; but their laughter was immense when on ascending to the garret they saw the hens and chickens running over the floor.

The next day, Sunday, we were constantly hearing of outrages inflicted on the towns people; breaking into houses and robbing them. I was too well used to those little affairs to think them very severe, but was intensely amused when I heard of their entry into Dr. Madison's neatly kept and well furnished house, carrying off molasses and preserves in pieces of old China, and wrapping up flour in Mrs. Madison's purple velvet cloak.

At sunset we saw a man led by with a file of soldiers. The children came in and told me that it was Capt. Matt White, that they were taking him out to shoot him.

[1] A kind officer who had spent some time in Winchester during its early occupation.

I thought they knew nothing about it and gave the matter no attention.

Sunday began a fearful work. The Virginia Military Institute with all the professors' houses was set on fire,[1] and the distracted families amid the flames were rushing about trying to save some of their things, when they were forced to leave them, officers standing by for the purpose. Not even their books and papers could they save, and scarcely any clothes. Col. Williamson was the only officer of the Institute who remained in the village, and he had to keep quiet and say nothing when his daughters were driven from their house and all its contents burned, even the old black mahogany desk where hidden away was a yellow lock of his wife's hair, and her letters tied up with a blue ribbon.

This one of his daughters told me, as if it was the greatest loss of all. One officer, Captain Prendergast,[2] knew Mrs. Gilham's brother, Col. Haydon, of the U.S. Army, and for his sake granted her the particular favor of removing some of her household goods, which after she had succeeded in removing, she was compelled to stay by with her little boys to guard. There she sat through the afternoon by her household goods, to keep them from being stolen by negroes and soldiers, and through the long night she remained at her post, and not a man dared to help her or offered to take her place. All the warehouses at the river, all the mills and buildings near were burned, all in flames at the same hour, and it really seemed as if the Evil One was let loose to work his will that day. The town people were so frightened that few dared to show themselves on the streets and Yankees and exultant negroes had their full satisfaction. Negroes were seen scudding away in

[1] General John D. Imboden says that Hunter ordered the torch to be applied also to Old Washington College, but his officers protested. It became Washington and Lee University, when General R. E. Lee ended his years as its president. (*Battles and Leaders*, IV, 486.)

[2] General Franz Sigel refers to "Captain R. G. Prendergast, commander of my escort." (*Battles and Leaders*, IV, 489.)

all directions bearing away the spoils of the burning barracks—books, furniture, trunks full of the clothes of the absent cadets were among the spoils. . . .

They all held high carnival. Gen. Crook had his headquarters on a hill near me, in a large handsome house belonging to Mr. Fuller and as it was brilliantly lighted at night and the band playing it was quite a place of resort for the coloured population. . . .

We were told that they would leave on Tuesday; and when the time arrived the signal was given to depart. Some had already gone when on looking down the street in the direction of Gov. Letcher's [1] house I saw it on fire. I instantly put on my bonnet and ran down there to help Mrs. Letcher as I was able, for though many persons were in town who knew her better than I did, none dared to leave their houses. I was too used to their ways to be afraid of them, and so in breathless haste got there in time to see the house enveloped in flames. Mrs. Letcher had consented to entertain two officers at her house, that she had been civilly asked to do. They had spent the night, and eaten breakfast with the family, sociably chatting all the while.

When they rose from breakfast, one of them, Capt. Berry, informed Mrs. Letcher that he should immediately set fire to her home. He took a bottle of benzine, or some inflammable fluid, and pouring it on the sofas and curtains in the lower rooms, applied a match, and then proceeded up stairs. Mrs. Letcher ran up stairs and snatching her sleeping baby from the cradle, rushed from the house with it, leaving everything she had to the flames. Lizzy ran up stairs and went into her father's room to secure some of his clothes, and had hung over her arm some of his linen, when Capt. Berry came near her with a lighted match, and set fire to the clothes as they hung on her arm. He then gathered all the family clothing and bedding into a pile in the middle of the room and set fire to them.

When I reached the scene, Mrs. Letcher was sitting on a stone in the street with her baby on her lap sleep-

[1] John Letcher, Governor of Virginia, 1860-1864.

ing and her other little children gathered around. She
sat tearless and calm, but it was a pitiable group, sitting there with their burning house for a background to
the picture.

Some officers who had stayed all night at Mr. Mat-
thew White's, and breakfasted there, had in reply to
the anxious inquiries of the poor old Mother about her
son who had been arrested some days before, assured
her that he was in the jail just opposite her house; that
he was temporarily detained, but would be immediately
released. That afternoon as I sat by the window I saw
a wagon pass on its way up the street, and in it a stiff,
straight form covered with a sheet. It was poor Matt
White on his way to his Mother. He had been taken
out to the woods and shot as the children had said,
and had been left where he fell. Mrs. Cameron's
daughters hearing the firing, went down to the place
when the party had left, and finding the poor body,
stayed there by it all night to keep it from being man-
gled by animals. No men were near to do it, and they
kept up their watch till word could be sent to his parents where to find him; and that was not done till Tuesday evening, for no one could pass to the town till the
troops had left.

The next day, Wednesday, was his funeral. Everybody who knew the family was there, I among the rest.
We went to the cemetery and saw the poor fellow
buried, and I turned and walked sadly away. . . . Soon
I met Mrs. Powell, my dearest and most intimate
friend. She looked very pale, and turned to me as if
she would speak, but passed on. I thought it strange
that she should pass me in that way but went on
home. . . . I sat on the porch in the twilight, and one
of the neighbors' little boys came and climbed up on
the porch till he reached my ear. Holding to the
balustrade he leaned over and whispered, "Did you
know that Col. McDonald and Harry were killed and
were lying in the woods fifteen miles from here?" I got
up and called Allan and sent him up town to ascertain
if there was any truth in what the child had said.

While Allan was gone the father of the child came and told me that it was true that they had been attacked, but that there was no certainty that they had been killed; that it was thought they were prisoners. . . .[1]

5. HENRIETTA BEDINGER LEE—"YOU BURNED MY HOME"

Colonel Edmund Lee and his wife lived at "Bedford" south of Shepherdstown far down in the Shenandoah Valley. On July 19, 1864, Mrs. Lee was alone with her young son Harry, a little daughter and the servants, when her home was burned by order of the invading General David Hunter. The next day, a refugee in Shepherdstown, Mrs. Lee, gentle, dignified lady that she was, wrote this bitter denunciation to General Hunter.

Late in July when General Jubal Early heard of the burning of the homes of Mrs. Lee, Colonel Boteler and Alexander Hunter, a state senator, he sent General John McCausland on a raid to Chambersburg, Pennsylvania, to demand an indemnity of $100,000 in gold. The money not being forthcoming, the town was fired.

Mrs. Lee lived to a ripe old age, blessed with children and grandchildren. Harry, the little boy who saw Bedford in flames, became a much-loved clergyman in the Episcopal church.

Jefferson County, Virginia
July 20, 1864

General Hunter:

Yesterday your underling, Captain Martindale, of the First New York Cavalry, executed your infamous order and burned my house. You have had the satis-

---

[1] Colonel McDonald and Harry were captured. Harry escaped, but the colonel was imprisoned in Cumberland, Maryland.

faction ere this of receiving from him the information that your orders were fulfilled to the letter; the dwelling and every out-building, seven in number, with their contents, being burned. I, therefore, a helpless woman whom you have cruelly wronged, address you, a Major-General of the United States army, and demand why this was done? What was my offence? My husband was absent, an exile. He had never been a politician or in any way engaged in the struggle now going on, his age preventing. This fact your chief of staff, David Strother, could have told you. The house was built by my father,[1] a Revolutionary soldier, who served the whole seven years for your independence. There was I born; there the sacred dead repose. It was my house and my home, and there has your niece (Miss Griffith), who has tarried among us all this horrid war up to the present time, met with all kindness and hospitality at my hands. Was it for this that you turned me, my young daughter, and little son out upon the world without a shelter? Or was it because my husband is the grandson of the Revolutionary patriot and "rebel," Richard Henry Lee, and the near kinsman of the noblest of Christian warriors, the greatest of generals, Robert E. Lee? Heaven's blessing be upon his head forever. You and your Government have failed to conquer, subdue, or match him; and disappointment, rage, and malice find vent on the helpless and inoffensive.

Hyena-like, you have torn my heart to pieces! for all hallowed memories clustered around that homestead, and demon-like, you have done it without even the pretext of revenge, for I never saw or harmed you. Your office is not to lead, like a brave man and soldier, your men to fight in the ranks of war, but your work has been to separate yourself from all danger, and with your incendiary band steal unaware upon helpless women and children, to insult and destroy. Two fair homes did you yesterday ruthlessly lay in ashes, giving not a moment's warning to the startled inmates of your wicked purpose; turning mothers and children out of

[1] Daniel Bedinger.

doors, you are execrated by your own men for the cruel work you give them to do.

In the case of Colonel A. R. Boteler, both father and mother were far away. Any heart but that of Captain Martindale (and yours) would have been touched by that little circle, comprising a widowed daughter just risen from her bed of illness, her three fatherless babies—the oldest not five years old—and her heroic sister. I repeat, any man would have been touched at that sight but Captain Martindale. One might as well hope to find mercy and feeling in the heart of a wolf bent on his prey of young lambs, as to search for such qualities in his bosom. You have chosen well your agent for such deeds, and doubtless will promote him.

A colonel of the Federal army has stated that you deprived forty of your officers of their commands because they refused to carry on your malignant mischief. All honor to their names for this, at least! They are men; they have human hearts and blush for such a commander!

I ask who that does not wish infamy and disgrace attached to him forever would serve under you? Your name will stand on history's page as the Hunter of weak women, and innocent children, the Hunter to destroy defenceless villages and refined and beautiful homes—to torture afresh the agonized hearts of widows; the Hunter of Africa's poor sons and daughters, to lure them on to ruin and death of soul and body; the Hunter with the relentless heart of a wild beast, the face of a fiend and the form of a man. Oh, Earth, behold the monster! Can I say, "God forgive you?" No prayer can be offered for you. Were it possible for human lips to raise your name heavenward, angels would thrust the foul thing back again, and demons claim their own. The curses of thousands, the scorns of manly and upright, and the hatred of the true and honorable, will follow you and yours through all time, and brand your name infamy! infamy!

Again, I demand why you have burned my home?

Answer as you must answer before the Searcher of all hearts, why have you added this cruel, wicked deed to your many crimes?

6. ISSA DESHA BRECKINRIDGE—"I AM AN EXILE"

Issa, daughter of Dr. John R. Desha and grand-daughter of Governor Joseph Desha of Kentucky, married Colonel William Campbell Preston Breckinridge of Lexington. Few families were so divided in allegiance. Within a year of the wedding the colonel was riding with John Hunt Morgan's cavalry, his father the Reverend Robert J. Breckinridge had become a prominent Unionist, his brother Joseph had enlisted in the Union Army and his brother Robert in the Confederate.

In the spring of 1864 Mrs. Breckinridge tried to get a pass into the Confederacy, but General W. T. Sherman wrote on April 24: "No person can now pass beyond our lines, save by making the circuit by some foreign country." In a few months she went to Canada; from there, in November, accompanied by her father, she journeyed to Washington. At last she got her pass —from President Lincoln—but by then all truce boats down the James River had ceased running. Back to Toronto she traveled, to stay till peace came.

When they were reunited in Lexington, Colonel Breckinridge resumed his law practice and edited the Observer. His election to Congress took them to Washington, where Issa died in 1892, survived by three children.

Queen's Hotel, Toronto, Canada
July 30, 1864

My own precious, loved and loving husband:

I hardly know where to begin. I am here an exile. On the night of the eighth Papa learned that the wives of all Rebel officers in Kentucky were to be sent South in the most disagreeable way and to land God knows where. He begged me to start the next day for Canada knowing that to go South at this season would be certain death to me and trembling at the thought at my being in the hands of our fiendish foes.

The night Papa heard of this, he saw General Stephen Burbridge [1] now Lord and Master of our poor suffering state. Burbridge told him the order was to be issued and to be indiscriminate and that it had come from Stanton. This was Sunday Morning. Monday noon I left home. Going forth a stranger in a strange land—all this was bitter but when I had to kiss our precious child [2] my last, long kiss, I felt that God had sent upon me more than I could bear—with every sorrow comes the thought I still have Willie and his love is everything to me.

I now count the days between this time and that in which I hope to go to you. Till then goodbye.

Your loving, trusting wife,

I. D. Breckinridge

7. SARA RICE PRYOR—IN BESIEGED PETERSBURG

During the siege, which began in the middle of June, the Pryor children had grown so accustomed to the differing boom of guns and varying screech of shells they amused themselves by naming them.

Roger Pryor was captured on November 27, 1864, and imprisoned in Fort Lafayette until a short time before the surrender at Appomattox.

After the Confederacy collapsed the Pryors went up to New York City on money raised by pawning Sara's jewelry. Roger embarked on a new career as a journalist and a distinguished career as a jurist, becoming a

[1] General Stephen Gano Burbridge, U.S.A., had been assigned on February 15, 1864, to the command of the District of Kentucky, with broad civil as well as military powers.

[2] Ella, her two-year-old daughter.

*justice of the Supreme Court of the state. Sara won
recognition for her stories and essays in national magazines and for her memoirs, published in 1904. She died
in 1912. They had seven children.*

Petersburg, Virginia, 1864

The month of August in the besieged city passed
like a dream of terror. The weather was intensely hot
and dry, varied by storms of thunder and lightning—
when the very heavens seemed in league with the
thunderbolts of the enemy. Our region was not shelled
continuously. One shot from "our own gun," as we
learned to call it, would be fired as if to let us know
our places; this challenge would be answered from one
of our batteries, and the two would thunder away for
five or six hours. We always sought shelter in Mr.
Campbell's bomb-proof cellar at such times, and the
negroes would run to their own "bum-proofs," as they
termed the cells hollowed under the hill.

My husband sent me a note by his courier, one hot
August day, to tell me that his old aide, Captain
Whitner, having been wounded, was now discharged
from the hospital, but was much too weak for service
in the trenches, so he had obtained for the captain
leave of absence for two weeks, and had sent him to
me to be built up. On the moment the sick man appeared in an ambulance. I was glad to see him, but
a gaunt spectre arose before my imagination and
sternly suggested: "Built up, forsooth! And pray, what
are you to build him up with? You can no more make
a man without food than the Israelites could make
bricks without straw."

However, the captain had brought a ration of bacon
and meal, with promise of more to come. I bethought
me of the flourishing garden of my neighbor, whose
onions and beets were daily gathered for her own
family. I wrote a very pathetic appeal for my wounded
Confederate soldier, now threatened with scurvy for
want of fresh food, and I fully expected she would be
moved by my eloquence and her own patriotism to

grant me a daily portion from her garden. She answered that she would agree to send me a dish of vegetables fourteen days for fourteen dollars. Gold was then selling at the rate of twenty-five dollars in our paper currency for one dollar in gold, so the dish was not a very costly one. But when it appeared it was a very small dish indeed,—two beets or four onions. Homoeopathic as were the remedial agents, they helped to cure the captain.

One morning, late in August, Eliza came early to my bedside. I started up in alarm.

"Shelling again?" I asked her.

"Worse," said Eliza.

"Tell me, tell me quick—is the General——"

"No, no, honey," said my kind nurse, laying a detaining hand upon me, "You cert'nly sleep sound! Didn't you hear a stir downstairs in the night? Well, about midnight somebody hallooed to the kitchen, and John ran out. There stood a man on horseback and a dead soldier lying before him on the saddle. He said to John, 'Boy, I know General Pryor would not refuse to take in my dead brother.'

"John ran up to my room and asked me what he must do. 'Take him in,' I told him. 'Marse Roger will never forgive you if you turn him away.' "

"You were perfectly right," I said, beginning to dress myself. "Where is he?"

"In the parlor," said Eliza. "He had a man-servant with him. John brought in his own cot, and he is lying on it. His brother is in there, and his man, both of them."

The children were hushed by their nurse's story, and gathered under the shade in the yard. When breakfast was served, I sent John to invite my guest in. He returned with answer that "the captain don' feel like eatin' nothin'."

"Captain?" I asked.

"No'm, he ain't a captain, but his dead brother was. He was Captain Spann of South Carolina or Georgia, I forget which. His man came into the kitchen for hot water to shave his dead master, but I didn't ask questions 'cause I saw he was troubled."

I went out to my ever blooming rose and found it full of cool, dewy blossoms. I cut an armful, and knocked at the parlour door myself. It was opened by a haggard, weary-looking soldier, who burst into tears at seeing me. I took his hand and essayed to lead him forth, but he brokenly begged I would place the roses upon his brother's breast. "Will you, for the sake of his poor wife and mother?"

Very calm was the face of the dead officer. His servant and his brother had shaven and cared for him. His dark hair was brushed from a noble brow, and I could see that his features were regular and refined. . . .

I persuaded the lonely watcher to go with John to an upper room, to bathe and rest for a few minutes; but he soon descended and joined us at our frugal breakfast, and then Mr. Gibson, my good rector, came in to help and advise, and in the evening my husband returned, much gratified that we had received and comforted the poor fellow.

As August drew to a close, I began to perceive that I could no longer endure the recurrence of such scenes; and I learned with great relief that my brother-in-law had moved his family to North Carolina and had placed Cottage Farm, three miles distant from the besieged city, at my disposal. Accordingly, I wrote to General Bushrod Johnson,[1] requesting an army wagon to be sent me early the next morning, and all night was spent in packing and preparing to leave.

The wagon did not come at the specified hour. All day we waited, all next night (without our beds), and the next day. As I looked out the window in the twilight, hoping and watching, the cannonading commenced with vigor, and a line of shells rose in the air, describing luminous curves and breaking into showers of fragments. Our gun will be next, I thought,

[1] Major-General Bushrod R. Johnson had helped Beauregard baffle Butler, and was constantly engaged in the defense of Petersburg.

and for the first time my strength forsook me, and I wept over the hopeless doom which seemed to await us. Just then I heard the wheels below my window, and there was my wagon with four horses. . . .

8. AGNES—"I AM FOR A TIDAL WAVE OF PEACE"

Since we heard from our anonymous friend Agnes in January 1863 she has witnessed a bread riot of hungry women and children in Richmond; learned to make ink from the crimson sap of gall-oak nuts; plaited straw for a new hat; mended her china with white lead; attended Mr. Davis's receptions and Tuesday "at-homes," and continued to keep Mrs. Pryor informed of life in the Confederate capital.

Richmond, August 26, 1864

You dear, obstinate little woman! What did I tell you? I implored you to get away while you could, and now you are waiting placidly for General Grant to blow you up. That awful crater! Do the officers around you consider it honorable warfare to dig and mine under a man and blow him up while he is asleep— before he has time to get his musket? I always thought an open field and a fair fight, with the enemy in front at equal chances, was the American idea of honest, manly warfare. To my mind this is the most awful thing that could be imagined. There is a strong feeling among the people I meet that the hour has come when we should consider the lives of the men left to us. Why let the enemy wipe us off the face of the earth? Should this feeling grow, nothing but a great victory can stop it. Don't you remember what Mr. Hunter [1] said to us in Washington? "You may sooner check

[1] R. M. T. Hunter of Virginia, who had been U. S. Senator with Jefferson Davis and was president *pro tem* of the Confederate Senate when President Davis was inaugurated in Richmond.

with your bare hand the torrent of Niagara than stop
this tidal wave of secession." I am for a tidal wave of
peace—and I am not alone. Meantime we are slowly
starving to death. Here, in Richmond, if we can afford
to give $11 for a pound of bacon, $10 for a small dish
of green corn, and $10 for a watermelon, we can have
a dinner of three course for four persons. Hampton's
cavalry [1] passed through town last week, amid great
excitement. Every man as he trotted by was cutting and
eating a watermelon, and throwing the rinds on the
heads of the little negro boys who followed in crowds,
on either side of the street. You wouldn't have dreamed
of war—such shouting and laughing from everybody.
The contrasts we constantly see look like insanity in
our people. The President likes to call attention to the
fact that we have no beggars on our streets, as evidence
that things are not yet desperate with us. He forgets our
bread riot which occurred such a little while ago. That
pale, thin woman with the wan smile haunts me. Ah!
these are the people who suffer the consequence of all
that talk about slavery in the territories you and I used
to hear in the House and Senate Chamber. Somebody,
somewhere, is mightily to blame for all this business,
but it isn't you nor I, nor yet the women who did not
really deserve to have Governor Letcher send the
mayor to read the Riot Act to them. They were only
hungry, and so a thousand of them loaded some carts
with bread for their children. You are not to suppose
I am heartless because I run on in this irrelevant
fashion. The truth is, I am so shocked and disturbed
I am hysterical. It is all so awful.

Your scared-to-death

AGNES.

---

[1] After General Stuart's death Major-General Wade Hampton of South Carolina had been promoted to command the
cavalry.

9. PHOEBE YATES PEMBER—
OUR EXCHANGE PRISONERS

Phoebe Yates, a native of South Carolina, married Thomas Pember of Boston, and was early left a widow. Possessed of executive ability and a tender heart, she made the journey to Richmond in the hope of helping the war wounded. She became superintendent of one of the wings of the immense Chimborazo Hospital. Dr. Freeman quotes T. C. de Leon, the Confederate commentator, who described her as "brisk and brilliant . . . with a will of steel, under a suave refinement, and [a] pretty, almost Creole accent [which] covered the power to ring in defi on occasion." Dr. Freeman adds: "The story of Mrs. Pember's war on waste and thievery, of her struggle with indifference, and of her battle to save the lives of individual soldiers would be heartbreaking were it not told with an odd humor." [1] *This distinctive humor flashes even in the autumn of 1864, amid the encircling gloom.*

Early in September our hearts were gladdened by the tidings that the exchange of prisoners was to be renewed. The sick and wounded of our hospital (but few in number just then), were transferred to other quarters, and the wards put in order to receive our men from Northern prisons.

Can any pen or pencil do justice to those squalid pictures of famine and desolation! Those gaunt, lank skeletons with the dried yellow flesh clinging to bones enlarged by dampness and exposure! Those pale, bluish lips and feverish eyes, glittering and weird when contrasted with the famine-stricken faces,—that flitting, piteous, scared smile which greeted their fellow creatures, all will live forever before the mental vision that then witnessed it.

---

[1] *The South to Posterity*, p. 115.

Living and dead were taken from the flag-of-truce boat, not distinguishable save from the difference of care exercised in moving them. The Federal prisoners we had released were in many instances in a like state, but our ports had been blockaded, our harvests burned, our cattle stolen, our country wasted. Even had we felt the desire to succor, where could the wherewithal have been found? But the foe,—the ports of the world were open to him. He could have fed his prisoners upon milk and honey, and not have missed either. When we review the past, it would seem that Christianity was but a name—that the Atonement had failed, and Christ had lived and died in vain.

But it was no time then for vague reflections. With beating heart, throbbing head and icy hands I went among this army of martyrs and spectres whom it was almost impossible to recognize as human beings; powerless to speak to them, choking with unavailing pity, but still striving to aid and comfort. There was but little variety of appearance. From bed to bed the same picture met the eye. Hardly a vestige of human appearance left.

The passion of sympathy could only impede my efforts if yielded to, for my hand shook too tremulously even to allow me to put the small morsels of bread soaked in wine into their mouths. It was all we dared to give at first. Some laid as if dead with limbs extended, but the greater part had drawn up their knees to an acute angle, a position they never changed until they died. Their more fortunate comrades said that the attitude was generally assumed, as it reduced the pangs of hunger and relieved the craving that gnawed them by day and by night. The Federal prisoners may have been starved at the South, we cannot deny the truth of the charge, in many instances; but we starved with them; we had only a little to share with any—but the subject had better be left to die in silence.

One among them lingered in patience the usual three days that appeared to be their allotted space of life on their return. He was a Marylander, heir to a name renowned in the history of his country, Richard Hammond Key, grandson of Francis Scott Key, author of "Star Spangled Banner," the last of seven sons reared in affluence, but presenting the same bluish, bloodless appearance common to them all. Hoping that there would be some chance of his rallying, I gave him judicious nursing and good brandy. Every precaution was taken, but the third day fever supervened and the little life left waned rapidly. He gave me the trinkets cut from gutta percha buttons that he had beguiled his captivity in making at Point Lookout,[1] to send to his family, handing me one of them for a souvenir; begged that he might be buried apart from the crowd in some spot where those who knew and cared for him might find him some day, and quietly slept himself to death that night. The next morning was the memorable 29th September, 1864, when the enemy made a desperate and successful attack, taking Fort Harrison,[2] holding it and placing Richmond in jeopardy for four hours. The alarm bells summoned the citizens together, and the shops being closed to allow those who kept them to join the city guards, there were no means of buying a coffin, or getting a hearse. It was against the rules to keep a body beyond a certain time on the hospital grounds, so little time was to be lost if I intended keeping my promise to the dead. I summoned a convalescent carpenter from one of the wards, made him knock together a rough coffin from some loose boards, and taking the seats out of my ambulance had

[1] U. S. prison in Maryland.
[2] An important point in the outer defense line southeast of Richmond, near the fortifications of Chapin's Bluff. On September 29, 1864, Federal troops captured it in a surprise move. Fearing that its loss might expose the capital, General Lee hastily gathered detachments for a counterattack and took the field in person. Three times the attack was delivered on the thirtieth, but to no avail. Lee had to extend his lines, which, with his depleted forces, was dangerous. During the fighting at Fort Harrison, Wade Hampton was stopping an advance of Federals that might have brought them to the Southside Railroad. See D. S. Freeman, *R. E. Lee*, III, 500-505.

it, with the body enclosed, put in. My driver was at his post with the guards, so taking the reins and kneeling in the little space at the side of the coffin I started for Hollywood cemetery, a distance of five miles.

The enemy were then in sight, and from every elevated point the masses of manoeuvering soldiers and flash of the enemy's cannon could be distinguished. Only stopping as I passed through the city to buy a piece of ground from the old cemetery agent, I reached Hollywood by twelve o'clock. Near the burying-ground I met the Rev. Mr. McCabe, requested his presence and assistance, and we stood side by side while the sexton dug the grave. The rain was pouring in torrents, while the clergyman repeated the Episcopal burial service from memory. Besides ourselves there were but two poor women, of the humblest class of life—Catholics, who passing casually, dropped upon their knees, undeterred by the rain, and paid their humble tribute of respect to the dead. He had all the honors of a soldier's burial paid to him unconsciously, for the cannon roared and the musketry rattled, mingling with the thunder and lighting of Heaven's artillery. The sexton held his hat over the small piece of paper on which I inscribed his name and birthplace (to be put on his headboard) to protect it from the rain, and with a saddened heart for the solitary grave we left behind I drove back to the city. The reverend gentleman was left at his home, and, perhaps, to this day does not know who his companion was during that strange hour.

I found the city in the same state of excitement, for no authentic news was to be heard, or received, except perhaps at official quarters; and it was well known that we had no troops nearer than Petersburg, save the citizens who had enrolled themselves for defense; therefore too anxious to return directly to the hospital, I drove to the residence of one of the cabinet ministers, where I was engaged to attend a dinner, and found the mistress of the establishment, surrounded by her servants and trunks preparing for a hasty retreat when necessary. Some persuasion induced her to desist, and the situa-

tion of the house commanding an extensive view of
the surrounding country, we watched the advance of
the enemy from the extreme northeast, for with the aid
of opera-glasses we could even distinguish the colors of
their uniforms. Slowly onward moved the bodies of
dark blue, emerging from and disappearing into the
woods, seeming to be skirting around them, but not to
be diminishing the distance between, although each
moment becoming more distinct, which proved their
advance, while not one single Confederate jacket could
be observed over the whole sweep of ground.

Half an anxious hour passed, and then, far away
against the distant horizon, one single mounted horse-
man emerged from a thick wood, looked cautiously
around, passed across the road and disappeared. He was
in gray, and followed by another and another, winding
around and cutting off the foe. Then a startling peal
at the bell, and a courier brought the news that Wade
Hampton and his cavalry were close upon the rear of
the enemy. There was no occasion for fear after this,
for General Hampton was the Montrose of the Southern army, he who could make any cause famous with
his pen and glorious with his sword. The dinner continued in course of preparation, and was seasoned,
when served, by spirits brightened by the strong re-
action.

The horrors that attended, in past times, the bombardment of a city, were experienced in a great degree
in Richmond during the fighting around us. The close
proximity to the scenes of strife, the din of battle, the
bursting of shells, the fresh wounds of the men hourly
brought in were daily occurrences. Walking through
the streets during this time, after the duties of the
hospital were over, when night had well advanced, the
pavement around the railroad depot would be crowded
with wounded men just brought in, and laid there waiting for conveyance to the receiving hospitals. Some on
stretchers, other on the bare bricks, or laid on a thin
blanket, suffering from wounds hastily wrapped around
with strips of coarse, unbleached, galling bandages of

homespun cotton, on which the blood had congealed and stiffened until every crease cut like a knife. Women passing accidentally, like myself, would put down their basket or bundle, and ringing at the bell of neighboring houses, ask for basin and soap, warm water, and a few soft rags, and going from sufferer to sufferer, try to alleviate with what skill they possessed, the pain of fresh wounds, change the uneasy posture, and allay the thirst. Others would pause and look on, till the labor appearing to require no particular talent, they too would follow the example set them, and occasionally asking a word of advice, do their duty carefully and willingly. Idle boys would get a pine knot or tallow-dip, and stand quietly and curiously as torchbearers, till the scene, with its gathering accessories, formed a strange picture, not easily forgotten. Persons driving in different vehicles would alight sometimes in evening dress, and choosing the wounded most in need of surgical aid, put them in their places, and send them to their destination, continuing their way on foot. There was little conversation carried on, no necessity for introductions, and no names ever asked or given. This indifference to personality was a peculiarity strongly exhibited in hospitals, for after nursing a sick or wounded patient for months, he has often left without any curiosity exhibited as regarded my name, my whereabouts, or indeed any thing connected with me. A case in point was related by a friend. When the daughter of our general had devoted much time and care to a sick man in one of the hospitals, he seemed to feel so little gratitude for the attention paid, that her companion to rouse him told him that Miss Lee was his nurse. "Lee, Lee?" he said. "There are some Lees down in Mississippi who keep a tavern there. Is she one of them Lees?"

Almost of the same style, although a little worse was the remark of one of my sick, a poor fellow who had been wounded in the head and who, though sensible enough ordinarily, would feel the effect of the sun on his brain when exposed to its influence. After advising him to wear a wet paper doubled into the crown of his hat more from a desire to show some interest in him than from any belief in its efficacy, I paused at the door long enough to hear him ask the wardmaster "who that was?" "Why, that is the matron of the hospital; she gives you all the food you eat, and attends to things." "Well!" said he, "I always did think this government was a confounded sell, and now I am sure of it, when they put such a little fool to manage such a big hospital as this."

The ingenuity of the men was wonderful in making toys and trifles, and a great deal of mechanical talent was developed by the enforced inaction of hospital life. Every ward had its draught-board and draughtsmen cut out of hard wood and stained with vegetable dyes, and sometimes chessmen would be cut out with a common knife, in such ornamentation that they would not have disgraced a drawing-room. One man carved pipes from ivy root, with exquisitely-cut shields on the bowls bearing the arms of the different States and their mottoes. He would charge and easily get a hundred and fifty dollars for a pipe (Confederate paper was then sixty cents for the dollar), and he only used his well-worn pocket-knife. Playing cards—the greatest comfort to alleviate the tedium of their sick life—were difficult to get a substitute for, so that the original packs had a hard time. They became, as may be supposed from the hands which used them, very dirty in a short time, and the corners in a particularly disreputable condition, but after the diffusion of the Oxford editions of the different books of the Bible sent from England as a donation, the soldiers took a lesson, and rounded the corners in imitation. A pack of cards after four years' use in a Southern hospital was beyond criticism.

The men had their fashions too, sometimes insisting upon having light blue pants drawn for them, and at other seasons preferring gray; but while the mania for either color raged, they would be dissatisfied with the other. When the quartermaster-general issued canvas shoes there was a loud dissatisfaction expressed in constant grumbling, till some original genius dyed the whitish tops by the liberal application of poke-berries. He was the Brummel of the day, and for many months crimson shoes were the rage, and long rows of unshod men would sit under the eaves of the wards, all diligently employed in the same labor and up to their elbows in red juice.

This fashion died out, and gave place to a button mania. Men who had never had a dream or a hope beyond a horn convenience to keep their clothing together, saved up their scanty means to replace them with gilt, and made neat little wooden shelves with a slit through the middle into which the buttons slid, so that they could be cleaned and brightened without taking them off, or soiling the jacket. With the glitter of buttons came the corresponding taste for gilt bands and tinsel around the battered hat, so that while our future was lowering darker and darker, our soldiers were amusing themselves like children who had no interest in the coming results.

The duty which of all others pressed most heavily upon me and which I never did perform voluntarily was that of telling a man he could not live, when he was perhaps unconscious that there was any danger apprehended from his wound. The idea of death so seldom occurs when disease and suffering have not wasted the frame and destroyed the vital energies, that there is but little opening or encouragement to commence such a subject unless the patient suspects the result ever so slightly. In many cases too, the yearning for life was so strong that to destroy the hope was beyond human power. Life was for him a furlough, family and friends once more around him; a future was all he wanted, and he considered it cheaply purchased if only for a month by the endurance of any wound, however painful or wearisome.

There were long discussions among those responsible during the war, as to the advisability of the frequent amputations on the field, and often when a hearty, fine-looking man in the prime of life would be brought in minus an arm or leg, I would feel as if it might have been saved, but experience taught me the wisdom of prompt measures. Poor food and great exposure had thinned the blood and broken down the system so entirely that secondary amputations performed in the hospital almost invariably resulted in death, after the second year of the war. The blood lost on the battle-field when the wound was first received would enfeeble the already impaired system and render it incapable of further endurance.

Once we received a strong, stalwart soldier from Alabama, and after five days' nursing, finding the inflammation from the wound in his arm too great to save the limb, the attending surgeon requested me to feed him on the best I could command; by that means to try and give him strength to undergo amputation. Irritability of stomach as well as indifference to food always accompanying gun-shot wounds, it was necessary, while the fever continued, to give him as much nourishment in as small a compass as possible, as well as easily digestible food, that would assimilate with his enfeebled condition. Beef tea he (in common with all soldiers and I believe men) would not, or could not take, or anything I suggested as an equivalent, so getting his consent to drink some "chemical mixture," I prepared the infusion. Chipping up a pound of beef and pouring upon it a half pint of water, the mixture was stirred until all the blood was extracted, and only a tea-spoonful of white fibre remained; a little salt was added, and favored by the darkness of the corner of the ward in which he lay, I induced him to swallow it. He drank without suspicion, and fortunately liked it, only complaining of its being too sweet; and by the end of ten days his pulse was fairly good, and there had been no accession of fever. Every precaution was taken, both for his sake and the benefit of the experiment, and the arm taken off by the most skillful surgeon we had. After the amputation, which he bore bravely, he looked as bright and well as before, and so on for five days—then the usual results followed. The system proved not strong enough to throw out the "pus" or inflammation: and this, mingling with the blood, produced that most fatal of all diseases, pyaemia, from which no one ever recovers.

He was only one of numerous cases, so that my heart beat twice as rapidly as ordinarily whenever there were any arrangements progressing for amputation, after any length of time had elapsed since the wound, or any effort made to save the limb. The only cases under my observation that survived were two Irishmen, and it was really so difficult to kill an Irishman that there was little cause for boasting on the part of the officiating surgeons. One of them had his leg cut off in pieces, amputation having been performed three times, and the last heard from him was that he had married a young wife and settled on a profitable farm she owned in Macon, Georgia. He had touched the boundary lines of the "unknown land," had been given up by the surgeons, who left me with orders to stimulate him if possible. The priest (for he was a Catholic) was naturally averse to my disturbing what he considered the last moments of a dying man who had made his confession and taken his farewell of this world, and which ought to have been devoted to less worldly temptations than mint juleps; and a rather brisk encounter was the result of a difference of opinion on the subject; for if he was responsible for the soul, so was I for the body, and I held my ground firmly.

It was hard for an Irishman and a good Catholic to have to choose at this supreme moment between religion and whiskey; but though his head was turned respectfully towards good Father T—— his eyes rested too lovingly on the goblet offered to his lips to allow me to make any mistake as to the results of his ultimate intentions. The interpretation put by me on that look was that Callahan thought that as long as first proof brandy and mint lasted in the Confederacy this world was good enough for him, and the result proved that

I was not mistaken. He always gave me the credit I have awarded to the juleps, and until the evacuation of Richmond kept me informed of his domestic happiness. . . .

10. KATE CUMMING—CHASING MY HOSPITAL

Stouthearted Kate has moved on with the Army of Tennessee into Georgia but her hospital has moved ahead of her and she is trying desperately to catch up with it.

General W. T. Sherman's plans of capturing Atlanta depended on the destruction of the railroads that centered there: the Georgia, running east to Augusta; the West Point, southwest to Montgomery; and the Central, south and southeast to Macon and Savannah. Late in July he marched down the Chattahoochee Valley to hit the West Point road. General Hood, fighting him at Ezra Church on the twenty-eighth, was repulsed and the line broken. At the same time expeditions by Federal cavalry under George Stoneman and Edward M. McCook against the railroads to Macon and Augusta did them a lot of damage, though the forces were dispersed and the leaders captured. No wonder Kate had railroad trouble.

She stuck to her job till the war was over.

[Americus, Georgia]

August 19, 1864

We started from Newnan on the 15th instant, and very much to our regret, as we had to leave so many of our old patients behind. . . .

Mr. Williams of the Ninth Kentucky, one of our old patients, tried to procure a permit to come with us, but he did not succeed. We were very sorry, as he was anxious to get away from Newnan for fear of being captured. He had been in the country at the time the hospital was moved. . . .

We arrived at West Point about sundown the same day. Dr. W. had put us under the care of the conductor, and he took us to a small hotel—the Exchange. The landlord was moving, but informed us we might lodge there for the night, as we had provisions with us; that was all for which we cared. He gave us a room without even a washbowl or pitcher in it; for the privilege of remaining in this delightful room we paid the moderate sum of ten dollars.

We walked around the place; it is like many other of our small towns—in a forlorn condition. . . .

There is quite a formidable fort built on a high hill, and from it we had a very fine view of the surrounding country. The fort is garrisoned by Massingale's battery. . . .

We had a pleasant walk on the bridge which the enemy were so desirous of destroying. I believe the guard on it were Governor Brown's [1] men. In the late raid through this portion of the country, the enemy's object was the destruction of this bridge, as it is a very important one to us. By its destruction we would lose one of the communications with the Gulf States, and at present they are the granary of the Tennessee army; and besides that, all communications between these states and both armies would be hindered, at least for awhile. The river at this point is very wide.

The late raiders did not come any further than Opelika, which is not many miles distance. There they destroyed a large portion of the railroad and government property. . . .

We were informed that morning that the Federals had cut the road between that point and Atlanta, and as the train did not come in at its usual time, we were confident the report was true, but the arrival of the train proved it false. We left about 4 P.M. on the 16th.

When a few miles beyond Opelika the locomotive ran off the track, and we came near having a very serious accident. I was reading, and knew nothing of

[1] Joseph E. Brown, Governor of Georgia, 1857-1865, was an almost fanatical defender of States' rights.

it until I heard some ladies scream. I then felt a motion as if the train was about to upset. I saw several of the cars ahead of us plunge off the road, and men jumping from them; many took to the woods, as they were fearful of an explosion.

We remained on the car all night. Next morning men who had come from Opelika were at work trying to clear the track, but the job looked like an endless one. Every car excepting the one we were on (it being the last) was off the track.

One of our old patients made us some coffee, and we, like all the rest, ate our breakfast on the roadside. We were in the woods, and no sign of a habitation near. As there was little or no hope of our leaving there for some time, a gentleman who had found an empty house a little ways back came and took his party, Mrs. W., and myself to it. We found it quite a nice retreat. It had been a school-house, and the benches and desks were left standing. We had books, and altogether had quite a pleasant day. Our gentleman friend was Senator Hill,[1] of Legrange, Georgia. . . . Mr. Hill gave us some nice biscuit and ham, his servant made our coffee for dinner; and altogether we had a most delightful repast.

Miss Augusta Evans,[2] the authoress, was on the train, going to Columbus, where she has a badly wounded brother. From her I learned that all was quiet in Mobile, although we have had a naval battle, and Forts Morgan, Powell, and Gaines were taken. The battle was a desperate one, and we have lost our splendid ram, the Tennessee. Admiral Buchanan was severely wounded; himself and whole crew are prisoners. . . .

About 3 P.M., a wood-car came from Columbus, on which we all got. We cut branches of trees and held them over us for protection from the sun. We reached Columbus without further accident in time to catch

[1] Senator Ben Hill was a much more liberal supporter of the Confederacy than Governor Brown.
[2] See page 211 *supra*.

the Macon train. We arrived at the latter place about
4 A.M., the 17th. Went to a hotel and paid ten dollars
for a bed, and as much more for breakfast. We called
on Drs. Bemiss and Stout, and learned from them that
our hospital had gone to Americus, Georgia. These two
gentlemen were low spirited; they do not like the idea
of coming so far South at this season, and think it will
be deleterious to the wounded. . . .

The train to Americus had already gone and Mrs.
W., being fearful that if we remained in the hotel
another day our exchequer would be empty, we called
on our old friend, Dr. Cannon, who has charge of the
Wayside Home. I knew he could tell us where we
could procure a boarding house more suited to our
means. His two daughters were with him, and were
keeping house in two rooms, refugee style: one of the
rooms was parlor, bed-room, and dining-room, the
other a kind of dressing-room. It astonishes me to see
how well every body manages now-a-days; they put
up with inconveniences as if they had been used to
them all their lives. The war seems to have raised the
minds of many above common every-day annoyances.
Dr. C. insisted on us remaining with his family, and
as Mrs. W. was half sick, and we were both worn out,
we were only too thankful to accept the kind invitation.
The family seem to be perfectly happy, as much so, I
expect, as they ever were in their home in Tennessee.

Dr. Nagle and an officer who is stationed at Andersonville, where the prisoners are kept, spent the evening with us. The prisoners and their behavior was the
principal topic of conversation, and from all we could
learn we did not like the prospect of being so near
them (Americus is ten miles below Andersonville).
This officer informed us that no less than a hundred
died daily. He said they were the most desperate set
of men that he had ever seen. There were two parties
among them, the black republicans and the copperheads, and they often have desperate fights, and kill
each other. This officer said it was revolting to be near
such men, and did not like his position.

Dr. C. sent us to the depot on the 19th in an ambulance. The train stopped a little while at Fort Valley, where the Buckner and Gamble Hospitals, of our post, have remained. There we saw a few familiar faces. The train remained about a half an hour at Andersonville, so we had time for a good view of the prisoners' quarters. I must say that my antipathy for prison-life was any thing but removed by the sight. My heart sank within me at seeing so many human beings crowded so closely together. I asked a gentleman near why we had so many in one place. He answered that we would not have men enough to guard them were they scattered. O, how I thought of him who is the cause of all this woe on his fellow-countrymen—Abraham Lincoln. What kind of a heart can he have, to leave these poor wretches here? To think how often we have begged for exchange; but this unfeeling man knows what a terrible punishment it is for our men to be in Northern prisons, and how valuable every one of them is to us. For this reason he sacrifices thousands of his own. May Heaven help us all! But war is terrible.

Arrived at Americus to-day, the 19th. . . .

11. MARY ANN HARRIS GAY—THE BATTLE FOR ATLANTA

Miss Gay was born in Jones County, Georgia, March 19, 1829. She and her mother were living in Decatur when war broke out. Her half sister, Missouri Stokes, taught school in the neighborhood, and her half brother, Thomas J. Stokes, was with the 10th Texas Infantry. Now in July 1864 the residence was being used as headquarters for Sherman's advance army.

Miss Gay wrote her book Life in Dixie during the War *especially for her only nephew, Thomie Stokes of Atlanta, but he died before it was published. Joel Chandler Harris supplied the introduction. "It is a gentle, a faithful and a tender hand that guides the pen," he says; "a soul nerved to sacrifice that tells the tale."*

Decatur, Georgia

No news from "the front;" no tidings from the loved ones in gray; no friendly spirit whispering words of cheer or consolation. Shut up within a narrow space, and guarded by Federal bayonets! not a ray of friendly light illuminated my environment.

The constant roaring of cannon and rattling of musketry; the thousand, yea, tens of thousands of shots blending into one grand continuous whole, and reverberating in avalanchan volume over the hills of Fulton, and the mountain heights of old DeKalb— told in thunder tones of the fierce contest between Federal and Confederate forces being waged without intermission for the possession of Atlanta.

The haughty, insolent boast of the enemy, now that Joe Johnston was removed from the command of the Army of the Tennessee, that they would make quick work of the rebellion, and of the complete subjugation of the South, had in no way a tendency to mitigate anxiety or to encourage hope. Thus surrounded, I sought and obtained permission to read Federal newspapers. The United States mail brought daily papers to the officers in command of the troops quartered in our yard; and through this medium I kept posted, from a Northern standpoint, concerning the situation of both armies. While there was little in these dispatches gratifying to me, there was much that I thought would be valuable to my people if I could only convey it to them; and I racked my brain day and night, devising ways and means by which to accomplish this feat. But the ways and means decided upon were, upon reflection, invariably abandoned as being impracticable.

In this dilemma, a most opportune circumstance offered an immediate solution of the difficult problem. In the midst of a deep study of the relative positions of the two armies, and of the hopes and fears animating both, a tall, lank, honest-faced Yankee came to the door of the portico and asked "if Miss Gay was in."

I responded that I was she, and he handed me a letter addressed to myself. I hastily tore it open and read the contents. It was written by a reverend gentleman whose wife was a distant relative of my mother, and told that she was very ill. "Indeed," wrote he, "I have but little hope of ever seeing her any better, and I beg you to come to see her, and spend several days."

I showed the letter to my mother, who was sitting near by, and, like myself, engaged in studying the situation. She strenuously objected to my going, and advanced many good reasons for my not doing so; but my reasons for going counteracted them all in my estimation, and I determined to go.

Taking Telitha with me, I carried the letter to the Provost Marshal, and asked him to read it and grant me the privilege of going. After reading the letter, he asked me how I obtained it, and received my statement. He then asked me if I could refer him to the party who brought it to me. Leaving the letter with him, I ran home and soon returned with the desired individual who had fortunately lingered in the yard in anticipation of usefulness. Convinced that the invitation was genuine, and for a humane purpose, this usually morose marshal granted me "a permit" to visit those poor old sick people, for the husband was almost as feeble as his wife. I told the obliging marshal that there was another favor I should like to ask of him, if he would not think me too presumptuous. "Name it," he said.

I replied: "Will you detail one or more of the soldiers to act as an escort for me? I am afraid to go with only this girl."

To this he also assented, and said it was a wise precaution. He asked when I wished to come home.

"Day after to-morrow afternoon," I told him, and received assurance that an escort would be in waiting for me at that time.

It now became necessary to make some important

preparations for the trip. A great deal was involved, and if my plans were successful, important events might accrue. A nice white petticoat was called into requisition, and, when I got done with it, it was literally lined with Northern newspapers. "The Cincinnati Enquirer," and "The New York Daily Times;" "The Cincinnati Commercial Gazette," and "The Philadelphia Evening Ledger," under the manipulation of my fingers, took their places on the inner sides and rear of the skirt, and served as a very stylish "bustle," an article much in vogue in those days. This preparatory work having been accomplished, it required but a few moments to complete my toilet, and, under the auspices of a clear conscience and a mother's blessing, doubtless, I started on a perilous trip. The ever-faithful Telitha was by my side, and the military escort a few feet in advance.

After a walk of a mile and a half, I reached my destination for that day. I found the old lady in question much better than I had expected. Nervous and sick himself, her husband had greatly exaggerated her afflictions. By degree, and under protest, I communicated to these aged people my intention of carrying information to Hood's headquarters, that might be of use to our army. Both were troubled about the possible result if I should be detected; but my plans were laid, and nothing could deter me from pursuing them.

The rising sun of another day saw Telitha and me starting on our way to run the gauntlet, so to speak, of Federal bayonets. These good old people had given me much valuable information regarding the way to Atlanta—information which enabled me to get there without conflict with either Confederate or Federal pickets. Knowing the topography of the country, I took a circuitous route to an old mill, Cobb's I believe, and from there I sought the McDonough road. I didn't venture to keep that highway to the city, but I kept within sight of it, and under cover of breast-works and other obstructions, managed to evade videttes and pickets of both armies. After walking fourteen or fifteen miles, I entered Atlanta at the beautiful home of Mrs. L. P. Grant, at the southern boundary of the city. That estimable lady never lost an opportunity of doing good. On this occasion, as upon every other offering an opportunity, she remembered to do good. She ordered an appetizing lunch, including a cup of sure-enough coffee, which refreshed and strengthened me after my long walk. Her butler having become a familiar personage on the streets of Atlanta, she sent him as a guide to important places. We entered the city unchallenged, and moved about at will. The force of habit, probably, led me to Mrs. McArthur's and to Mrs. Craig's on Pryor Street. The head of neither of these families was willing to accompany me to Confederate headquarters, and without a guide I started to hunt them for myself. What had seemed an easy task now seemed insurmountable. I knew not in what direction to go, and the few whom I asked seemed as ignorant as myself. Starting from Mrs. Craig's, I went towards the depot. I had not proceeded very far before I met Major John Y. Rankin. I could scarcely restrain tears of joy. He was a member of the very same command to which my brother belonged. From Major Rankin I learned that my brother, utterly prostrated, had been sent to a hospital, either in Augusta or Madison.

Preferring not to stand upon the street, I asked Major Rankin to return with me to Mrs. Craig's, which he did, and spent an hour in pleasant conversation. Mrs. Craig was a delightful conversationalist, and while she was entertaining the major with that fine art, I retired to a private apartment, and with the aid of a pair of scissors ripped off the papers from my under-skirt and smoothed and folded them nicely, and after re-arranging my toilet, took them into the parlor as a trophy of skill in outwitting the Yankee. Telitha, too, had a trophy to which she had clung since we left home with the tenacity of an eel, and which doubtless she supposed to be an an offering to "Marse Tom," and was evidently anxious that he should receive it. Having

dismissed Mrs. Grant's butler as no longer necessary
to my convenience, Major Rankin, myself and Telitha
went direct to the headquarters of his command. The
papers seemed to be most acceptable, but I noticed
that the gleanings from conversation seemed far more
so. The hopefulness and enthusiasm of our soldiers
were inspiring. But alas! how little they knew of the
situation, and how determined not to be enlightened.
Even then they believed that they would hold Atlanta
against Herculean odds, and scorned the idea of surrender. At length the opening of Telitha's package
devolved on me. Shirts, socks and soap, towels, gloves,
etc., formed a compact bundle that my mother had
sent to our soldiers.

I now turned my thoughts to our negroes, who were
hired in different parts of the city. Rachel, the mother
of King, hired herself and rented a room from Mr.
John Silvey. In order that I might have an interview
with Rachel without disturbing Mr. Silvey's family, I
went to the side gate and called her. She answered
and came immediately. I asked her if she realized the
great danger to which she was continually exposed.
Even then "shot and shell" were falling in every direction, and the roaring of cannon was an unceasing
sound. She replied that she knew the danger, and
thought I was doing wrong to be in Atlanta when I
had a home to be at. I insisted that she had the same
home, and a good vacant house was ready to receive
her. But she was impervious to every argument, and
preferred to wait the coming of Sherman in her present
quarters. Seeing that I had no influence over her, I
bade her good-bye and left.

Telitha and I had not gone farther than the First
Presbyterian Church, not a square away from the gate
upon which I had leaned during this interview with
Rachel, before a boomshell fell by that gate and
burst into a thousand fragments, literally tearing the
gate into pieces. After this fearfully impressive adventure, unfortified by any "permit" I struck a bee line
to Mrs. Grant's. An old negro man belonging to Mrs.

Williams, who had "come out" on a previous occasion, was there, and wanted to return under my protection to his home within the enemy's lines. Very earnest assurances from Mrs. Grant to that effect convinced me that I had nothing to fear from betrayal by him, and I consented that he should be a member of my company homeward bound. Two large packages were ready for the old man to take charge of, about which Mrs. Grant gave him directions, *sotto voce*. Putting one of them on the end of a walking cane he threw it over his right shoulder, and with his left hand picked up the other bundle. Telitha and I were unencumbered. We had not proceeded very far before we encountered our pickets. No argument was weighty enough to secure for me the privilege of passing the lines without an official permit. Baffled in this effort, I approved the action of the pickets, and we turned and retraced our steps in the direction of Atlanta, until entirely out of sight of them, and then we turned southward and then eastward, verging a little northward. Constant vigilance enabled me to evade the Yankee pickets, and constant walking brought me safely to the home of my aged and afflicted friends, from which I had started early in the morning of that day. These friends were conservative in every act and word, and, it may be leaned a little out of the perpendicular towards that "flaunting lie," the United States flag; therefore they were favorites among the so-called defenders of the Union, and were kept supplied with many palatable articles of food that were entirely out of the reach of rebels who were avowed and "dyed in the wool."

A few minutes sufficed to furnish us with a fine pot of soup (and good bread was not lacking), of which we ate heartily. The old negro man was too anxious to get home to be willing to spend the night so near, just for the privilege of walking into Decatur under Yankee escort, and said he was "going home," and left me.

The next day my escort was promptly on hand, and in due time I was in Decatur. . . .

Not many mornings subsequent to the adventure just related, I discovered upon opening the door that the Yankee tents seemed to be vacant. Not a blue-coat was to be seen. What could it mean? Had they given up the contest and ignominiously fled? As if confirmatory of the gratifying suggestion, the booming of cannon in the direction of Atlanta was evidently decreasing. Then again I thought perhaps the wagon train had been sent out to forage upon the country, and as it would now have to go forty-five and fifty miles to get anything, it required an immense military escort to protect it from the dashing sanguinary attacks of the "rebels."

Before the sun had attained its meridian height, a number of our scouts appeared on the abandoned grounds; and what joy their presence gave us! But they left us as suddenly as they came, and on reflection we could not think of a single encouraging word uttered by them during their stay. Suspense became intolerable. With occasional lulls, the roaring of cannon was a continuous blending of ominous sound.

In the midst of this awful suspense, an apparition, glorious and bright, appeared in our presence. It was my brother. He had left Madison a few days before, where he had been allowed to spend a part of his furlough, instead of remaining at the Augusta hospital. His mother's joy at meeting her beloved son, and under such circumstances, was pathetic indeed, and I shall never forget the effort she made to repress the tears and steady the voice as she sought to nerve him for the arduous and perilous duties before him. . . .

The shades of night came on, and darker grew until complete blackness enveloped the face of the earth, and still the low subdued tones of conversation between mother, son and daughter, mingled with unabated interest. Hark! Hark! An explosion! An earthquake? The angry bellowing sound rises in deafening grandeur, and reverberates along the far-off valley and distant hill-tops. What is it—this mighty thunder that never ceases? The earth is ablaze—what can it be?

This illumination that reveals minutest objects? With blanched face and tearful eye, the soldier said:

"Atlanta has surrendered to the enemy. The mighty reports are occasioned by the blowing up of the magazines and arsenals."

Dumbfounded we stood, trying to realize the crushing fact. Woman's heart could bear no more in silence, and a wail over departed hopes mingled with the angry sounds without. . . .

12. MARY RAWSON—"THEY TOOK POSSESSION OF ATLANTA QUIETLY"

The young daughter of E. E. Rawson of Atlanta kept a war diary which ended with the occupation by Sherman at the beginning of September 1864. Her father was a member of the city Council. When Sherman sought to justify his order of evacuation he addressed himself to James M. Calhoun, Mayor, E. E. Rawson, and S. C. Wells. Mary married Captain John D. Ray of the 1st Georgia Volunteers.

Atlanta, Georgia August 31, 1864

This day witnessed the downfall of the hopes of the citizens of Atlanta. Today Gen. Hood commenced his evacuation of our city. The gentlemen who did not wish to fall into the hands of the federals might have been seen in the afternoon of this day in company of the last of the soldiers, wending their way slowly out of the now desolate Atlanta; as night threw around our home its sable shadows, silence reigned broken only by pleasant converse with our now absent friends. How different from the few last nights preceeding; the pleasure and repose of these evenings was disturbed by the noise of exploding shells and the sharp crack of the death-dealing musketry. Oh! how much more pleasure there would have been had it not been for the expectation of the scene of the coming morrow. Nine oclock comes and we retire for the night, but sleep and dreams were soon interrupted by rapid and loud explosions. On arising a most beautiful spectacle greeted our sight. The Heavens were in a perfect glow while the atmosphere seemed full of flaming rockets, crash follows crash and the swift moving locomotives were rent in pieces and the never tiring metalic horse lay powerless while the sparks filled the air with innumerable spangles. This great exhibition was occasioned by the burning of the military stores which could not be removed with the soldiers. This crashing had scarcely ceased when our attention was called in another direction by a bright light which proved to be the burning of some more Government provisions.

After a time, it seemed to us an unending time, the morning dawned and the bright sun arose which ushered in another eventful month, September 1864. Although the commencement of this day was outwardly so pleasant, language falls short in expressing the suspense and anxiety experienced by everyone. Time after time had we been told of the severity of Gen. Sherman until we came to dread his approach as we would that of a mighty hurricane which sweeps all before it caring naught for justice or humanity.

The forenoon passed slowly with nothing of importance transpiring except a visit from Mr. Tenny, informing us that a few cavalry had been left to dispute every inch of ground through the city, as he said. With dinner time came Father, who said that the Federals had taken possession of the city. Oh! What a relief to me, I had expected them to enter in disorder exulting loudly in the success of their enterprise. Atlanta was taken possession of quietly. About ten oclock in the morning the mayor, two councilmen with the principle citizens went out to invite them in. After some hesitation they marched in under the command of Gen. Slocume.[1] Gen. Sherman was at this time preparing to

---

[1] Major-General Henry W. Slocum, corps commander.

encounter Gen. Hood near Jonesboro.[1] Immediately upon entering the town the stars and stripes were seen floating from the flag pole on the Franklin building. Father's store was used as a signal station; the signals were given with a blue flag having a large white star in the center and in the evening they used beautiful lanterns which were moved in different directions. . . .

Friday 2d. passed without particular event occurring. Saturday, this morning the sun and the bright azure are shut out by lowering clouds from which the rain pours in torrents. At ten this morning Father had a visit from the provost marshal and several other officers, who wished us to give up our beautiful home for headquarters for the general. This request Father told him it was impossible to comply with for where could we find another home of any kind? They finally gave up the idea of taking it from us and seemed much pleased with our old school house instead. Oh how I felt to see the beloved old playground in front of the school covered with tents and the beautiful little shade tree cut down. Besides how could I see Miss Maria's and Miss Anne's cherished pet flowers trampled down by those who could not appreciate their beauty and fragrance. Oh it was too much and Mattie and I shed tears to think of the desolation. We were the only ones left of the pleasant class of seven who used to assemble daily at the Pine Hill seminary. How many friends were scattered in the great stampeed previous to the desertion of Atlanta. Many of the girls had gone further South with their parents and one dear class mate left us for another and I hope better world, during the enclosure of our city by both Armies. But I forget myself. I was speaking of the visit of the officers. When they prepared to leave I was amused as well as astonished to see the behavior of the grooms. One of them

[1] Sherman had moved twenty-two miles southwest of Atlanta to strike the Central Railroad near Jonesboro. On August 31, General William J. Hardee, facing west from Jonesboro, attempted, without success, to drive the Federals into Flint River, but the next day drove Sherman back from Jonesboro.

happening to be in our bomb-proof, his master called "Jack come out of that proof and get my horse" and how he did fly to obey his orders, brought his horse and equiped him for his rainy journey by buttoning on his oilcloth coat and after much elaborate brushing he gently placed him on his saddle and they went away. All this I witnessed from the dining room window. . . .

The darkness now set in and I had a fine view of Gen. Gearys [1] headquarters with the tents surrounding it—my window presenting a good prospect of the city. The house was illuminated from the basement to the attic and the camp fires spread all over the hills filling the atmosphere with a light smoke with the piramid of light issueing from the windows of the generals home. . . . It grows late and I must retire to bed not having a very flattering anticipation of the coming Sabbath and carried to dreamland by the music of the bugle.

Sunday. At ten today our hearts were made sad by hearing the familiar chimes of the church bells. How often has this been the signal to us for leaving our homes to hear the word of God expounded. Today these peals serve only to send innumerable squads of soldiers to our own loved churches. The hills as well as the once crowded thorough-fare of Atlanta are covered with blue-coats wending their way to the different places of worship. Noon and dinner time come and afterwards Capt. Seymore called. Pa told him of the frequent depredations committed on our potato patch and he immediately sent us a guard. This afternoon as we stood in the upper front veranda, we noticed a great dust and what appeared to be a vast number of soldiers marching; besides, for the first time since the city was taken we heard the air of Yankee-doodle. After watching the soldiers some time one of

[1] General John W. Geary, U. S. A. He had been first postmaster, first alcalde, first mayor of San Francisco, and governor of Kansas. Sherman was accustomed to entrust civil affairs to him.

the guards came around the terrace and saluted his fellow with the interrogation did you see the Johnnies? They were bringing in some captured Confederates and by close observation we could distinguish the two bodies of infantry, prisoners and the victors. These men were taken to one of the freight depots where a great many of the ladies visited them carrying delicacies.

Monday has been a quiet day for us. This evening George Zimmerman came over to request that Father would call the next morning to see his mother, and Gen. Sherman had ordered all ladies whose husbands were in "Rebel service," as he said, to leave the city in five days and Mr. Zimmerman being absent he had no one to advise with.

Tuesday. While we were at breakfast this morning Grand-father came and told us that Aunty had been ordered to leave her beautiful home to give place to a *Yankee colonel* who had given her only half a day to move all her property. O cruel soldier. I concluded I would go with Father and see Miss Delia and as Grand-pa urged me I would go to Grand-Mas on my return. I found Miss Delia indignant at the thought of being driven from home. O, she said, I would not live among them and if I had had any idea of them coming I would have gone ere this. But not withstanding her anger I had a very pleasant visit. I went according to promise to see Grand-Ma. The house was all in confusion, occasioned by the bringing in of Aunty's furniture. Then I went to Aunty's to see if I could not render some assistance and by constant running to and fro we succeeded in getting most of her valuables removed. But all this time the officers were there dictating as to what should be carried away and what should remain and continually repeating the injunction of haste, haste, forgetting that haste makes waste. Tongue cannot express her trouble in leaving, she has no home to go to elsewhere.

On returning to my home I found Mother in great
anxiety, caused by the information derived from the
guard first and confirmed by Mr. Tenny and Mr. Andrews that all citizens should be compelled to vacate the
city, though they still had choice of which home they
would prefer. We could be sent farther down in Dixie
or we could attempt the ice and snow of the Northern
winter. Father did not think the report at all reliable,
but went to the provost marshal to inquire, but on
reaching the office the door was closed; and a notice
tacked on the door, saying that no one would be admitted until the next day, he then called on Gen. Geary
and asked him concerning the order but he had heard
nothing of it. So wearied out by walking and anxiety
he returned home without any cheering news.

Wednesday. 7th. Today the first report on leaving
the breakfast room was a confirmation of the one received yesterday. Father immediately set out for the
headquarters of Gen. Slocume and afterwards to the
provost and afterwards home again. At noon we
gathered around Father to hear Gen. Shermans order
read. During the forenoon he had seen Gen. Geary,
Col. Beckworth, Capt. Forbes and Capt. Seymore.
These had all expressed it as their opinion that the
command referred to these men who in some way had
been in the Confederate service and that all others
could remain quietly in their home. The question now
was. What explanation to give the order. There was
also another law written forbidding any person to sell
cotton or tobacco, as such comodities would be impressed for the government use. Pa was kept constantly moving to and fro trying to get authority to
dispose of his tobacco for some mere pittance though
this was finally proved to be impracticable, unless a
special permit could be obtained from Sherman.

Thursday. 8th. The order compelling all persons to
evacuate the city was today plainly written out. All
those whose husbands were in the service were to leave

on Monday, while the remainder were given fifteen days to pack and leave.

Fathers property mostly consisted in land and Confederate money so we had not means enough to venture North, unless Pa could get something for his tobacco.

Friday. 9th. Father made a visit to Col. Beckworth and Col. Cason to find if no disposition could be made of the tobacco, but ill fated weed though much loved and longed for by Yankee soldiery, you seem as ever to be only a source of trouble to those who possess and use you. No success was experienced and evening found us as undecided as in the morning.

Saturday dawns and another day of continued exertion and restless anxiety slowly passes. All of this time we had been wasting our precious fifteen days. Another appeal was made today to Col. Beckworth and he promised to see Gen. Sherman and obtain a written paper allowing us to dispose of our provisions and tobacco if he could. With this assurance we prepared to spend the approaching Sabbath.

Sunday. This morning Mother concluded that although we had not the slightest idea of our future home, we had better commence the task of packing. Scarcely was the work begun when we heard that all those who went South would have their trunks searched and all goods not ready made be removed. Now came the question as to how we could secrete them and so take them with us. We finally prepared two trunks to go either way by folding pieces of goods between ready made clothes and by tearing the cloth into pieces of sufficient length to make dress skirts and a great many other ways we found of hiding our goods. While we were in the midst of our work Aunt Charlotte came over from Grandmas and told us they had already opened Auntys trunks twice and came to perform the same detestable office again, when Aunty refused de-

cidedly to open her baggage any more and Col. Beckworth coming in at that moment gave him a sound
cudgening. Aunt Charlotte expressed her determination to follow her master and mistress wherever they
go. Dear old Granny may you be well protected and
carefully nursed during your old age and when life
is over be laid gently to rest by those who can and
do appreciate you.

This afternoon on hearing martial music, we looked
up from the front porch where were were sitting to
see the street filled with cavalry and infantry pack
mules and army wagons and cattle crowded promis-
cously together, the cavalry and infantry ensigns floating in unison together. The musicians all riding on
white horses. After making the signal for the march to
commence they rode silently along until they passed
in front of Gen. Gearys headquarters when simultane-
ously they broke into the old soul stirring "Hail Columbia"; the suddenness of the music startled me. They
then, (after finishing the piece) slowly and silently
marched through the city. A few minutes after this
Mother went over to see my Grandparents and Aunty;
and I went to have a little talk with Mattie; her father
had determined to go to the North and so it seemed
probable that the friends of seven years would be separated. We finally parted, I with a beautiful sprig of
honeysuckle in my hair, placed there by Mr. Andrews
who remarked that this would be the last time he would
deck my hair for me.

Monday. 12th. This morning on leaving the breakfast table I hastily tied on my hat and veil previous
to going to bid my dear kindred goodbye, for this was
the day appointed for them to go. Arriving at the house
I found two huge Army wagons and two ambulances
at the gate and men hurrying to and fro with trunks
and other baggage. At last they all came out and took
their places in the ambulance and after a sad adieu
they slowly departed. Then I returned home and all
along the street in front of Mrs. Zimmermans I no-

ticed many vehicles for taking them away and even more sadly than at first if possible I continued my walk.

Tuesday. 13th. This morning Father concluded to go himself to see Gen. Sherman and ask if he could get a written order permitting him to sell his provisions. About ten oclock he came back bringing the papers signed by the General, then came a long conversation with Mother which terminated in the resolve to brave the severities of the cold North West. We immediately prepared to emigrate to the prairies of Iowa. . . .

13. HENRIETTA HUNT MORGAN—
"A BETTER SON NEVER LIVED"

On September 4, 1864, four days after John Hunt Morgan left Mattie in Abington, Virginia, for his last raid, he was shot by a Union soldier in Greeneville, Tennessee. Now it is his mother's turn to speak—to speak to the bereft wife whom she had never seen. She writes from Hopemont, her home in Lexington, Kentucky.

The daughter of John Wesley Hunt and widow of Calvin Morgan of Lexington, Henrietta was the mother of eight children. Her namesake daughter was the wife of General Basil Duke, John Hunt Morgan's right hand and chronicler; her daughter Kitty, the wife of the great General Ambrose P. Hill. Besides John Hunt, Henrietta gave four sons to the Confederacy: Richard, Charlton, Calvin and Thomas. Thomas had been killed only three months ago—and now there is this culminating grief! Key, her youngest son, named for kinsman Francis Scott Key, was a boy of fifteen.

A daughter was born to Mattie Ready Morgan after John Hunt's death. Some years later Mattie married

*James Williamson, a Confederate veteran who became
a circuit judge at Lebanon, Tennessee.*

October 1st 1864

My Dear Dear Mattie, What words of comfort can I
offer, my precious one, when my own heart is lashed
and torn bleeding with this last terrible wound? Weak
and worn and not at all healed from the great sorrow
that has weighed me down the past eighteen months,
my heart is faint, my nerves shattered, I lie awake
night after night, count each strike of the clock, dread
both night and day, tremble to open a letter. How
gladly would I gather you and all together and fly to
some far-off land, where there would be no sound of
strife, but Oh! the dear ones can never be restored.
How hard it is to resign my children. God gave them
to me, to lose. It cannot be wicked that I feel the struggle so great to resign them. God forgive me if it is!
I love you, dear Mattie, as having been a part of my
boy. I hope the time may someday come when I can
evince to you my full appreciation of the love you
bore my noble son. A better son and brother never
lived, so gentle, watchful to guard me from the dis-
agreeables of life. From his youth to the last time I
saw him he considered his mother!

Poor dear Charlton truly says he has lost a father,
brother and friend. Trust in my love, dear child. I shall
cherish it, for his sake and your own. My children are
my all—are you not one? Although the circle is getting
smaller and smaller, we must be a united family. Consider me as your own mother. Command my services
in any way at any time. You have my heart.

For two weeks, although confined to my room and
on the bed, I could not help hoping there was some
mistake. If a servant would step in and remark, "Miss
Henrietta, many persons think it is not so," I felt like
falling on my knees to embrace them with a feeling of
gratitude for those little words of comfort. I wanted
every hour to pour out my heart to God, and plead
for his life to be spared a few years longer. After my

prayers for a little while I would be comforted, but when the terrible letters came from dear Dick and Basil, it was all over, my hope was all all gone. I had to bow my head to the rod. It is selfish in me so to indulge and not try to comfort you. Forgive it, for it is my nature. After a while my letters should be more tranquil, I will try not to indulge in such lamentations! My children are sincerely attached to you; command them at all times as brothers and sisters. I had a letter from dear Dollie of the 18th, the first for a long time; I was happy to know she and the children were well and comfortable. How anxious she must be all the time about her husband. I hear Henrietta has left Abingdon. Her whereabouts I do not know, poor dear child. I hoped Basil and Dick would have recruited a little before going into active service. Frank, my baby—do use your sisterly influence to keep him from the front. I heard you were going to Augusta; I was very glad you would be with your relations. I have a dear kind brother who will do all in his power to comfort you. I trust, my dear, there may still be a *blessing* in store for you and all. The last letter from you was the 1st of September. Your dear husband had left the day before soon to be back. How well it is the veil cannot be lifted from the future. God bless you and shield you from all future sorrow is the unceasing prayer of your unknown, tho devoted Mother.

HENRIETTA MORGAN

III

WINTER OF DESPERATION

November 1864–March 1865

The recent antagonists, Hood and Sherman, now marched away from each other. Hood was going northwest to destroy Sherman's lines of communication, to recapture Nashville and perhaps keep on to the Ohio River.

Sherman dispatched first Thomas and then Schofield to hold Nashville. Schofield might have been destroyed at Spring Hill, Tennessee, on November 29, but somehow his army was allowed to slip by. When Hood attacked him the next day at Franklin, in a charge that for desperate valor rivaled Pickett's at Gettysburg, 4,500 Confederates were killed or wounded in an hour. Schofield proceeded to Nashville. There George H. Thomas waited patiently till he had assembled a massive force, twice as strong as Hood's. Then at the Battle of Nashville, December 15 and 16, he overwhelmed Hood and put his army to rout all the way back to the Tennessee River, the only complete rout suffered by any major Confederate force.

Meanwhile Atlanta was put to the torch on November 15. Sherman took up his march to Savannah and the sea; four infantry corps, one cavalry, 68,000 men, spread wide on four great roads. He had no reason to worry about supply lines. He had accumulated vast stores and had a rich and fertile country to live on. The orders for foraging were liberal, and at that were abused. The general effect of pillage and demolition was like that created by Sheridan in the Shenandoah. Through that broad swath was a scene of desolation

*"where stood chimneys only, amid ruins. The very
birds of the air and the beasts of the field had fled."*

General Hardee was in charge of the defense of
Savannah, but with so small a force that he could not
make it effective. On December 20 he took his men
across the river into South Carolina, and the next day
Sherman was in the city. He wired Lincoln, "I beg to
present you, as a Christmas gift, the city of Savannah."

After recuperating for a month, Sherman turned
north. His army found a gruesome satisfaction in pun-
ishing South Carolina for the part she had played in
starting the war, and the destruction wreaked was worse
than in Georgia. On February 17 Charleston was evacuated and Columbia went up in flames. Wilmington,
North Carolina, last port of the Confederacy, was surrendered on the twenty-second.

Meanwhile, in Virginia the armies of Grant and Lee
stayed locked in the siege of Petersburg. Sheridan's
cavalry ranged far and wide.

On February 3, 1865, Alexander Stephens, Robert
M. T. Hunter and John A. Campbell met President
Lincoln and Secretary of State Seward on a steamer at
Hampton Roads for an informal peace talk. It came to
nothing.

And on February 6 Robert E. Lee was appointed
general-in-chief of all Confederate armies.

1. MARY ANN HARRIS GAY—"LEAD, BLOOD AND TEARS"

"All who cannot support themselves without ap-
plying to the United States Commissary for assistance,"
Sherman had ordered, "must go outside our lines, either
north or south. . . . But Mary Ann Gay and her
mother did not leave their home in Decatur. She writes
now of the situation in late November after Sherman's
departure from the burned city and countryside of
Atlanta for the March to the Sea.

Could Winston Churchill have read Miss Gay's book before he warned the British people to expect "blood, sweat and tears"?

After mingling renewed vows of allegiance to our cause, and expressions of a willing submission to the consequences of defeat—privations and evil dire, if need be—with my morning orison; yet I could not be oblivious to the fact that I was hungry, very hungry. And there was another, whose footsteps were becoming more and more feeble day by day, and whose voice, when heard at all, was full of the pathos of despair, who needed nourishment that could not be obtained, and consolation, which it seemed a mockery to offer.

In vain did I look round for relief. There was nothing left in the country to eat. Yea, a crow flying over it would have failed to discover a morsel with which to appease its hunger; for a Sheridan [1] by another name had been there with his minions of destruction, and had ruthlessly destroyed every vestige of food and every means of support. Every larder was empty, and those with thousands and tens of thousands of dollars were as poor as the poorest, and as hungry too. Packing trunks, in every house to which refugees had returned, contained large amounts of Confederate money. We had invested all we possessed except our home, and land and negroes, in Confederate bonds, and these were now inefficient for purchasing purposes. Gold and silver had we none. A more favored few had a little of those desirable mediums of purchase, and sent a great distance for supplies; but they offered no relief to those who had stayed at home and borne the brunt of battle, and saved their property from the destroyers' torch.

What was I to do? Sit down and wait for the inevitable starvation? No; I was not made of such stuff. I had heard that there had been a provision store opened in Atlanta for the purpose of bartering provisions for

[1] In the Shenandoah, Sheridan had "burned, blasted, slaughtered, destroyed."

munitions of war—anything that could be utilized in warfare. Minie balls were particularly desirable. I therefore took Telitha by the apron and had a little talk with her, and when I was through she understood that something was up that would bring relief to certain organs that had become quite troublesome in their demands, and she was anxious to take part in the performance, whatever that might be. I went also to my mother, and imparted to her my plans of operation, and she took the pathetic little backward step peculiar to herself on occasions which tried her soul, and with quivering lip she assented in approving, thought almost inaudible words.

With a basket in either hand, and accompanied by Telitha, who carried one that would hold about a peck, and two dull case-knives, I started to the battle-fields around Atlanta to pick up the former missiles of death to exchange for food to keep us from starving.

It was a cold day. The wind was very sharp, and over the ground, denuded of forest trees and undergrowth, the wind was blowing a miniature gale. Our wraps were inadequate, and how chilled we became in that rude November blast! But the colder we were, the faster we walked, and in an incredibly short time we were upon the battle-field searching for lead.

I made it a point to keep very near the road in the direction of Atlanta, and soon found myself on the very spot where the Confederate magazine stood, the blowing up of which, by Confederate orders, shook the very earth, and was distinctly heard thirty-five or forty miles distant. An exclamation of glad surprise from Telitha carried me to her. She had found a bonanza, and was rapidly filling her basket with that which was more valuable to us than gold. In a marshy place, encrusted with ice, innumerable bullets, minie balls, and pieces of lead seemed to have been left by the irony of fate to supply sustenance to hungry ones, and employment to the poor, as all the winter those without money to send to more favored and distant points found sure returns from this lead mine. It was so cold! our feet were almost frozen, and our hands had commenced to bleed, and handling cold, rough lead cramped them so badly that I feared we would have to desist from our work before filling the baskets.

Lead! Blood! Tears! O how suggestive! Lead, blood and tears, mingled and commingled. In vain did I try to dash the tears away. They would assert themselves and fall upon lead stained with blood. "God of mercy, if this be Thy holy will, give me fortitude to bear it uncomplainingly," was the heart-felt invocation that went up to the throne of grace from over lead, blood and tears, that fearful day. For relief, tears did not suffice. I wanted to cry aloud; nature would not be satisfied with less, and I cried like a baby, long and loud. Telitha caught the spirit of grief, and cried too. This ebullition of feelings on her part brought me to a realization of my duty to her, as well as to my poor patient mother to whom the day must seem very long, and I tried to stifle my sobs and lamentations.

At length our baskets were filled, and we took up our line of march to the desolated city. There were no labyrinths to tread, no streets to follow and an occasional question secured information that enabled us to find the "commissary" without delay. Telitha was very ambitious that I should appear a lady, and wanted me to deposit my load of lead behind some place of concealment, while we went on to deliver hers, and then let her go back for mine. But I was too much a Confederate soldier for that, and walked bravely in with my heavy, precious load.

A courteous gentleman in a faded grey uniform, evidently discharged because of wounds received in battle, approached and asked what he could do for me. "I have heard that you give provisions for lead," I replied, "and I have brought some to exchange." What seemed an interminable silence ensued.

"What would you like in exchange?" he asked.

"If you have sugar, and coffee, and meal, a little of

each if you please," I timidly said. "I left nothing to eat at home." The baskets of lead were removed to the rear and weighed, and in due time returned to me filled to the brim with sugar, flour, coffee, meal, lard, and the nicest meat I had seen in a long time.

"O, sir," I said, "I did not expect so much."

Joy had gone out of my life, and I felt no thrill of that kind; but I can never describe the satisfaction I experienced as I lifted two of those baskets, and saw Telitha grasp the other one, and turned my face homeward. . . .

2. A SOLDIER'S WIFE—"THINGS IS WORSE AND WORSE"

This poor woman lived in Nansemond County, Virginia, near the girlhood home of LaSalle Corbell. She was the mother of four small children. Her husband was on duty with General Pickett.

B —— N ——, Dec. 17, 1864

My Dear B ——: Christmus is most hear again, and things is worse and worse. I have got my last kalica frock on, and that's patched. Everything me and children's got is patched. Both of them is in bed now covered up with comforters and old pieces of karpet to keep them warm, while I went 'long out to try and get some wood, for their feet's on the ground and they have got no clothes, neither; and I am not able to cut the wood, and me and the children have broke up all the rails 'roun' the yard and picked up all the chips there is. We haven't got nothing in the house to eat but a little bit o' meal. The last pound of meet you got from Mr. G——is all eat up, and so is the chickens we raised. I don't want you to stop fighten them yankees till you kill the last one of them, but try and get off and come home and fix us all up some and then you can go back and fight them a heep harder than you ever fought them before. We can't none of us hold out much longer down here. One of General Mahone's [1] skouts promise me on his word to carry this letter through the lines to you, but, my dear, if you put off a-comin' 'twon't be no use to come, for we'll all hands of us be out there in the garden in the old graveyard with your ma and mine.[2]

3. REBECCAH C. RIDLEY—HOOD IS DEFEATED AT NASHVILLE

Chancellor Bromfield Lewis Ridley of Fair Mont plantation near Murfreesboro, Tennessee, and his wife Rebeccah had a daughter Bettie who kept a war journal. When Bettie died from "congestion of the lungs" in November 1864, Mrs. Ridley carried it on. She names in this entry the five sons whom she gave to the Confederate cause. Bromfield, the youngest, was a lieutenant on the staff of General A. P. Steward at the age of nineteen and after the war wrote Battles and Sketches of the Army of Tennessee. *Mrs. Ridley had witnessed the Battle of Stone's River at New Year's 1863. Her husband had to leave home, taking the young daughter Sallie with him. Fair Mont was burned in February and Mrs. Ridley moved into the only building spared, the old kitchen.*

Jefferson, Tennessee
December, 18, 1864

After my Dear Bettie's death Lavinia C. came over to stay with me. O how lonely and desolate I felt, hus-

---

[1] The fiery Major-General William Mahone.

[2] After he got her letter the husband of a "Soldier's Wife" went home without a furlough, and on his return to camp was arrested as a deserter and found guilty. He appealed to Mrs. Pickett, who in turn appealed to her husband. The execution was postponed and three days later an order came from Richmond, reprieving all deserters.

band far away in North Carolina, Sallie in Georgia, my 5 sons all in the Army, exposed to mortal peril, by bullit, and I desolate, my houses burned, and nearly all my household treasures in ashes—my negroes refractory and insolent and not supporting themselves—what little they make I have to divide with them, and the Yankees get the balance. The negroes are so utterly worthless they will not put up fences and burn the rails to keep from cutting wood. I employed Mr. Brown to live with me another year.

Lavinia and I have employed our time in sewing, knitting and reading until December 1, when the booming of cannon toward Columbia told us hostilities had commenced and Hood's Army was advancing on Nashville. A series of battles took place all along—on Friday a terrible battle was fought at Franklin. Hood took the place but lost 13 Generals 6 killed 7 wounded. The Southerners pressed the Yankees back to Nashville and Murfreesboro. I heard Brom was on the way and went to meet him and how rejoiced I was to see him after 2 years absence—grown to be a large fine looking man. He came home with me, but was running about so I saw but little. We went up to the hill—Brom with us—in a short time a company of Yanks who had escaped from the stockade passed by retreating rapidly to Murfreesboro. We had a big scare fearing they would come by and catch Brom, but they were running for life. He rode after them with 3 others—took a shot at them. He stayed until 8th when he returned to his command. We have had a severe sleet for 3 days. The ground has been covered with snow and ice—freezing our poor unprotected soldiers—some of them I understand are barefooted, none have tents—or a sufficiency of blankets and all have to depend on the country for subsistance—poor fellows, how my heart bleeds for them. They come in at the houses to warm, and get something to eat, and some of our citizens who pretend to be very Southern grudge them the food they eat—say they will be eat out. In these terrible conditions Hood attacked Nashville on Wed-

nesday 14th.[1] The noise of cannon was terrific all day
—we all felt as if our fate was at stake. . . . At night
all was still, about 1 o'clock someone woke me, it was
Brom! My Heart died within me. I asked hastily what
is the matter? He said "I came for my clothes and
servant. The waggons are ordered to Franklin. I rode
all night and went into Battle, it raged all day, we were
driven back, lost 20 pieces of cannon. I have eat
nothing."

I got him something to eat, he looked so sad, had
traversed the road between our house and camp 60
miles in all, and galloped all day in the Battle Field
carrying dispatches, got off his horse to deliver a message to Gen. Seares,[2] when a cannon ball passed between them, taking a pice out of Gen. S. leg, and the
concussion knocked Brom down, without injury, tho
thank God. He got leave to ride home that night—30
miles for his clothes and servant—threw himself on
the bed—took 2 hours sleep, the first he had in 36—
rode 4 miles in the morning, bought a horse and returned by 9 o'clock, and went off with his servant behind him. He looked so sad at parting—said "farewell,
Mama, I hope I will see you again." I was satisfied
Hood was defeated—but they fought all day Thursday
—the soldiers and waggons passed rapidly by—such
gloom and sorrow in every heart. Nature seems to
mourn with us—it has been dark, and lowering and
drizzling for 2 days—not a ray of sunshine, and but
little hope in our hearts. The Yankees we hear are visiting their wrath on the defenseless citizens, taking off
their food, bed clothes, breaking their table ware. We
have looked for them all day, but suppose they are all
after Hood's Army, and I fear awfully they will overtake and destroy a good many at the river before they
cross. Only one of my sons poor Brom is with Hood's
Army. George, I hear is sick at Withville [Wythe-

[1] The battle began at six in the morning of the fifteenth,
the Federals attacking, and lasted through the sixteenth.

[2] Brigadier-General C. W. Sears.

ville], Va. Luke in Macon, Ga. Jerome in Newnan,
Ga. Charlie in N.C. with his papa. Farewell to my
hope of seeing husband and daughter. . . .

4. MARY ELLEN ARNOLD—RUNNING THE BLOCKADE

*Mary Ellen Lyman of Massachusetts married
Amory Appleton of the same state. They had one son,
George Lyman Appleton—the George of her diary.
After Amory Appleton's death in the early 1850s she
married Charles S. Arnold of Savannah. He died in
1856.*

*George while serving in the Confederate Army was
taken seriously ill with measles and incapacitated for
further duty. When Sherman laid siege to Savannah
early in December 1864 Mrs. Appleton and George
escaped to Wilmington, North Carolina. They got passage on the blockade-running steamer Hansa bound
for the Bahamas. From Nassau they went on to St.
Thomas in the Virgin Islands and from there got a
ship to Europe, where they remained till November
1869.*

*Mrs. Appleton's journal is barely legible. It is written
in short, clipped notations, evidencing the excitement
she was under. A sense of danger emerges dramatically
from the pages of the dilapidated little book.*

St. Thomas—West Indies
Feb. 16th 1865

Left Wilmington, N. Carolina, Thursday, Dec. 31—
at noon—pouring rain—on the Hansa—blockade running steamer anchored at mouth of Cape Fear River,
until Sunday evening Jan. 3, 1865. Everything being
ready lights put out etc. start at midnight, papers,
money & valuables in small packages, ready to be saved
or destroyed should the blockading vessels overtake us
or drive us ashore—pass safely through however, the

small steamer heavily laden with cotton in the hands
of a daring crew—resolved to lose all rather than be
caught—goes on safely till Wednesday morning at daylight when a sail is discovered. A Yankee cruiser the
Vanderbilt sees us, & starts in pursuit. All steam is
crowded on, over the safety valve, a heavy weight
placed, and on we rushed. Shot after shot is fired at us
but we keep our distance—the coral reefs appear in
sight under the green water. Our Bahama pilot sits
like a statue on the wheel house—first raising one hand,
then the other to guide the helmsman at the wheel.
Bale after bale of cotton, worth nearly its weight in
gold is thrown into the sea to lighten us, accompanied
by the sighs of men at such a sacrifice—about 80 bales
are over. The water becomes too shallow for our pur-
suers and we are safe. The 20th shot is fired and falls
harmless behind us. The crew of the Hansa give cheer
after cheer and dip their flag, Confederate, three times
to the discomfited foe.

Our names had been written down before leaving
Cape Fear River, in the order in which we were to
have taken to the boats in case of need. Mine was in
the Starboard Life boat with George and 22 others,
under the charge of Cannop—1st mate, a man calm
resolved, kind and gentlemanly. Captain Atkinson,
English; first mate Cannop, English; 2nd mate Mc-
Leod, Scotch. Crew and passengers in all nearly one
hundred souls and I the only woman on board. 3 mate
Dickson—Doveton, Chief Engineer, and Wells, Bahama pilot. At 11 o'clock A.M. on Wed. Jan. 6th 1865,
reach Nassau, New Providence.

5. MRS. WILLIAM LAMB—FORT FISHER IS
BOMBARDED

*Wilmington, North Carolina, was the last open
port of the Confederacy. On a sandy peninsula guarding the Cape Fear River, entrance to the port, was Fort
Fisher. On December 20, 1864, appeared Admiral*

*David Porter's fleet and land forces led by Ben Butler
and Godfrey Weitzel. At midnight on the twenty-third
an old gunboat stocked with powder was exploded near
the fort. General Butler pinned great faith to this con-
traption but it was a complete fizzle. Christmas morning, while sixty Union vessels threw their shells, troops
were landed for attack. But the Federals heard that
Confederate reinforcements were expected from Wilmington. Butler got scared and withdrew that afternoon. He was relieved, as big a fiasco as his "power
ship" and bustled off to Massachusetts.*

*Commandant of the fort was handsome, gallant,
thirty-year-old Colonel William Lamb. A Norfolk boy,
he had married a Providence, Rhode Island, girl. He
enlisted as a captain in a Virginia regiment and rose to
the rank of colonel. Mrs. Lamb was living in Norfolk
with her father-in-law, the mayor of the city, when it
was occupied by the Federals in May 1862. About the
same time her third child was born and soon after they
joined the colonel at Fort Fisher. The little boy Willie
was sent to Providence to be with the grandparents. For
a while Mrs. Lamb lived in the upper room of a pilot's
house near the fort and then in a cottage built by garrison soldiers. It was to this cottage that the body of
Rose Greenhow was brought when it was washed
ashore, and it was Mrs. Lamb who dried Rose's clothes
before a pine-knot fire.*

Confederate Point, North Carolina
"The Cottage," January 9th, 1865

My Own Dear Parents:

I know you have been anxious enough about us all,
knowing what a terrible bombardment we have had, but
I am glad that I can relieve your mind on our behalf
and tell you we are all safe and well, through a most
merciful and kind providence. God was with us from
the first, and our trust was so firm in him that I can
truly say that both Will and I "feared no evil."

I stayed in my comfortable little home until the fleet
appeared, when I packed up and went across the river

to a large but empty house, of which I took possession; a terrible gale came on which delayed the attack for several days, but Saturday it came at last in all its fury; I could see it plainly from where I was, I had very powerful glasses, and sat on a stile out doors all day watching it—an awful but magnificent sight. . . .

The shelling was even more terrific on Sunday, and I, not knowing how long it might continue concluded to go to Fayetteville, and started Sunday noon in a small steamer, with the sick and wounded, to Wilmington, where I was obliged to stay for several days in great suspense, not able to get away and not able to hear directly from Will, as the enemy had cut the wires—and then a martyr to all kinds of rumors—one day heard that Will had lost a leg, &c., &c., but I steadfastly made up my mind to give no credit to anything bad. At last, I heard again, that we had driven our persecutors off, and I returned again to the place I went first, and the next day Will came over for me and took me to the fort, which I rode all over on horseback, but we did not move over for nearly a week. The fort was strewn with missiles of all kinds, it seemed a perfect miracle how any escaped, the immense works were literally skinned of their turf, but not injured in the slightest; not a bomb-proof or a magazine—*and there are more then one*—touched; the magazine the enemy thought they had destroyed was only a caisson; the men had very comfortable quarters in the fort—pretty little whitewashed houses—but the shells soon set fire to them, making a large fire and dense smoke, but the works are good for dozens of sieges—plenty of everything; particularly plenty of the greatest essential—*brave hearts*. Our beloved General Whiting was present, but gave up the whole command to Will, to whom he now gives, as is due, the whole credit of building and defending his post, and has urged his promotion to brigadier-general, which will doubtless be received soon, though neither of us really care for it.

We expect the Armada again, and will give him a

warmer reception next time. The fort, expecting a longer time of it, was reserving their heaviest fire for nearer quarters. Butler's "gallant troops" came right under one side of the fort, but our grape and canister soon drove them off, and *not* Porter's shell, which did not happen to be falling that time; they left their traces sufficiently next morning.

The "gallant fellow" who stole the horse from inside the fort, was doubtless so scared he didn't know much *where* he was. The *true* statement of the thing is, that an officer, unauthorized by Will or the general, sent a courier outside the fort with a message to some troops outside, and soon after he left the fort, was attacked and killed by a Yankee sharpshooter hidden under a bridge. The poor body fell and the *horse* was taken, and the flag spoken of, in the same way, was shot from the parapet and blew outside, when it was taken. When any of them see the *inside* of the fort they'll never live to tell the tale.

Ah, mother! you all, at home peacefully, do not know the misery of being driven from home by a miserable, cruel enemy! 'Tis a sad sight to see the sick and aged turned out in the cold to seek a shelter. I cannot speak feelingly because of any experience myself, as God is so good to us, and has so favored us with life, health and means, and my dear, good husband has provided me a comfortable home in the interior, where I can be safe.

Will has worried so much about you, dear mother, thinking you would be so anxious about us. He often exclaims, when reading some of the lying accounts: "How that will worry Ma!"

How is my darling Willie? We do so want to see our boy. I think Will will have to send for him in the spring. Kiss the dear one dozen of times for his father and mother.

Though it was a very unpleasant Christmas to me, still the little ones enjoyed theirs. Will had imported a crowd of toys for them and they are as happy as possible with them.

I have not heard from my dear home since last August, and you can imagine how very anxious I am to hear, particularly of dear sister Ria. Is she with George? Do write me of all the dear ones I love so much. How I would love to see you all, so much, and home!

I forgot to tell you of the casualties in the fight. Ours were only three killed; about sixty wounded; they were all.[1]

6. JUDITH BROCKENBROUGH McGUIRE—
"I THOUGHT OF THE GAYETY OF PARIS"

Mrs. McGuire had hoped to make Christmas cheerful for her small family in Richmond. She had even aspired to a turkey, but turkeys were priced from $50 to $100 and so were out of the question. Her son John was in a Northern prison, and her daughters were refugees some distance from Richmond. For many months her diary had been written on brown wrapping paper; now even scraps of that were hard to find.

Richmond, Virginia
January 8th, 1865.—Some persons in this beleaguered city seem crazed on the subject of gayety. In the midst of the wounded and dying, the low state of the commissariat, the anxiety of the whole country, the troubles of every kind by which we are surrounded, I am mortified to say that there are gay parties given in the city. There are those denominated "starvation parties," where young persons meet for innocent enjoyment, and retire at a reasonable hour; but there are others where the most elegant suppers are served—

[1] The Federals renewed the attack on Fort Fisher on January 15, 1865, and this time meant business. After contesting every redoubt, the noble little band of defenders fell before the heavy bombardment of a great fleet and the assault of a large land force. Colónel Lamb, wounded in the left hip, was captured. Through the efforts of General Bragg, Mrs. Lamb was able to follow him to his Northern prison.

cakes, jellies, ices in profusion, and meats of the finest kinds in abundance, such as might furnish a meal for a regiment of General Lee's army. I wish these things were not so, and that every extra pound of meat could be sent to the army. When returning from the hospital, after witnessing the dying scene of a brother, whose young sister hung over him in agony, with my heart full of the sorrows of hospital-life, I passed a house where there were music and dancing. The revulsion of feeling was sickening. I thought of the gayety of Paris during the French Revolution, of the "cholera ball" in Paris, the ball at Brussels that night before the battle of Waterloo, and felt shocked that our own Virginians, at such a time, should remind me of scenes which we were wont to think only belonged to the lightness of foreign society. The weddings, of which there are many, seem to be conducted with great quietness. There seems to be a perfect mania on the subject of matrimony. Some of the churches may be seen open and lighted almost every night for bridals, and wherever I turn I hear of marriages in prospect.

January 16th.—Fort Fisher has fallen; Wilmington will of course follow.[1] This was our last port into which blockade-runners were successful in entering, and which furnished us with immense amount of stores. What will be the effect of this disaster we know not; we can only hope and pray.

January 21st.—We hear nothing cheering except in the proceedings of Congress and the Virginia Legislature, particularly the latter. Both bodies look to stern resistance to Federal authority. The city and country are full of rumours and evil surmising; and while we do not believe one word of the croaking, it makes us feel restless and unhappy.

[1] Wilmington fell on the twenty-second.

7. MALVINA BLACK GIST—THE TREASURY
NOTE DEPARTMENT LEAVES COLUMBIA

John Black of Newberry, South Carolina, had a daughter Malvina, born on November 12, 1842, and brought her as a child to live in Columbia. When she grew up she married the son of Governor William H. Gist, Major William Moreno Gist, who within a few months was killed in a skirmish the day before the Battle of Chickamauga and buried in an unknown grave. Then the sprightly, intelligent Malvina took a job in the Treasury Note Department. Bills bearing the signature "M. Gist" are still extant. Her brother, a scout, was a prisoner in the North.

She began a diary five days after Sherman left Savannah on his march through South Carolina and continued it through May 5, 1865.

Columbia, S.C., February 6, 1865.—This wild talk about the Federal Army and what it's going to do is all nonsense. Coming here! Sherman! Why not say he's going to Paramaribo? One is about as likely as the other, notwithstanding that papa shakes his head so solemnly over it, and mamma looks so grave. He is always shaking his head over something, it seems to me, and she forever looking grave. I do hope I shall be able to get around being old, somehow. Old people's weather is all bad weather; their horoscope all background; their expectation all disappointment; their probabilities all failures. No doubt I am foolish— mamma says I am—but there's a certain satisfaction in being young and foolish rather than old and wise.

February 7.—While I cannot sign the bills as rapidly as Nannie Giles can, today I finished up four packages of the denomination of fifty dollars. Mr. Tellifiere says I am a treasury girl worth having, and that I did a big day's work, and a good day's work. Took my vocal lesson and paid Signor Torriani for my last quarter. He is gloriously handsome in the Italian way, which is a very striking way. I also sent check to the milliner for the $200 due on my new bonnet, and paid $80 for the old lilac barege bought from Mary L——. Miss P—— does not yet agree to let me have the congress gaiters for $75, and unless she does she may keep them herself, to the end of time! 'Tis a pretty come to pass when $75 of Confederate currency is not the equivalent of an ordinary pair of Massachusetts made shoes! J. C. called this evening. He is pleasant, but stops right there, and that isn't the place to stop. A man must know how to be disagreeable to be dangerously attractive, I think.

February 8.—Saw that young Englishman again today. He isn't half the idle dreamer he pretends to be. In truth (but let me whisper it softly), *I believe he's a spy!* I can't see, otherwise, why he is so tremendously and eagerly interested in matters Confederate. Nor is he smart enough to make me believe it's *me!* . . .

February 10.—This being German day, I went as usual for my lesson. If I must say it, old Frau's dressing is all top-dressing, and her conversation never more than a mild diversion. Its absorbing theme today was the same as with every one else—Sherman's movements; is he coming here? And what will he do when he does? These are the questions which embody the vague foreboding, the monstrous prophecies that fill the air. I marvel at the ease with which some people lose their heads. You would think Sherman was a three-tailed bashaw, to hear some of them talk.

February 11.—The dawning of a doubt is a troublesome thing, for if a doubt does not out and out destroy faith, it assuredly chastens it to an uncomfortable degree. Is he coming, that terrible Sherman, with all his legions? Well, and if he does, Beauregard is coming

too, and Hampton [1] and Butler [2] are already here, so
where's the sense of getting worried? I shall continue
to possess my soul in peace.

February 12.—The situation becomes more alarm-
ing—that much I am fain to confess. My father's head
is not the only one shaking now; they are all shaking—
all the men's heads in town. No one can tell what a
day will bring forth. Steady, now, nerves! Courage
now, heart! My grandsires fought for liberty in the war
of the Revolution; my great-grandmother faced the
British, nor quailed so much as an eyelash before them!
Is it for me to be afraid? I am not afraid.

February 13.—We were greatly startled yesterday
by the firing of cannon in the upper part of the city.
It proved to be a call for Colonel Thomas' Regiment
of Reserves. I am sorry the weather is so cold. Our
ill-clothed, ill-fed troops must suffer acutely in such
bitter weather. Today I accompanied my mother to the
Wayside Hospital, carrying some jelly and wafers for
the sick. One of the inmates, a convalescent soldier,
played with much taste and skill on the banjo. Came
home to find my father much excited about me, having
heard Mayor Goodwyn [3] say that he has no hope at
all of holding the city. And my father does not consider the track of a great army the safest place for
young women; hence he wants me to leave; go; get out
of the way! But where? Where shall I fly from Sherman's army?

Tuesday, February 14.—Such a day! It was like "a
winnowing of chaos." Very little work was done at the
Treasury Department in the midst of such excitement

---

[1] On January 6, 1865, while on leave of absence, General
Hampton, commander of the Cavalry Corps, Army of Northern Virginia, was assigned to the command of all the cavalry
in the operations against Sherman.

[2] Major-General M. Calbraith Butler, C. S. A.

[3] Colonel F. J. Goodwyn.

and confusion. We are to remove at once to Richmond, and I am told Colonel Joseph Daniel Pope, Mr. Jamison, and many of the employees of the printing establishment, have already departed. I do not know if this be true; I hear too many contradictory reports for all of them to be true. One thing, however, appears to be quite true—*Sherman is coming!* And I never believed it before. This afternoon, we could distinctly hear firing in the distance, and at this writing (8:30 P.M.) we can see the sky arched with fire in the direction of the Saluda factory. Must I go with the department to Richmond? In such case, my parents will be entirely alone, Johnny having gone, also, to the front. Does this not clearly show the dire extremity to which we are reduced, when boys of sixteen shoulder the musket? There are other reasons why I should like to remain here to receive Sherman: it is high time I was having some experiences out of the ordinary, and if anything remarkable is going to happen, I want to know something about it; it might be worth relating to my grandchildren! Anyhow, it is frightfully monotonous, just because you are a woman, to be always tucked away in the safe places. I want to stay. I want to have a taste of danger. *Midnight.*—But I am overruled; I must go. My father says so; my mother says so. Everything is in readiness—my trunks packed, my traveling clothes laid out upon the chair, and now I must try to catch a little sleep. And then on the morrow—what? What will be the next stroke upon the *Labensuhr?* God only knows.

February 15.—(Waiting at the depot). Going as usual to the department this morning, I found orders had been issued for our immediate removal to Richmond. Barely had I time to run home, dash a few articles into my trunk, say good-bye, and join the others here. We girls are all together—Elise, Ernestine, Sadie, Bet, and myself. We have been seated in the train for hours and hours. Oh! this long waiting; it is weary work! A reign of terror prevails in the city, and the scene about me will ever live in memory. Government employees are hastening to and fro, military stores are being packed, troops in motion, aids-de-camp flying hither and thither, and anxious fugitives crowding about the train, begging for transportation, All kinds of rumors are afloat, every newcomer bringing a new version. The latest is that Hardee[1] had refused to evacuate Charleston, and will not combine forces with Hampton in order to save the capital. I am strangely laden; I feel weighted down. Six gold watches are secreted about my person, and more miscellaneous articles of jewelry than would fill a small jewelry shop —pins, rings, bracelets, etc. One of my trunks is packed with valuables and another with provisions. Shelling has begun from the Lexington heights, and under such conditions this waiting at the depot has a degree of nervousness mixed with impatience. We catch, now and again, peculiar whizzing sounds—shells, they say. Sherman has come; he is knocking at the gate. Oh, God! turn him back! Fight on our side, and turn Sherman back!

8. EMMA FLORENCE LeCONTE—
"POOR OLD COLUMBIA!"

Young Emma LeConte was the daughter of the distinguished scientist Joseph LeConte, friend and pupil of Agassiz of Harvard. He lived at Midway, Georgia, and then at Athens, where he was professor of geology and natural history in the state university. In 1856 he was called to the faculty of the South Carolina state

[1] General Hardee, in command of the department of South Carolina, Florida and Georgia, had escaped from Sherman at Savannah and moved north. Beauregard arriving to take charge, Wade Hampton urged on him the importance of evacuating Charleston and transferring the garrison of 16,000 men to a stand before Columbia. Instead, when the city was abandoned on the seventeenth the garrison was sent on a long march to North Carolina. The last troops to leave were those from Fort Sumter.

university at Columbia. When the university was turned into a hospital in June 1862 Emma remained on the campus with her mother and sister Sallie, while her father carried out one of the notable powder-making enterprises attempted by the Confederacy. She was sixteen when Sherman came. Her journal runs from December 1864 to August 1865.

Columbia, South Carolina

February 14, 1865. What a panic the whole town is in! I have not been out of the house myself, but Father says the intensest excitement prevails on the street. The Yankees are reported a few miles off on the other side of the river. How strong no one seems to know. It is decided if this be true that we will remain quietly here, father alone leaving. It is thought Columbia can hardly be taken by raid as we have the whole of Butler's cavalry here—and if they do we have to take the consequences. It is true some think Sherman will burn the town, but we can hardly believe that. Besides these buildings, though they are State property, yet the fact that they are used as a hospital will, it is thought, protect them. I have been busily making large pockets to wear under my hoopskirt—they will hardly search our persons. Still everything of any value is to be packed up to go with father. I do not feel half so frightened as I thought I would. Perhaps because I realize they are coming. I hope still this is a false report. Maggie Adams and her husband have promised to stay here during father's absence. She is a Yankee and may be some protection and help. . . . I look forward with terror, and yet with a kind of callousness to their approach. . . .

February 15. Oh, how is it possible to write amid this excitement and confusion! We are too far off to hear and see much down here in the Campus, but they tell me the streets in town are lined with panic-stricken crowds, trying to escape. All is confusion and turmoil. The Government is rapidly moving off stores—all day the trains have been running, whistles blowing and wagons rattling through the streets. All day we have been listening to the booming of cannon—receiving conflicting reports of the fighting. All day wagons and ambulances have been bringing in the wounded over the muddy streets and through the drizzling rain, with the dark clouds overhead. All day in our own household has confusion reigned too. The back parlor strewed with clothing etc., open trunks standing about, while a general feeling of misery and tension pervaded the atmosphere. Everything is to go that can be sent— house linen, blankets, clothing, silver, jewelry—even the wine—everything movable of any value. Hospital flags have been erected at the different gates of the Campus—we hope the fact of our living within the walls may be of some protection to us, but I fear not. I feel sure these buildings will be destroyed. I wish mother could have sent more furniture to different friends in town, but it is too late now. . . . I have destroyed most of my papers, but have a lot of letters still that I do not wish to burn, and yet I do not care to have them share the fate of Aunt Jane's and Cousin Ada's in Liberty Co., which were read and scattered along the roads. I will try to hide them. One of my bags is filled. The other I will pack tonight. Henry will stay with us, and vows he will stand by us through thick and thin—I believe he means it, but do not know how he will hold on. It is so cold and we have no wood. The country people will not venture in town lest their horses should be impressed. So we sit shivering and trying to coax a handful of wet pine to burn. Yonder come more wounded—poor fellows—indeed I can write no more.

Night. Nearer and nearer, clearer and more distinctly sound the cannon—Oh, it is heart-sickening to listen to it! . . . Just now as I stood on the piazza listening, the reports sounded so frightfully loud and near that I could not help shuddering at each one. And yet there is something exciting—sublime—in a cannonade. But the horrible uncertainty of what is before us! My great fear now is for father—Oh, if he were only gone—were only safe!

The alarm bell is ringing. Just now when I first heard it clang out my heart gave a leap, and I thought at once, "It's the Yankees." So nervous have I grown that the slightest unusual sound startles me. Of course I knew it was fire, yet it was with a beating heart I threw open the window to see the western horizon lit up with the glow of flames. Although we are composed, our souls are sick with anxiety. . . .

Later—They have passed our first line of breastworks. No firing tonight. Father and Uncle John leave tonight or tomorrow morning.

February 16. How can the terror and excitement of today be described! I feel a little quieter now and seize the opportunity to write a few lines. Last night, or rather early this morning, father left. After the last lines in my entry last evening, I went downstairs and and found in the back parlor with father a man calling himself Davis. I had heard father speak of him before. He met him in Georgia while making his way back home with Sallie, and he was kind to them during that difficult journey. He calls himself a Confederate spy or scout and is an oddity. I only half trust him—he evidently is not what he pretends to be. He says he is a Kentuckian and is both coarse and uneducated, but wonderfully keen and penetrating. . . . He has taken an unaccountable fancy to father—as shown by his hunting him up—and he assures him again and again that he will have us protected during the presence of the Yankees here. He claims great influence with the Yankee officers and entire knowledge of the enemy's movements. All the evening he seemed exceedingly uneasy that Father should so long have deferred his departure and very impatient to get him off. He offered to lend him a horse if that would facilitate his leaving. Father is not uneasy, for our authorities assure him that all is right, but I do not like this man's evident anxiety. Can he know more than the Generals? About half-past twelve father took leave of us. Thus to part! Father starting on an uncertain journey—not knowing whether he may not be captured in his flight, and leaving us to the mercy of the inhuman beastly Yankees —I think it was the saddest moment of my life. Of course father feels very anxious about us, and the last words the man Davis said to him were to assure him that he might feel easy about us. I wonder if there is any confidence to be put in what he says! Hardly, I suppose. We said goodbye with heavy hearts and with many presentiments of evil.

After father was gone I sat up still, talking with Davis. I could not sleep, and besides I wanted to hear that father was safely off. We asked our guest how he thought Columbia would be treated—he said he would not tell us—it would alarm us too much. Does he really know all he pretends, or is he only guessing? It was three o'clock before I lay down and fell into a disturbing doze which lasted until seven. Davis stayed and slept on the ground floor, but was gone before we awoke.

The breakfast hour passed in comparative calm. About nine o'clock we were sitting in the dining room, having just returned from the piazza where we had been watching a brigade of cavalry passing to the front. "Wouldn't it be dreadful if they should shell the city?" someone said. "They would not do that," replied mother, "for they have not demanded its surrender." Scarcely had the words passed her lips when Jane, the nurse, rushed in crying out that they were shelling. We ran to the front door just in time to hear a shell go whirring past. It fell and exploded not far off. This was so unexpected. I do not know why, but in all my list of anticipated horrors I somehow had not thought of a bombardment. I leaned against the door, fairly shivering, partly with cold, but chiefly from nervous excitement. After listening to them awhile this wore off and I became accustomed to the shells. They were shelling the town from the Lexington heights across the river, and from the campus their troops could be seen drawn up on the hill-tops. Up the street this morning the Government stores were thrown open to the people and there was a general scramble. Our negroes were up there until frightened home by the shells. The shelling was discontinued for an hour or two and then renewed with so much fury that we unanimously resolved to adjourn to the basement and abandon the upper rooms. Sallie and I went up to our rooms to bring down our things. I was standing at my bureau with my arms full when I heard a loud report. The shell whistled right over my head and exploded. I stood breathless, really expecting to see it fall in the room. When it had passed I went into the hall and met Sallie, coming from her room, pale and trembling. "Oh Emma" she said, "this is dreadful!"

We went downstairs—mother stood in the hall looking very much frightened. "Did you hear——" "Yes indeed"—and at that instant another whistled close overhead. This was rather unpleasant and we retreated to the basement without further delay, where we sat listening as they fell now nearer, and now farther off. Sallie suffered most—she would not be left alone, and would not allow me to go to the outer door to look about, but would call me back in terror. The firing ceased about dinner time. . . .

During the afternoon a rapid cannonade was kept up and I do not think the forces could have been more than half a mile from here. Dr. Thomson says they are only skirmishing. Davis says we have received re-inforcements, but he thinks we cannot hold the town as we have given up the strongest position. He was here this morning during the shelling and stood talking to me in the dining room for some time, giving me a picture of the confusion in town. Our soldiers had opened and plundered some of the stores. He brought me a present of a box of fancy feathers and one or two other little things he had picked up. He says the bridge will be burned and the towns evacuated tonight.

10 o'clock P.M.—They are in bed sleeping, or trying to sleep. I don't think I shall attempt it. Davis was

here just now to tell the news—it is kind of him to come so often to keep us posted. I went up to see him—made Henry light the gas and sat talking to him in the hall, while through the open door came the shouts of the soldiery drawn up along the streets ready to march out. Perhaps the Yankees may be in tonight—yet I do not feel as frightened as I thought I would. . . . We have moved into the back basement room. I opened the door which gives from our present sleeping room on the back yard just now, and the atmosphere was stifling with gun-powder smoke. Henry had to cut down a tree in the yard today for fuel. . . .

February 17. . . . At about 6 o'clock while it was still quite dark and all in the room were buried in profound slumber, we were suddenly awakened by a terrific explosion. The house shook—broken window-panes clattered down, and we all sat up in bed, for a few seconds mute with terror. . . . We lit the candle, and mother sent Jane to inquire of Henry the cause. Of course he did not know. I went out of doors. The day was beginning to break murkily and the air was still heavy with smoke. All continuing quiet we concluded that the authorities had blown up some stores before evacuating. . . . After breakfast the cannon opened again and so near that every report shook the house. I think it must have been a cannonade to cover our retreat. It did not continue very long. The negroes all went uptown to see what they could get in the general pillage, for all the shops had been opened and provisions were scattered in all directions. Henry says that in some parts of Main Street corn and flour and sugar cover the ground. An hour or two ago they came running back declaring the Yankees were in town and that our troops were fighting them in the streets. This was not true, for at that time every soldier nearly had left town, but we did not know it then. . . . Mother is downright sick. She had been quite collected and calm until this news, but now she suddenly lost all self-control and exhibited the most lively terror—indeed I thought she would grow hysterical. . . . By-and-by the firing ceased and all was quiet again. It was denied that the Yankees had yet crossed the river or even completed their pontoon bridge, and most of the servants returned up town. They have brought back a considerable quantity of provisions—the negroes are very kind and faithful—they have supplied us with meat and Jane brought mother some rice and crushed sugar for Carrie, knowing that she had none. How times change! Those whom we have so long fed and cared for now help us. . . . A gentleman told us just now that the mayor had gone forward to surrender the town.

One o'clock P.M.—Well, they are here. I was sitting in the back parlor when I heard the shouting of the troops. I was at the front door in a moment. Jane came running and crying, "O Miss Emma, they've come at last!" She said they were marching down Main Street, before them flying a panic-stricken crowd of women and children who seemed crazy.

I ran upstairs to my bedroom window just in time to see the U.S. flag run up over the State House. O what a horrid sight! What a degradation! After four long bitter years of bloodshed and hatred, now to float there at last! That hateful symbol of despotism! I do not think I could possibly describe my feelings. I know I could not look at it. I left the window and went downstairs to mother. In a little while a guard arrived to protect the hospital. They have already fixed a shelter of boards against the wall near the gate—sentinels are stationed and they are cooking their dinner. The wind is very high today and blows their hats around. This is the first sight we have had of these fiends except as prisoners. The sight does not stir up very pleasant feelings in our hearts. We cannot look at them with anything but horror and hatred—loathing and disgust. The troops now in town is a brigade commanded by Col. Stone.[1] Everything is quiet and orderly. Guards have been placed to protect houses, and Sherman has promised not to disturb private property. . . .

[1] Colonel George A. Stone, with men from Iowa.

Later—Gen. Sherman has *assured* the Mayor, "that he and all the citizens may sleep as securely and quietly tonight as if under Confederate rule. Private property shall be carefully respected. Some public buildings have to be destroyed, but he will wait until tomorrow when the wind shall have entirely subsided." . . .

February 18. What a night of horror, misery and agony! It even makes one sick to think of writing down such scenes. Until dinner-time we saw little of the Yankees, except the guard about the campus, and the officers and men galloping up and down the street. . . . We could hear their shouts as they surged down Main Street and through the State House, but were too far off to see much of the tumult. . . . I hear they found a picture of President Davis in the Capitol which was set up as a target and shot at amid the jeers of the soldiery. From three o'clock till seven their army was passing down the street by the Campus, to encamp back of us in the woods. Two Corps entered the town —Howard's and Logan's [1]—one, the diabolical 15th which Sherman has hitherto never permitted to enter a city on account of their vile and desperate character. Slocum's Corps remained over the river, and I suppose Davis' also. The devils as they marched past looked strong and well clad in dark, dirty-looking blue. The wagon trains were immense. Night drew on. Of course we did not expect to sleep, but we looked forward to a tolerably tranquil night. . . . At about seven o'clock I was standing on the back piazza in the third story. Before me the whole southern horizon was lit up by camp-fires which dotted the woods. On one side the sky was illuminated by the burning of Gen. Hampton's residence a few miles off in the country, on the other side by some blazing buildings near the river. Sumter Street was brightly lighted by a burning house so near our piazza that we could feel the heat. By the red glare we could watch the wretches walking—generally stag-

[1] Major-General O. O. Howard and Major-General John A. Logan.

gering—back and forth from the camp to the town—
shouting—hurrahing—cursing South Carolina—swear-
ing—blaspheming—singing ribald songs and using such
obscene language that we were forced to go indoors.
The fire on Main Street was now raging, and we
anxiously watched its progress from the upper front
windows. In a little while, however, the flames broke
forth in every direction. . . . Guards were rarely of any
assistance—most generally they assisted in the pillag-
ing and the firing. The wretched people rushing from
their burning homes were not allowed to keep even the
few necessaries they gathered up in their flight—even
blankets and food were taken from them and destroyed.
The firemen attempted to use their engines, but the
hose was cut to pieces and their lives threatened.

The wind blew a fearful gale, wafting the flames
from house to house with frightful rapidity. By midnight the whole town (except the outskirts) was
wrapped in one huge blaze. Still the flames had not
approached sufficiently near us to threaten our immediate safety, and for some reason not a single Yankee
soldier had entered our house. . . . Henry said the
danger was over, sick of the dreadful scene, worn out
with fatigue and excitement, we went downstairs to
our room and tried to rest. I fell into a heavy kind of
stupor from which I was presently roused by the bustle
about me. Our neighbor Mrs. Caldwell and her two
sisters stood before the fire wrapped in blankets and
weeping. Their house was on fire, and the great sea of
flame had again swept down our way to the very Campus walls. . . . Jane came in to say that Aunt Josie's
house was in flames—then we all went to the front
door—My God! what a scene! It was about four o'clock
and the State House was one grand conflagration.

Imagine night turning into noonday, only with a
blazing, scorching glare that was horrible—a copper
colored sky across which swept columns of black rolling smoke glittering with sparks and flying embers,
while all around us were falling thickly showers of
burning flakes. Everywhere the palpitating blaze wall-

ing the streets with solid masses of flames as far as the
eye could reach—filling the air with its terrible roar.
On every side the crackling and devouring fire, while
every instant came the crashing of timbers and the
thunder of falling buildings. A quivering molten ocean
seemed to fill the air and sky. The Library building
opposite us seemed framed by the gushing flames and
smoke, while through the windows gleamed the liquid
fire.

The College buildings caught. . . . All the physicians
and nurses were on the roof trying to save the buildings, and the poor wounded inmates left to themselves,
such as could crawled out while those who could not
move waited to be burned to death. The Common opposite the gate was crowded with homeless women and
children, a few wrapped in blankets and many shivering
in the night air. Such a scene as this with the drunken
fiendish soldiery in their dark uniforms, infuriated,
cursing, screaming, exulting in their work, came nearer
the material ideal of hell than anything I ever expect
to see again. . . .

The State House of course is burned, and they talk
of blowing up the new uncompleted granite one. . . .
We dread tonight. O, the sorrow and misery of this
unhappy town! From what I can hear their chief aim,
while taunting helpless women, has been to "Humble
their pride—Southern pride." "Where now," they would
say, "is all your pride—see what we have brought you
to. This is what you get for setting yourselves up as
better than other folks." . . .

Sunday, February 19. The day has passed quietly as
regards the Yankees. . . . I rose, took off my clothes
for the first time in three days, and after bathing and
putting on clean clothes felt like another being. This
morning fresh trouble awaited us. We thought the
negroes were going to leave us. While we were on the
piazza Mary Ann came to us weeping and saying she
feared the Yankees were going to force Henry to go
off with them, and of course she would have to go with

her husband. He did not want to go and would not unless forced. . . . The others, Maria and her children, want to go I think. They have been dressed in their Sundays best all day. . . .

February 20. . . . Shortly after breakfast—O joyful sight—the two corps encamped behind the Campus back of us marched by with all their immense wagon trains on their way from Columbia. They tell us all will be gone by tomorrow evening. . . .

Of course there was no Service in any of the churches yesterday—no Church bells ringing—the Yankees riding up and down the streets—the provost guard putting up their camp—there was nothing to suggest Sunday. . . .

February 21. A heavy curse has fallen on this town— from a beautiful city it is turned into a desert. How desolated and dreary we feel—how completely cut off from the world. No longer the shrill whistle of the engine—no daily mail—the morning brings no paper with news from the outside—there are no lights—no going to and fro. It is as if a city in the midst of business and activity were suddenly smitten with some appalling curse. One feels awed if by chance the dreary stillness is broken by a laugh or too loud a voice. . . .

February 22. I have seen it all—I have seen the "Abomination of Desolation." It is even worse than I thought. The place is literally in ruins. The entire heart of the city is in ashes—only the outer edges remain. On the whole length of Sumter Street not one house beyond the first block after the Campus is standing, except the brick house of Mr. Mordecai. Standing in the centre of town, as far as the eye can reach nothing is to be seen but heaps of rubbish, tall dreary chimneys and shattered brick walls, while "In the hollow windows, dreary horror's sitting." Poor old Columbia—where is all her beauty—so admired by strangers, so loved by her children! . . .

Everything has vanished as if by enchantment—stores, merchants, customers—all the eager faces gone—only three or four dismal looking people to be seen picking their way over heaps of rubbish, brick and timbers. The wind moans among the bleak chimneys and whistles through the gaping windows of some hotel or warehouse. The market a ruined shell supported by crumbling arches—its spire fallen in and with it the old town clock whose familiar stroke we miss so much. After trying to distinguish localities and hunting for familiar buildings we turned to Arsenal Hill. Here things looked more natural. The Arsenal was destroyed but comparatively few dwellings. Also the Park and its surroundings looked familiar. As we passed the old State House going back I paused to gaze on the ruins—only the foundations and chimneys—and to recall the brilliant scene enacted there one short month ago. And I compared that scene with its beauty, gayety and festivity, the halls so elaborately decorated, the surging throng, to this. I reached home sad at heart and full of all I had seen. . . .

February 23. . . . Somehow I feel we cannot be conquered. We have lost everything, but if all this—negroes—property—all could be given back a hundredfold I would not be willing to go back to them. I would rather endure any poverty than live under Yankee rule. . . . I would rather far have France or any other country for a mistress—anything but live as one nation with the *Yankees*—that word in my mind is a synonym for all that is mean, despicable and abhorrent. . . .

9. CHARLOTTE ST. JULIEN RAVENEL—
"THE ENEMY COMES TO OUR PLANTATION"

The young daughter of Henry William Ravenel, well-known botanist, lived at Pooshee plantation in Berkeley County, South Carolina. The plantation and the surrounding countryside were protected only by a few old men and young boys. After the Federal occupation of Charleston and the burning of Columbia in the middle of February 1865 roving bands of Union soldiers, white and black, burned and pillaged the neighborhood, as Charlotte tells in her journal.

Mrs. Chesnut says: "Potter's raid . . . ruined us. It burned our mills and gins, and a hundred bales of cotton. Indeed, nothing is left now but the bare land, and debts incurred for the support of these hundreds of Negroes during the war." This was Brigadier-General Edward E. Potter who commanded the Beaufort District in South Carolina after January 1865.

Pooshee

The 1st of March is a day which we will never forget; everything went on as usual until nine o'clock at night when we heard several pistol shots in the negro yard. I ran up stairs to tell Pennie who had gone to bed and by the time I got back we heard a noise at the back door; our hearts sank when we heard them talking, for they were negroes without an officer, what we had always dreaded. They asked for the master of the house, and when Grand Pa went out, they asked in the most insolent manner for his horses, wagons, meat and poultry. They then asked if there were any fire arms in the house, and told there was none but a plantation gun. They said they would not believe that such a house could be without a gun and that they would have it or shed blood. They then went off into the yard to get the things. They emptied the smokehouse; took what poultry they wanted, and then went to the store room under the house, took a few things from there and told the negroes to go in and take the rest;—which they did, cleaning out the store room and meat room. There were a great many things there for Aunt Bet had moved over her provisions. The plantation negroes took about twenty bushels of salt; twenty of rice; fifteen of grist, besides several jars of lard, molasses; all of Hennie's soap, a box of Pineland crockery and a good many other things. They left us with one quart of salt in the house and would not bring any of it back, until Pa stated the case to a *white* Yankee the next day and he went around and made them bring some of it back.

When the negro soldiers first went to the store room they sent for Grand Pa. It made our blood curdle to hear our aged relative spoken to in the manner they did. We were all in the hall and could hear everything that went on below. After some very impudent language we heard a gun click. I will never forget that moment as long as I live. The wretch had his gun pointed at Grand Pa, and though we found out afterwards that they did not dare to take life, we did not know it at the time.

After this they called up the negroes and told them they were free, and if they worked for Grand Pa again they would shoot them. They then went off with three horses, a wagon and a buggy. They told the negroes that the army would be through the next day to take our clothes and other things. Three of us set up in the hall for the rest of the night, and though the others retired to their rooms there was rest for no one. It must have been too mortifying to poor Grand Pa for his negroes to behave as they did, taking the bread out of our mouths. I thought better of them than that. I have attempted to describe that dreadful night, but nothing can come up to the reality.

The next morning everything looked so desolate that it made us feel sad, most of the house servants came in crying, and said they were willing to do for us, but were afraid. Of course we would not put them in any danger, so sent them all off. We sat down to breakfast to a plate of hominy and cold corn bread that had been cooked the day before for one of our soldiers. The very night before we had sat down to an elaborate supper;—such are the fortunes of war! We cleaned up the house and cooked dinner, looking all the time for our *friends* for such we considered the officers. Just as our dinner was put on the table a party rode up; we were so glad to see them that we all went in the piazza. The officer came forward and bowed very politely. Pa then told him how we had been treated the the night before and asked what guarantee we would have against such treatment in the future.

Capt. Hurlbut who was in command of the party said that the black soldiers had no authority to come without an officer and if found, they would be punished. He said that Gen'l. Potter would be along soon and we might get a protection from him, but afterwards he said that he would write a paper which might do us good, and certainly would do no harm. I do not remember the words; but the sense of it was, that we had very wisely remained at home, while many had flocked to other parts of the Confederacy. He said that everything had already been taken from us, and he would advise that we would not be further molested. He then spoke to the negroes, told them they were free and could either go away or stay at home, but if they remained on the place, they must work, for no one could live without working. He told them they would be better off if they stayed at home.

Soon after Col. Hartwell and staff arrived. They all agreed in saying that the marauders would be punished and the Colonel signed the paper. One of his staff got quite familiar; played with Aunt Ria's baby, little Maria, and ended by kissing her. We laugh and tell the baby she has caught a Yankee beau, and she always laughs and seems to enjoy the joke. In a very short time Gen'l Potter and his staff came up in the piazza. Then the army commenced passing through the yard, about three regiments of infantry, one white and two colored passed through, besides artillery and cavalry. Each one stopped and the men ran in every direction after poultry. They marched the colored regiment right by the piazza; I suppose as an insult to us. The negroes were collected in the yard and cheered them on. Hennie and Sister asked the General if he could not leave us a guard that night, but he said there was no use; his army did not straggle, and that he could not leave a guard at every place he passed. The General did not make a favorable impression on us; he was very short in his manner, but his staff were very polite. One of them told us to try the General again.

You must not be too surprised at our staying out in the piazza with so many men, for there were a great many of us to keep company, and then we had never seen such a sight in our lives before. The last of the army had not left the yard before we saw the General returning; he said he had determined to take up his headquarters here that night. We were all, of course, delighted for we could not have been better guarded. They had the parlor for their sitting room, and one chamber for the General. The wagon train camped just in front of the house, and two regiments in the field in front. There was a sentinel at the front and one at the back door all night. The camp fires looked very pretty at night. Did we ever imagine that Pooshee would be headquarters for a Yankee army? About two hundred head of poultry and a great many sheep were killed; the negroes' own did not escape! We recognized one of the prisoners (that our scouts had here the first of the week) driving a cart, and Lieut. Bright and his men were prisoners that night in the wash room, one of them asked to be allowed to speak to some of the girls who were at the back door; he seemed to be a gentleman.

During the course of the next day soldiers were continually passing through. Our protection paper was of great use, for we were not molested again and from that day to this 9th of March we have been in comparative quiet.

Wantoot house has been burned, also seven unoccupied houses in Pineville. Some of the residents there were shamefully treated, even their clothes taken from them. Uncle Rene was among the fortunate ones; he only had a ham stolen from his house but all of his poultry. They went into the house at Woodboo, though a Mrs. Williams was living there to protect it, opened every drawer and box in the house; dressed themselves

in Uncle Thomas's and the boys' new clothes, leaving
their old ones behind.

At Northampton they were told by the negroes that
a good many things were hid in the house, so made a
thorough search. They actually threatened to hang Mr.
Jervey, and had the rope brought. For some time they
had been told the treasure had been buried. The people
about here would not have suffered near as much if it
had not been for these negroes; in every case they have
told where things have been hidden and they did most
of the stealing. The negroes here have behaved worse
than any I have heard of yet.

Daddy Sandy is as faithful as ever. He is sorry that
the Yankees have been here. George still comes about
the house, but does not do much. Daddy Billy, who
we all thought so much of, has not come in since they
were made free. He pretends to be hurt because Hennie
told him he could go if he wanted to. Hennie's maid
Annette has taken herself off. Kate comes in regularly
to attend in the bed rooms night and morning.

We have to do our own cooking now, and you don't
know how nicely we do it. We take it by turns to cook
dinner in the pantry, two going together every day. I
have not touched my needle for a week; would you
believe that? The field negroes are in a dreadful state;
they will not work, but either roam the country, or sit
in their houses. At first they all said they were going,
but have changed their minds now. Pa has a plan to
propose to them by which they are to pay Grand Pa
so much for the hire of the land and houses; but they
will not come up to hear it. I do not see how we are to
live in this country without any rule or regulation. We
are afraid now to walk outside of the gate.

IV

OUR CONFEDERACY IS GONE WITH A CRASH

March–May, 1865

In Richmond on March 18 the Confederate Congress adjourned. As Sherman marched north from ruined Columbia desperate efforts were made to concentrate against him. Hardee's men came from Savannah, Bragg's from Wilmington, the garrison from Charleston, and what was left of the noble Army of Tennessee all the way from Tupelo. But only 20,000 could be mustered. Under Joseph E. Johnston they fought Sherman's 80,000 in a three-day battle at Bentonville, North Carolina (March 19-21). Undefeated, they retired in good order and spirit toward the center of the state.

In the entrenchments at Petersburg Lee's army had spent an agonizingly cold and hungry winter. Supplies—what there were of them—came over the only line still open, South Side Railroad. Young General John B. Gordon made a gallant attempt, on March 25, to break through at Fort Stedman and wreck Grant's own supply line. He nearly succeeded, but in confused fighting was driven back to the trenches. On March 31 Sheridan, with a great detachment of infantry and cavalry, went out four miles west of the entrenchments, encountered Pickett and Bushrod Johnson at Dinwiddie Court House, was repulsed; but the next day, coming on with his immoderately superior forces, won the Battle of Five Forks, the last important battle of the war.

Petersburg and Richmond were evacuated on April 2. The President and his government fled south with

*the treasury and the records. Lee moved his men west-
ward seeking to reach the Richmond & Danville Railroad for the southwest. Thwarted, he turned toward
Lynchburg, and the skeleton army marched and fought
and struggled on, until the hopelessness of it all became
ineluctable. Then Appomattox and the surrender on
April 9.*

*In the last bivouac General Lee issued his Farewell
Address to his soldiers:*

"After four years of arduous service marked by un-
surpassed courage and fortitude, the Army of Northern
Virginia has been compelled to yield to overwhelming
numbers and resources. . . . I determined to avoid the
useless sacrifice of those whose past services have endeared them to their countrymen. . . . Officers and men
can return to their homes and remain until exchanged.
. . . I bid you all an affectionate farewell."

*Mobile fell on April 12. An the eighteenth General
Johnston surrendered to Sherman near Durham, North
Carolina. On May 4 General Richard Taylor surrendered the troops in the Deep South, and on the same
day, meeting at Washington, Georgia, the Cabinet decided it was useless to continue the struggle anywhere.
On May 26 General Kirby Smith surrendered his Trans-
Mississippi Department. A total of 157,000 Confederate soldiers surrendered to a total of 797,800 Federals.*

*But 258,000 gray ghosts were marching from Fort
Sumter to Appomattox in the Army of Confederate
Dead.*

*And the Southern women, who had danced with them
and worked and prayed for them, shed tears that were
both sad and proud.*

1. MALVINA BLACK GIST—"WE MAY HAVE TO FLY FROM RICHMOND"

Arriving at Richmond after their flight from the doomed city of Columbia, Malvina and the other members of the Confederate Note Department were established in the Ballard Hotel. They became protegées of George A. Trenholm of Charleston, who had succeeded Christopher G. Memminger as Secretary of the Treasury in June 1864.

In 1867 Malvina married Clark Waring and spent the rest of her life in Columbia. She wrote three novels, a number of short stories and several books of verse. She died in 1930 at the age of eighty-eight, survived by three children.

BALLARD HOUSE, RICHMOND, March 1, 1865—We have taken Richmond, if the Yankees haven't! Yes, we are here; but had some trouble to get settled. The fashionable mode of living is room-keeping, and we are strictly in the fashion. And now how nicely comes in that trunk of provisions my thoughtful papa made me bring, much against my own wishes. On opening it, we found meal, hominy, flour, a side of bacon, some coffee, tea, and a quantity of potatoes. They will help us along wonderfully, as all food products bring a tremendous price in this beleaguered city. Ernestine went to market this morning and paid $10 for a steak for our breakfast. At that rate we can only afford to take a savory smell occasionally! Ernie is simply angelic in spirit—she never loses patience, never gets cross, never says anything she oughtn't to say, even against the Yankees! The city is crowded to suffocation, the streets thronged with soldiers in uniform, officers gaily caparisoned, and beautiful women, beautifully dressed, though not in the latest Parisian toilettes. I should say there is no more brilliant capital among all the nations. Are there great and somber tragedies going on around us? Is there a war? I thought so before I reached Richmond!

March 2.—Our department quarters here are not nearly so comfortable as those left behind in Columbia. They do well enough, however. I have not had a chance to mention that handsome officer we saw on the train after leaving Greensboro. He was of the blonde type, with tawny, flowing mustache, and hair bright as "streaks from Aurora's fingers." Tall and broad-shouldered, he was attired in a captain's uniform, and deeply absorbed in reading a book. What was the book? Lise and I were wild to find out. We did find out, and, I hope, without exciting the least suspicion on his part. The book was "Quits." Knowing the story so well, and his face being so expressive, we could almost guess the contents of the pages as he turned them over. But after awhile he did not appear so deeply interested in it, and when our train had to be exchanged for another he stepped forward, raised his hat, and asked to be allowed to remove our packages. He was very grave and dignified. Were we wrong in accepting the attention? Sadie says we must not accept the slightest attention from unknown men while thus traveling. We have been thrust forth from the safe environment of our homes and cannot afford to take any risks. Sadie is as proper as a dowager duchess of eighty. But, ah! the strange exigencies of these times! What is to become of us? There is no longer the shadow of a doubt—our homes are in ashes.

March 3.—I find myself regarding Lise with increasing admiration and affection. She is surely the most graceful girl in existence, combining a lot of downright amiability with a vast amount of tact. Also, she has a deal of fun and mischief. That blond stranger must have noticed all of this with his eyes, so darkly blue.

March 4.—A letter from home! It reached me by
hand through the department—is most reassuring and
at the same time most delightfully comprehensive. They
are all safe—thank God, my dear ones. Johnny came
through without a scratch, and so did my new Stein-
way. It was a night of untold horrors (the 17th), but
in the general conflagration our house was saved. My
father and mother made friends even among their
enemies, and through their exertions and old Maum
Nancy's the family were fed and protected during the
whole time. A number of Federal officers were quartered with the family until the morning of the 20th.
One of them, whom mamma describes as "a most attractive young lieutenant," examined my music, tried
my piano, playing with no little skill, and then inquired, "Where is she; the young lady who plays?"
And when my father answered, "Gone to Richmond,"
he laughingly rejoined, "Ran away from the Yankees!
Now, where was the use of that? We are just as sure
to catch her there as here." Are you, Mr. Lieutenant?
I fancy not; Sherman's army can't expect to over-run
the whole earth; we are safe enough in Richmond. And
yet I regret again not being there. I might have conducted the argument on both sides, for a while, with
that attractive young lieutenant, and who knows?
perchance make one Yankee's heart ache a little. What
fun! What an opportunity! What a chance to get even
have I lost!

March 5.—Oh! the seduction, the novelty, the fas-
cination of this life in Richmond! If patriotism is its
master-chord, pleasure is no less its dominant note,
and while it is as indescribable as the sparkle of cham-
pagne, it is no less intoxicating. Last night the parlor
was full of visitors, and the same may be said of almost
every night—officers, privates, congressmen, senators,
old friends and new ones, from all parts of the country. They are finding out our whereabouts and paying
their devoirs. And what do you think, my little book?
The blonde captain was among them. Strange things

are the most natural, I have begun to think, for our
strange acquaintance has come about in the most natural way. Dr. S—— knows his relatives in Maryland,
and we are acquainted with his relatives in Carolina,
so not even Sadie could gainsay the fitness of the acquaintance—nor Ernestine, who is an anxious mother
to the last one of us.

March 7.—He is just as charming a gentleman as I
thought he would be—I refer to the captain, of course.
Last night I saw him gazing at Bet's hair in the most
admiring manner. It is' magnificent. I should be awfully vain of it, were it mine—but she is not. Bet is as
levelheaded as a girl can be, and as sweet and modest
as a violet.

March 8.—Wish I had been taught to cook instead
of how to play on the piano. A practical knowledge of
the preparation of food products would stand me in
better stead at this juncture than any amount of information regarding the scientific principles of music. I
adore music, but I can't live without eating—and I'm
hungry! I want some chicken salad, and some charlotte
russe, and some oxpalate, and corn muffins! These are
the things I want; but I'll eat anything I can get. Hon-
estly, our cuisine has become a burning question. Dear,
sweet Ernie bears the brunt, and has to, because the
rest of us are simpletons! She'll be canonized some of
these days, or deserves to be, if she isn't.

March 9.—Little book, give me your ear. Close!
There! Promise me never to breathe it! Blank loves
Blank! Yes, he does! And she doesn't care for him—
not a pennyworth! It is a dreadful state of affairs, to be
sure. Why must there be so much loving and making
of love? How much nicer to just keep on being friends
with everybody (except one) and nothing more. It
is a shame that I have so little time to devote to my
journal. We meet so many delightful people and so
many famous people. The other day, attended a re-

view of Gray's Brigade, by Generals Fitzhugh Lee and
Longstreet, in an open field between the Nine Mile
and Darby Town roads. We went in an army ambulance, attended by a number of our gentlemen friends.
Fitz. Lee passed very near us. It was the sight of a
lifetime; it thrilled and pulsated all through me. When
the review was over, we were speedily surrounded by
a throng of gallants, officers and privates—the noble
privates, heroes, I love them! They bear the yoke and
do the fighting, while some of the officers don't do anything but ornament the army. Mind, I don't say all—
some. Do you think we women give no heed to these
things? I know what kind of a heart a man carries under his brass buttons. We spoke to many of our own
State troops, some of them gaunt and battle-scarred
veterans, and some of them young in service but with
the courage of veterans in them. Whether we get
whipped in this fight or not, one thing will be forever
indisputable—our soldiers are true soldiers and good
fighters. Sometimes I fear that we are going to get the
worst of it—but away with all fears!

> To doubt the end were want of trust in God.

So says Henry Timrod, in his *Ethnogenesis*, and he
is a poet, and the poet has a far-seeing eye. It opens
beautifully—this poem, I mean—

> Hath not the morning dawned with added light?
>   And shall not evening call another star
> Out of the infinite regions of the night
>   To mark this day in Heaven?

I hear Timrod's health is poor. What a pity! I hope
he will live to sing us many songs.[1] I must not forget
to chronicle the fact that I saw my gallant cousin,
Robert D——, out at the review. We greeted each
other with unfeigned pleasure.

[1] He died in Columbia, South Carolina, October 6, 1867.

March 10.—The drawing room was again crowded last night, and we got up an important dance on the spur of the moment. General Kershaw,[1] General Gary,[2] and General Ruggles [3] were present; also our friends, the congressman, the captain, the major, and the M.P. Oh! yes. We know Mr. Connelly, an Irish M.P. and Southern sympathizer. He seems to have plenty of money, and lives here in great style for war times; owns a steam yacht, and we are to have an outing on it before long. There are so many interesting things I could and ought to write about, but I just can't, because I am so hungry! And having nothing to eat, I am going to bed to fill up on sleep.

March 11.—Thank goodness! I'm not hungry tonight, and for a very good reason; we dined with the Secretary of the Treasury and his family, the Trenholms. It was a symposium to us poor Treasury girls, attractive and impressive. We discussed the varied menu, elegantly prepared and daintily served, with a Confederate appetite sharply whetted for long-denied delicacies. Mr. Morgan, the young midshipman, was there, quite *en famille*. I did not hear when the wedding is to be. I suppose after the war. Everything is going to take place after the war. As we arose from the table, President and Mrs. Davis were announced. This famous man *honoris causa,* I had already seen before in Columbia, but this was my first glimpse of his wife. She was graciousness itself. Some people whom I have heard talk, and who look upon Mr. Davis as a mere function of government, are disposed to regard him as a conspicuous failure, but, in the name of reason, how can one man please everybody? His role is certainly one of great difficulty. Socially, he may rub some persons the wrong way, but not so with us. He was pleasant, polished and entertaining.

---

[1] Major-General Joseph B. Kershaw.
[2] Major-General M. W. Gary.
[3] Brigadier-General Daniel Ruggles.

March 15.—The Trenholms are exceedingly kind to us. Whenever that majordomo of theirs makes his appearance with that big basket of his, plenty prevails in this section of the Ballard. Heaven bless them! To demolish the contents of that basket is like getting into a home kitchen. Will the time ever come when we can have real coffee to drink again? Our trunk of provisions is gone, and we often feel *gone* without them! Ernestine says Lise and I are completely spoiled for any other life than this surging, intoxicating stream of brass buttons, epaulettes, and sword-belted manhood. It may be so; I am afraid it is. There is an air of military inspiration around us; it pervades our being; we exist in a tremor of ecstasy, or else foreboding. Our Richmond life holds a little of everything, save *ennui*—not a grain of that in it.

March 16.—It is a hard thing to say, but I am going to say it. I don't admire all the men who wear the Confederate uniform! I would rather dig holes in the ground than talk to some of them!

March 17.—I could eat a tallow candle if I had a good one. But I have accepted an invitation to dine with the Trenholms—in my dreams! . . .

March 20.—A great joy has come to me this day, an unlooked-for, an inexpressible joy! A card was brought to me, and I took it with a sigh, because so many cards are brought in and we have so little time for rest. But the name upon that particular card made my heart thump and thump so fast I thought it would thump clean out of my body. It was my dear brother's name —the scout, who has been in prison two years, first at Camp Chase [1] and recently at Fort Delaware.[2] Without stopping as usual to give a last touch to my hair, I rushed into his presence and into his arms. He's the rowdiest, shabbiest, patchiest looking fellow you ever

[1] In Ohio.
[2] In Delaware.

saw, but as handsome as ever, and the same old darling. We talked and talked; we crowded the talk of two long years of separation into two short hours of face to face. It is a thrilling romance, the way he escaped from prison. In a dead man's shoes it was! That man's name was Jesse Tredway, and he died in his bunk after his name had been entered on the list of exchange. My brother put his dead comrade in his own bunk and said nothing. He answered to his name in the roll call and quietly took his place in the ranks of the outgoing prisoners. The details of that journey homeward, the recital of his adventures and narrow escapes from detection all along the route, is something to be heard from his own lips in order to be appreciated. The recital made the blood tingle in my veins and then suddenly run cold; made my pulses throb and then suddenly cease almost to throb at all. Think of it! The recklessness of the deed, and his subsequent anxiety and fear of detection every moment. In the soft veil of the night, in the white light of the morning, under the noonday sun, under the midnight stars, even in the stillness of sleep, never to be rid of the fear of detection. His very life hung upon the issue, for he had made up his mind to shoot down the first man who remanded him back to prison. Thank God! he was never detected, never remanded back! He will now journey on without delay, on foot, for the most part. He has no money to pay his passage—but what of that? It is a pleasure to him to walk on God's fair earth again, no longer a shut-up animal in a cage; the earth is full of a new glory for him, the glory of sweet liberty. The exile has returned to his home.

March 23.—Congressman Farrow asked me today if I were feeling well. Come to think of it, I do not feel well. My nerve forces seem to be all out of tune, and my digestion is impaired—in fact, a general *malaise* appears to be the result of hardtack on my constitution.

March 25.—My head aches; I have no appetite (and nothing fit to eat, either); my senses are dull. Heaven grant I may not be ill in Richmond! At this particular epoch, it is the place for everything else, but no place to be sick in.

March 29.—Mr. Duncan brings us the weightiest news. The Confederacy is going to the dogs—or, did he say the devil? That young lieutenant was right. We may have to fly from Richmond as we did from Columbia. It is a profound secret as yet; but he warns us to be ready to leave on quick notice. Are we to be driven to the wall? I can't believe it! But somehow—somehow—my heart is as barren of hope tonight as the great Sahara of water.

March 30.—Indeed, something very serious is astir in military circles. After arranging everything, the M.P. has had to give up the projected outing on the James? It is not safe—a fight is brewing. Doubtless I should worry more if I felt better; when the head is so confused with pain, and the nerves unstrung, all other matters are secondary.

March 31.—Feel better today. Mr. Connelly gave us a collation in the hotel in lieu of the abandoned picnic. Very swell, despite the blockade. Must have cost him a pretty sum. I told Mr. Duncan I would not leave Richmond, so full of a certain charm is the life here; but of course have had to give in, and now am ready for another flight as soon as he notifies us. . . .

2. JUDITH BROCKENBROUGH McGUIRE—
"THE SOUND OF CANNON IS EVER IN OUR EARS"

Mrs. McGuire has now been a refugee for four years and is fifty-two years old. She keeps up her vocation in the Commissary Department and her avocation in the hospitals.

March 10th, 1865. Still we go on as heretofore, hoping and praying that Richmond may be safe. I know that we ought to feel that whatever General Lee and the President deem right for the cause must be right, and that we should be satisfied that all will be well; but it would almost break my heart to see this dear old city, with its hallowed associations, given over to the Federals. Fearful orders have been given in the offices to keep the papers packed, except such as we are working on. The packed boxes remain in the front room, as if uncertainty still existed about moving them. As we walk in every morning, all eyes are turned to the boxes to see if any have been removed, and we breathe more freely when we find them still there.

To-day I have spent in the hospital.

March 11th. Sheridan's raid through the country is perfectly awful, and he has joined Grant, without being caught. Oh, how we listened to hear that he had been arrested in his direful career! It was, I suppose, the most cruel and desolating raid upon record—more lawless, if possible, than Hunter's. He had an overwhelming force, spreading ruin through the Upper Valley, the Piedmont country, the tide-water country, until he reached Grant.[1] His soldiers were allowed to commit any cruelty on non-combatants that suited their rapacious tempers—stealing every thing they could find; earrings, breastpins, and finger-rings were taken from the first ladies of the land; nothing escaped them which was worth carrying off from the already deso-

---

[1] "As the spring opened, Grant called to himself Sheridan's force, which had wintered in the Valley. Sheridan marched through that unhappy country; struck the remnants of Early's little army at Waynesboro, on March second; drove and scattered them, with large captures; crossed the Blue Ridge, destroyed miles of the Virginia Central Railroad and the James River canal, and, with little opposition, marched eastward through Virginia to the White House on the Pamunkey. From there, on March nineteenth, he reported his troops for duty with the armies immediately under Grant."—*The Story of the Confederacy*, by Robert S. Henry, pp. 453, 454.

lated country. And can we feel patient at the idea of such soldiers coming to Richmond, the target at which their whole nation, from their President to the meanest soldier upon their armyrolls, has been aiming for four years? Oh, I would that I could see Richmond burnt to the ground by its own people, with not one brick left upon another, before its defenceless inhabitants should be subjected to such degradation!

Fighting is still going on; so near the city, that the sound of cannon is ever in our ears. Farmers are sending in their produce which they cannot spare, but which they give with a spirit of self-denial rarely equalled. Ladies are offering their jewelry, their plate, any thing which can be converted into money, for the country. I have heard some of them declare, that, if necessary, they will cut off their long suits of hair, and send them to Paris to be sold for bread for the soldiers. . . . Some gentlemen are giving up their watches, when every thing else has been given. . . .

March 12th.—A deep gloom has just been thrown over the city by the untimely death of one of its own heroic sons. General John Pegram fell while nobly leading his brigade against the enemy in the neighborhood of Petersburg. But two weeks before he had been married in St. Paul's Church. . . . All was bright and beautiful. Happiness beamed from every eye. Again has St. Paul's been opened to receive the soldier and his bride [1]—the one coffined for a hero's grave, the other, pale and trembling, though still by his side, in widow's garb. . . .

March 31st.—A long pause in my diary. Every thing seems so dark and uncertain that I have no heart for keeping records. The croakers croak about Rich-

---

[1] She was the beautiful Hetty Cary, Constance's cousin, who came to Richmond from Baltimore early in war days and immediately became the toast of the town. General Chestnut said, "If there was no such word as 'fascinating,' you would have to invent it to describe Hetty Cary."

mond being evacuated, but I can't and won't believe it. . . .

There is hard fighting about Petersburg, and General A. P. Hill has been killed.[1] . . .

3. MARY D. WARING—"THEY MARCHED INTO MOBILE TO THE TUNE OF 'YANKEE DOODLE' "

After the Battle of Mobile Bay (August 5, 1864), in which Admiral Franklin Buchanan's great ram the Tennessee had, practically alone, engaged Admiral Farragut's fleet, Union forces had taken the two great Confederate forts, Morgan and Gaines, guarding the bay. Piles driven into the Mobile River rendered the city itself safe for the time being. General Dabney H. Maury, Betty Maury's cousin, was in command at the barricade, which was protected by Spanish Fort. After the Battle of Nashville he was reinforced by four brigades, including General Randall L. Gibson's, from Hood's army. General Maury surrendered to the Union fleet and land forces under General Gordon Granger on April 12.

Mary was the young daughter of Moses and Ellen Smoot Waring of Mobile. In her war diary she made note of personal affairs, events in the city, war news. Like Esther Alden and many another Southern girl, she could not bring herself to record the fall of the Confederacy. Her journal ended abruptly on April 16 in the middle of a sentence.

Mary married Lieutenant Thomas Locke Harrison, a graduate of the Naval Academy at Annapolis, who had served under Buchanan at Mobile Bay. They had two children. She and her husband are buried in Magnolia Cemetery at Mobile.

Mobile, Alabama

Mar. 27th, 1865. Today the enemy commenced

[1] On the last day of fighting in the trench lines at Petersburg.

operations by an attack on Spanish Fort, where some of our best troops under Gen. Gibson, were stationed. The firing was heavy and continuous, while the booming of heavy Artillery was heard distinctly on this side, rendering us very uneasy as to the fate of our brave and gallant boys stationed in and around the fort. Being unaccustomed to such heavy firing, we were, of course, much startled and excited until we gradually became used to the sound.

Tuesday March 28th. Heavy firing is still kept up at the Fort, from both sides. The wharves and all high places in the city, filled with persons, impelled, some by curiosity, but many more by anxiety, watching the firing. It has been impossible to do work of any description, or to compose the mind, for reading, writing, practicing or any thing else. I have been wandering around, like a restless spirit, trying to compose myself, but finding every effort to do so, impossible, finally give up the attempt, so great is my anxiety about Marion, and many of my friends stationed there.

Wednesday March 29th/65 Tidings from the Eastern Shore, relative to the proceedings of yesterday, are very encouraging, our boys still frustrating all efforts of the enemy to take the fort. Our casualties, considering the heavy cannonading, are slight, and our wounded receive the kindest care and attention at the Hospitals. This morning, as I started down town, I met Fanny, who being desirous of seeing the firing at Spanish fort, went with me round to Cousin Pidge's, where we had a very good view from the third story. We each stationed ourselves at the windows with an opera-glass apiece, and spent our whole morning in gazing at different objects on the bay. We could very readily discern the vessels of the enemy, also many of their transports coming in with fresh troops, and we imagined that we could see the "Nashville" [1] tho' I hardly imagine our sight was keen enough for that. Af-

[1] Confederate gunboat.

ter passing an hour or two, in this manner, we went down to Cousin P's room, where she had a nice lunch prepared for us, & which we did full credit. . . .

Thursday, March 30th, 1865.   The cannonading last eve, was fierce and heavy in the extreme, the firing, as we learned this morning, being *chiefly our gunboats* shelling the woods. So rapid and so distinct was the booming of the "big guns" that our fears and anxiety were not a little excited, tho' very little damage was done. . . .

Monday, Apr. 3rd.   Just one week today since the bombardment commenced, and our *dear,* gallant men fought hard and bravely. They certainly deserve our highest commendation and admiration, and all the encouragement we can heap upon them. Our thoughts are constantly for them and with them, and I trust that we may ever succeed in our noble cause.

Tuesday April 4th.   The fighting all last night and today has been excessively heavy, and makes us feel much anxiety and fear for our brothers and friends. This evening the firing is terrific, not a moment elapsing between the booming of "heavy artillery." I trust our noble little fort will stand defiant to the assaults of the enemy.

Wednesday, April 5th.   Our casualties of yesterday were very small, considering the tremendous bombardment of the whole day. All will end well, I trust, for us.

Thursday, April 6th.   Today I have been exceedingly busy, making a tobacco-bag, for one of the soldiers to whom our Society are preparing to send a handsome present in the form of a box of provisions. It was filled with every thing which these war times was capable of sending. I also busied myself with making a large sponge cake for Cousin Tom.

Friday, April 7th. It has been comparatively quiet and uneventful today, only we are still kept excited and uneasy about the firing. Tonight we meet at Mrs. Muldons' and, I fear, will not be permitted long to meet and work for our dear Confederate soldiers, as things begin to look threatening. After picking considerable lint and rolling bandages, we dispersed hoping to have, at least, one more meeting in peace and in Confederate lines. . . .

Sunday April 9th. Bright and early this morning I was awakened with "Spanish Fort is evacuated" while I could hardly believe it. Still I had to believe the evidence of my own eyes, for our soldiers were passing by in squads, from an early hour, dirty, wet and completely worn out, having been compelled to march through a marsh for a distance of four miles, in order to make their escape. Poor fellows, how discouraging it must have been to abandon the fort after having so bravely defended it for two weeks. All day long they have been coming in. . . . Mrs. Hall came in with any quantity of bad news—viz:—that the enemy had charged the breast works, at Blakely, taking them & capturing the whole garrison, which was sad news, indeed, for us. Our course was now clear to us, and we felt distressed at the idea of the occupation of our dear little city, by our detested enemy. We sat up until late, brooding over our misfortune. . . .

Monday, Apr. 10th 1865. This morning, we were much startled by the ringing of the alarm bell: the object of which was to call troops together to prepare for evacuation. Never have I experienced such feelings as now take possession of me—perfectly miserable, as may be imagined. Everybody is excited and running around, gathering what information they can. . . . It is with a heavy heart that I bid my friends "good bye" not knowing whether I shall ever see them again or not. . . .

Tuesday, April 11th 1865.   All excitement still this morning. We are all perfectly miserable at the idea of being separated, for an indefinite period of time, from our dear brothers and friends. . . . The day has passed away without my accomplishing a thing except watching our soldiers as they passed by, and now and then seeing a friend and saying *Adieu*. How sad the word. . . . This afternoon about dinner time, the 1st La. Regiment which has been stationed in Mobile for the past six or eight months, passed by on their way to the boat, seemingly in good spirits. . . .

Wednesday, April 12th.   I awoke this morning with a most deserted and desolate feeling. All our troops got off some time during the night, and the city is entirely free of "gray coats" except some few Scouts who will decamp upon the entrance of the enemy.

Our feelings can be better imagined than described, as we were momentarily expecting the intelligence that the enemy were nearly to the city. Meanwhile, quite a commotion has sprung up, down the street, and the people threatened with a *mob*. A quantity of commissary stores having been left by our military authorities, and being turned over to the poor, each one of that class, helping himself freely, and endeavoring to carry off as much as possible—each one tries to be first, and consequently much scuffling and rioting ensues—which is soon quelled by the citizens, who appear with loaded guns & various weapons.

About 12 o'clock, the Mayor, accompanied by many gentlemen, went down the bay to surrender the city to Gen. Granger, and soon they were on their way to the city. The Yankee troops did not come in until about four o'clock in the afternoon, when they were marched in to the tune of "Yankee Doodle." When I heard *that*, and the cheering of the men, I began to realize what *had* and was taking place, as before *that*, I had been so much excited that I hardly had time for thought. . . . My feelings this afternoon and tonight, have been any thing but pleasant. I believe I was never so gloomy—but there will be a bright day for us yet.

Thursday, April 13th. The city is filled with the hated Yanks, who differ in the greatest degree from our poor dear soldiers. Really I feel quite strange in my own city, seeing so many new and strange countenances. To do them justice, however, I must admit, though reluctant to do so, that they are very quiet and orderly, and they entered the city with extra-ordinary order and quiet, so different from what we had anticipated, from the numerous accounts of their behavior in captured cities. We are thankful for it and hope such conduct will be preserved throughout their stay here.

4. VARINA HOWELL DAVIS—"WITH HEARTS BOWED DOWN BY DESPAIR WE LEFT RICHMOND"

Except for a brief while in the spring of 1862 when Richmond was first threatened, Mrs. Davis had been in the city. In the White House she had borne two children. A little son, as we have seen, had been killed by falling from the north balcony.

The last photograph of the First Lady was taken in the winter of 1864. It shows her in a cheap muslin dress; her face is gaunt and lined but she bears herself proudly. She maintained her receptions down to the final weeks.

"Providence has seen fit," said Mrs. Chesnut, "that I should have known three great women, and Mrs. Jefferson Davis is one of them."

She was captured with her husband on May 10, 1865, at Irwinville, Georgia. She shared with him the last months of his two-year imprisonment in Fortress Monroe; she nursed him and cleaned his cell in the casemate dungeon. On his release she went with him to Canada and to England. They lived for several years in Memphis and finally retired to a new home, "Beau-

voir," *near Biloxi, Mississippi. After his death on December 6, 1889, she devoted herself to writing a tribute to him,* Jefferson Davis: ex-president of the Confederate States of America.

She died in New York on October 16, 1906, and was buried beside her husband in Hollywood Cemetery, Richmond, where so many of the Confederate great rest in peace.

Darkness seemed now to close swiftly over the Confederacy, and about a week before the evacuation of Richmond,[1] Mr. Davis came to me and gently, but decidedly, announced the necessity for our departure. He said for the future his headquarters must be in the field, and that our presence would only embarrass and grieve, instead of comforting him. Very averse to flight, and unwilling at all times to leave him, I argued the question with him and pleaded to be permitted to remain, until he said: "I have confidence in your capacity to take care of our babies, and understand your desire to assist and comfort me, but you can do this in but one way, and that is by going yourself and taking our children to a place of safety." He was very much affected and said, "If I live you can come to me when the struggle is ended, but I do not expect to survive the destruction of constitutional liberty."

He had a little gold, and reserving a five-dollar piece for himself he gave it all to me, as well as all the Confederate money due to him. He desired me not to request any of the citizens of Richmond to take care of my silver plate, of which we possessed a large quantity, for, said he, "They may be exposed to inconvenience or outrage by their effort to serve us."

All women like bric-a-brac, which sentimental people call their "household goods," but Mr. Davis called it "trumpery." I was not superior to the rest of my sex in this regard. However, everything which could not be readily transported was sent to a dealer for

[1] Richmond was evacuated April 2.

sale, and we received quite a large draft on a Richmond bank as the proceeds, but in the hurry of departure the check was not cashed.

Leaving the house as it was, and taking only our clothing, I made ready with my young sister and my four little children, the eldest only nine years old, to go forth into the unknown. Mr. Burton N. Harrison,[1] the President's private secretary, was to protect and see us safely settled in Charlotte, where we had hired a furnished house. Mr. George A. Trenholm's lovely daughters were also to accompany us to remain with friends there.

I had bought several barrels of flour, and intended to take them with me, but Mr. Davis said, "You cannot remove anything in the shape of food from here, the people want it, and you must leave it here."

The deepest depression had settled upon the whole city. . . .

The day before our departure Mr. Davis gave me a pistol and showed me how to load, aim, and fire it. He was very apprehensive of our falling into the hands of the disorganized bands of troops roving about the country, and said, "You can at least, if reduced to the last extremity, force your assailants to kill you, but I charge you solemnly to leave when you hear the enemy are approaching; and if you cannot remain undisturbed in our own country, make for the Florida coast and take a ship there for a foreign country."

---

[1] Burton Harrison was to be imprisoned with President Davis at Fortress Monroe. His fiancée, Constance Cary, who was staying with relatives in New Jersey, had no news of him for months. She went to Washington and worked to secure his release. At last she succeeded and he visited her and her mother there. Constance went to Europe late in 1866 and on her return she and Burton were married, November 26, 1867, in Saint Ann's Church at Morrisania, New York, where her aunt lived. Burton practiced law in New York City, and Constance became popular as a writer of vivacious short stories, novels, plays, essays. Her autobiography, *Recollections Grave and Gay*, appeared in 1911. She died in Washington November 21, 1920, survived by two sons.

With hearts bowed down by despair, we left Richmond. Mr. Davis almost gave way, when our little Jeff begged to remain with him, and Maggie clung to him convulsively, for it was evident he thought he was looking his last upon us.

As we pulled out from the station and lost sight of Richmond, the wornout engine broke down, and there we sat all night. There were no arrangements possible for sleeping, and at last, after twelve hours' delay, we reached Danville. A hospitable and wealthy citizen of that place invited me to rest with his family, but we gratefully declined and proceeded to Charlotte.

The baggage cars were all needing repairs and leaked badly. Our bedding was wet through by the constant rains that poured down in the week of uninterrupted travel which was consumed in reaching our destination. Universal consternation prevailed throughout the country, and we avoided seeing people for fear of compromising them with the enemy, should they overrun North Carolina. We found everything packed up in the house we had rented, but the agent, Mr. A. Weill, an Israelite, came to meet us there, and gave us every assistance in his power; and when he found there were no conveniences for cooking, he sent our meals from his own house for several days, refusing, with many cordial words, any offer to reimburse him for the expense incurred, and he offered money or any other service he could render.

Mr. Harrison, after seeing us safely established in Charlotte, fearing he might be separated from Mr. Davis, and hoping to be of use, set out for Richmond to rejoin him. . . .

5. PHOEBE YATES PEMBER—"THE WOMEN OF THE SOUTH STILL FOUGHT THEIR BATTLE"

Her four years' labor as matron in Chimborazo Hospital ably concluded, Mrs. Pember set down her impressions of the occupation of Richmond. Then she

*went to live with relatives in Savannah, carrying with
her all she possessed—a box of Confederate money
and one silver ten-cent piece.*

*Her account of hospital experiences was published
in 1879—*A Southern Woman's Story. *It is introduced
by this quotation:*

"Whatsoever is beginning that is done
   by human skill;
Every daring emanation of the mind's imperfect will;
Every first impulse of passion, gush of love or
   twinge of hate;
Every launch upon the waters, wide-horizoned
   by our fate;
Every venture in the chances of life's sad,
   aye, desperate game;
Whatsoever be our object, whatsoever be our aim—
      'Tis well we cannot see
      What the end will be."

Richmond, Virginia
April 2, 1865

No one slept during that night of horror, for added
to the present scenes were the anticipations of what the
morrow would bring forth. Daylight dawned upon a
wreck of destruction and desolation. From the highest
point of Church hill and Libby hill, the eye could range
over the whole extent of city and country—the fire
had not abated, and the burning bridges were adding
their flame and smoke to the scene. A single faint explosion could be heard from the distance at long intervals, but the *Patrick Henry* was low to the water's
edge and Drewry but a column of smoke. The whistle
of the cars and the rushing of the laden trains still continued—they had never ceased—and the clouds hung
low and draped the scene as morning advanced.

Before the sun had risen, two carriages rolled along
Main street, and passed through Rocketts just under
Chimborazo hospital, carrying the mayor and corpora-
tion towards the Federal lines, to deliver the keys of

the city, and half an hour afterwards, over to the east, a single Federal blue-jacket rose above the hill, standing transfixed with astonishment at what he saw. Another and another sprang up as if out of the earth, but still all remained quiet. About seven o'clock, there fell upon the earth the steady clatter of horses' hoofs, and winding around Rocketts, close under Chimborazo hill, came a small and compact body of Federal cavalrymen, on horses in splendid condition, riding closely and steadily along. They were well mounted, well accoutered, well fed—a rare sight in Southern streets,— the advance of that vaunted army that for four years had so hopelessly knocked at the gates of the Southern Confederacy.

They were some distance in advance of the infantry who followed, quite as well appointed and accoutered as the cavalry. Company after company, regiment after regiment, battalion after battalion, and brigade after brigade, they poured into the doomed city—an endless stream. One detachment separated from the main body and marching to Battery No., 2, raised the United States flag, their band playing the Star Spangled Banner. There they stacked their arms. The rest marched along Main Street through fire and smoke, over burning fragments of buildings, emerging at times like a phantom army when the wind lifted the dark clouds; while the colored population shouted and cheered them on their way.

Before three hours had elapsed, the troops had been quartered and were inspecting the city. They swarmed in every highway and byway, rose out of gullies, appeared on the top of hills, emerged from narrow lanes, and skirted around low fences. There was hardly a spot in Richmond not occupied by a blue coat, but they were orderly, quiet and respectful. Thoroughly disciplined, warned not to give offense by look or act, they did not speak to any one unless first addressed; and though the women of the South contrasted with sickness of heart the difference this splendidly-equipped army, and the war-worn, wasted aspect of their own defenders, they were grateful for the consideration shown them; and if they remained in their sad homes, with closed doors and windows, or walked the streets with averted eyes and veiled faces, it was that they could not bear the presence of invaders, even under the most favorable circumstances.

Before the day was over, the public buildings were occupied by the enemy, and the minds of the citizens relieved from all fears of molestation. The hospitals were attended to, the ladies being still allowed to nurse and care for their own wounded; but rations could not be drawn yet, the obstructions in the James river preventing the transports from coming up to the city. In a few days they arrived, and food was issued to those in need. It had been a matter of pride among the Southerners to boast that they had never seen a greenback, so the entrance of the Federal army had thus found them entirely unprepared with gold and silver currency. People who had boxes of Confederate money and were wealthy the day previously, looked around in vain for wherewithal to buy a loaf of bread. Strange exchanges were made on the street of tea and coffee, flour and bacon. Those who were fortunate in having a stock of household necessaries were generous in the extreme to their less wealthy neighbors, but the destitution was terrible. The sanitary commission shops were opened, and commissioners appointed by the Federals to visit among the people and distribute orders to draw rations, but to effect this, after receiving tickets, required so many appeals to different officials, that decent people gave up the effort. Besides, the musty corn-meal and strong cod-fish were not appreciated by fastidious stomachs—few gently nurtured could relish such unfamiliar food.

But there was no assimilation between the invaders and invaded. In the daily newspaper a notice had appeared that the military bands would play in the beautiful capital grounds every afternoon, but when the appointed hour arrived, except the Federal officers, musicians and soldiers, not a white face was to be seen. The negroes crowded every bench and path. The next week another notice was issued that the colored population would not be admitted; and then the absence of everything and anything feminine was appalling. The entertainers went along to their own entertainment. The third week still another notice appeared: "colored nurses were to be admitted with their white charges," and lo! each fortunate white baby received the cherished care of a dozen finely-dressed black ladies, the only drawback being that in two or three days the music ceased altogether, the entertainers feeling at last the ingratitude of the subjugated people.

Despite their courtesy of manner, for however despotic the acts, the Federal authorities maintained a respectful manner—the newcomers made no advance towards fraternity. They spoke openly and warmly of their sympathy with the sufferings of the South, but committed and advocated acts that the hearers could not recognize as "military necessities." Bravely-dressed Federal officers met their former old class-mates from colleges and military institutions and inquired after the relatives to whose houses they had ever been welcome in days of yore, expressing a desire to "call and see them," while the vacant chairs, rendered vacant by Federal bullets, stood by the hearth of the widow and bereaved mother. They could not be made to understand that their presence was painful. There were few men in the city at this time; but the women of the South still fought their battle for them; fought it resentfully, calmly, but silently! Clad in their mourning garments, overcome but hardly subdued, they sat within their desolate homes, or if compelled to leave that shelter went on their errands to church or hospital with veiled faces and swift steps. By no sign or act did the possessors of their fair city show that they were even conscious of their presence. If they looked in their faces they saw them not: they might have supposed themselves a phantom army. There was no stepping aside with affection to avoid the contact of dress, no feigned humility in giving the inside of the walk: they simply totally ignored their presence.

Two particular characteristics followed the army in possession—the circus and booths for the temporary accommodation of itinerant venders. The small speculators must have supposed that there were no means of cooking left in the city, from the quantity of canned edibles they offered for sale. They inundated Richmond with pictorial canisters at exorbitant prices, which no one had money to buy. Whether the supply of greenbacks was scant, or the people were not disposed to trade with the new-comers, they had no customers.

In a few days steamboats had made their way to the wharves, though the obstructions still defied the ironclads, and crowds of curious strangers thronged the pavements, while squads of mounted male pleasure-seekers scoured the streets. Gayly-dressed women began to pour in also, with looped-up skirts, very large feet, and a great preponderance of spectacles. The Richmond women sitting by desolated firesides were astonished by the arrival of former friends, sometimes people moving in the best classes of society, who had the bad taste to make a pleasure trip to the mourning city, calling upon their heart-broken friends of happier days in all the finery of the newest New York fashions, and in some instances forgiving their entertainers the manifold sins of the last four years in formal and set terms.

From the hill on which my hospital was built, I had sat all the weary Sunday of the evacuation, watching the turmoil, and bidding friends adieu, for even till noon many had been unconscious of the events that were transpiring, and now when they had all departed, as night set in, I wrapped my blanket-shawl around me, and watched below me all that I have here narrated. Then I walked through my wards and found them comparatively empty. Every man who could crawl had tried to escape a Northern prison. Beds in which paralyzed, rheumatic, and helpless patients had lain for months were empty. The miracles of the New

Testament had been re-enacted. The lame, the halt, and the blind had been cured. Those who were compelled to remain were almost wild at being left in what would be the enemy's lines the next day; for in many instances they had been exchanged prisoners only a short time before. I gave all the comfort I could, and with some difficulty their supper also, for my detailed nurses had gone with General Lee's army, and my black cooks had deserted me.

On Monday morning, the day after the evacuation, the first blue uniforms appeared at our quarters—three surgeons inspecting the hospital. As our surgeon was with them, there must have been an amicable understanding. One of our divisions was required for use by the new-comers, cleared out for them, and their patients laid by the side of our own sick so that we shared with them, as my own commissary stores were still well supplied. Three days afterwards an order came to transfer my old patients to Camp Jackson. I protested bitterly against this, as they were not in a fit state for removal, so they remained unmolested. To them I devoted my time, for our surgeons had either then left or received orders to discontinue their labors.

Towards evening the place was deserted. Miss G. had remained up to this time with me, but her mother requiring her presence in the city, she left at sunset, and after I had gone through all my wards, I returned to my dear little sitting-room, endeared by retrospection, and the consciousness that my labors were nearly over, but had been (as far as regarded results) in vain. . . .

6. JUDITH BROCKENBROUGH McGUIRE—
"LIKE A VIVID, HORRIBLE DREAM"

"My heart would break if the Federals occupied Richmond," Mrs. McGuire had said. *Now the Union flag waved from the roof of the Capitol, and the in-*

*vading General Godfrey Weitzel had moved into the
White House.*

Richmond, Virginia

April 3.—Agitated and nervous, I turn to my diary
to-night as the means of soothing my feelings. We
have passed through a fatal thirty-six hours. Yesterday morning we went, as usual, to St. James's Church,
hoping for a day of peace and quietness, as well as of
religious improvement and enjoyment. The sermon
being over, as it was the first Sunday in the month,
the sacrament of the Lord's Supper was administered.
While the sacred elements were being administered,
the sexton came in with a note to General Cooper,
which was handed him as he walked from the chancel,
and he immediately left the church. It made me anxious; but such things are not uncommon, and caused
no excitement in the congregation. The services being
over, we left the church, and our children joined us,
on their way to the usual family gathering in our room
on Sunday. . . .

John remarked to his father, that he had just returned from the War Department, and that there was
sad news—General Lee's lines had been broken, and
the city would probably be evacuated within twenty-
four hours. . . .

In an hour J. received orders to accompany Captain
Parker to the South with the Corps of Midshipmen.
Then we began to understand that the Government
was moving, and that the evacuation was indeed going
on. The office-holders were now making arrangements
to get off. Every car was ordered to be ready to take
them south. Baggage-wagons, carts, drays, and ambulances were driving about the streets; every one going
off that could go. The people were rushing up and
down the streets, vehicles of all kinds were flying
along, bearing goods of all sorts and people of all ages
and classes who could go beyond the corporation lines.
We tried to keep ourselves quiet. We could not go

south, nor could we leave the city at all in this hurried way. . . .

Last night, when we went out to hire a servant to go to Camp Jackson for our sister, we for the first time realized that our money was worthless here, and that we are in fact penniless. About midnight she walked in, escorted by two of the convalescent soldiers. We collected in one room, and tried to comfort one another. . . .

Oh, who shall tell the horror of the past night! Union men began to show themselves; treason walked abroad. About two o'clock in the morning we were startled by a loud sound like thunder; the house shook and the windows rattled; it seemed like an earthquake in our midst. It was soon understood to be the blowing up of a magazine below the city. In a few hours another exploded on the outskirts of the city, much louder than the first, and shivering innumerable plate-glass windows all over Shockoe Hill. It was then daylight, and we were standing out upon the pavement. The lower part of the city was burning.

About seven o'clock I set off to go to the central depot to see if the cars would go out. As I went from Franklin to Broad Street, and on Broad, the pavements were covered with broken glass; women, both white and coloured, were walking in multitudes from the Commissary offices and burning stores with bags of flour, meal, coffee, sugar, rolls of cotton cloth, etc., coloured men were rolling wheelbarrows filled in the same way. I went on and on towards the depot, and as I proceeded shouts and screams became louder. The rabble rushed by me in one stream. "Who are those shouting? What is the matter?" I seemed to be answered by a hundred voices, "The Yankees have come." I turned to come home, but what was my horror, when I reached Ninth Street, to see a regiment of Yankee cavalry come dashing up, yelling, shouting, hallooing, screaming! All Bedlam let loose could not have vied with them in diabolical roarings. I stood riveted to the spot; I could not move nor speak. Then

I saw the iron gate of our time-honoured and beautiful Capitol Square, on the walks and greensward of
which no hoof had been allowed to tread, thrown open
and the cavalry dash in. I could see no more. . . . I
came home. . . .

The Federal soldiers were roaming about the streets;
either whiskey or the excess of joy had given some of
them the appearance of being beside themselves. We
had hoped that very little whiskey would be found in
the city, as, by the order of the Mayor, casks were
emptied yesterday evening in the streets, and it flowed
like water through the gutters; but the rabble had managed to find it secreted in the burning shops, and bore
it away in pitchers and buckets. . . .

The fire was progressing rapidly, and the crashing
sound of falling timbers was distinctly heard. Dr. Read's
church was blazing. The War Department was falling
in; burning papers were being wafted about the streets.
The Commissary Department, with our desks and papers, was consumed already. Warwick & Barksdale's
mill was sending its flames to the sky. Cary and Main
Streets seemed doomed throughout; Bank Street was
beginning to burn, and now it had reached Franklin. . . . Almost every house is guarded; and the
streets are now (ten o'clock) perfectly quiet. The
moon is shining brightly on our captivity. God guide
and watch over us!

April 5.—I feel as if we were groping in the dark;
no one knows what to do. The Yankees, so far, have
behaved humanely. . . .

April 6th.—Mr. Lincoln has visited our devoted city
to-day. His reception was any thing but complimentary.
Our people were in nothing rude or disrespectful; they
only kept themselves away from a scene so painful.
There are very few Unionists of the least respectability
here; these met them (he was attended by Stanton and
others) with cringing loyalty, I hear, but the rest of the
small collection were of the low, lower, lowest of crea-

tion. They drove through several streets, but the greeting was so feeble from the motley crew of vulgar men and women, that the Federal officers themselves, I suppose, were ashamed of it, for they very soon escaped from the disgraceful association. . . .

April 10th.—Another gloomy Sabbath-day and harrowing night. We went to St. Paul's in the morning, and heard a very fine sermon from Dr. Minnegerode—at least so said my companions. My attention wandered continually. I could not listen; I felt so strangely, as if in a vivid, horrible dream. Neither President was prayed for; in compliance with some arrangement with the Federal authorities, the prayer was used as for all in authority! How fervently did we all pray for our own President! Thank God, our silent prayers are free from Federal authority. . . .

Thursday Night.—Fearful rumours are reaching us from sources which it is hard to doubt, that it is all too true, and that General Lee surrendered on Sunday last, the 9th of April. . . . We do not yet give up all hope. General Johnston is in the field, but there are thousands of the enemy to his tens. The citizens are quiet. The calmness of despair is written on every countenance. . . .

Good-Friday.—As usual, I went to the hospital, and found Miss T. in much trouble. A peremptory order has been given by the Surgeon-General to remove *all* patients. . . . The ambulances were at the door. Miss T. and myself decided to go at once to the Medical Director and ask him to recall the order. We were conducted to his office, and, for the first time since the entrance of Federal troops, were impolitely treated.

We had no service in our churches to-day. An order came out in this morning's papers that the prayers for the President of the United States must be used. How could we do it? . . .

Sunday Night.—Strange rumours are afloat to-night. It is said and believed, that Lincoln is dead, and Seward much injured.[1] As I passed the house of a friend this evening, she raised the window and told me the report. Of course I treated it as a Sunday rumour; but the story is strengthened by the way which the Yankees treat it. I trust that, if true, it may not be by the hand of an assassin, though it would seem to fulfil the warnings of Scripture. His efforts to carry out his abolition theories have caused the shedding of oceans of Southern blood. . . . But what effect will it have on the South? We may have much to fear.

7. MRS. W. T. SUTHERLIN—PRESIDENT DAVIS IN DANVILLE

Major Sutherlin and his wife opened their home in Danville, Virginia, to President Davis in flight from Richmond on April 3, 1865. A Cabinet meeting was held there, Secretary of War John C. Breckinridge alone being absent, and there the President's last proclamation was written. A marker on the house claims it as the "last capitol of the Confederacy, April 3-10, 1865."

When President Davis had been at our house for three days he said that he could not impose on our hospitality longer, and made arrangements to establish his headquarters at the old Benedict house, on Wilson Street. I told him that he might take his cabinet to any place he pleased, but as for himself he must be our guest so long as he remained in the city, and he yielded to the request. He remained here five days after that time, and was, of course, in a most anxious frame of

[1] Lincoln was shot in Ford's Theater the night of April 14 and died a little after seven o'clock Saturday morning the fifteenth. Secretary of State Seward was assaulted in his bedroom but was able to resume his duties in May.

mind, but was always pleasant and agreeable. One morning he and Mr. Sutherlin went down town and soon returned in an excited manner, and I knew something had happened. I met them at the door and President Davis told me almost in a whisper that Lee had surrendered and that he must leave town as soon as possible.

Making a few hurried arrangements, he offered his hand to me to say good-by, and I asked him the question: "Mr. Davis, have you any funds other than Confederate money?" and he replied in the negative. "Then," said I, offering him a bag of gold containing a thousand dollars, "take this from me." I offered the money without having consulted Mr. Sutherlin, but knew it would be all right with him.

Mr. Davis took my hand and the tears streamed down his face. "No," said he, "I cannot take your money. You and your husband are young and will need your money, while I am an old man, and," adding after a pause, "I don't reckon I shall need anything very long."

He then put his hand in his pocket and took out a little gold pencil which he asked me to keep for his sake. . . .

8. JUDITH BROCKENBROUGH McGUIRE— "GENERAL LEE HAS RETURNED"

With a breaking heart Mrs. McGuire closes the pages of her diary. It was published anonymously shortly after the war, as "By a Lady of Virginia."

Richmond, Virginia

April 16, 1865.—General Lee has returned. He came unattended, save by his staff—came without notice, and without parade; but he could not come unobserved; as soon as his approach was whispered, a crowd gathered in his path, not boisterously, but respectfully, and increasing rapidly as he advanced to his home on Franklin Street, between 8th and 9th, where, with a courtly bow to the multitude, he at once retired to the bosom of his beloved family.

When I called in to see his high-minded and patriotic wife, a day or two after the evacuation, she was busily engaged in her invalid's chair, and very cheerful and hopeful. "The end is not yet," she said, as if to cheer those around her; "Richmond is not the Confederacy." To this we all most willingly assented, and felt very much gratified and buoyed by her brightness. I have not the heart to visit her since the surrender, but hear that she still is sanguine, saying that, "General Lee is not the Confederacy," and that there is "life in the old land yet." He is not the Confederacy; but our hearts sink within us when we remember that he and his noble army are now idle, and that we can no longer look upon them as the bulwark of our land. He has returned from defeat and disaster with the universal and profound admiration of the world, having done all that skill and valour could accomplish.

The scenes at the surrender were noble and touching. General Grant's bearing was profoundly respectful; General Lee's as courtly and lofty as the purest chivalry could require. The terms, so honourable to all parties, being complied with to the letter, our arms were laid down with breaking hearts, and tears such as stoutest warriors may shed. "Woe worth the day!" . . .

[Final entry] May 4.—General Johnston surrendered on the 26th of April. "My native land, good-night!"

9. MARY CUSTIS LEE—"OUR POOR UNHAPPY COUNTRY"

After she left beloved Arlington and near-by Ravensworth there had been months of weary wandering for Mrs. Lee. She had visited relatives or friends at

Chantilly; in Loudoun, Fauquier, Clarke counties, at Kinloch, Annefield, Meida and Audley; at Hot Springs, Shirley and Marlbourne; at Hickory Hill in Hanover County and elsewhere. At times she had been within the Federal lines. In October 1863 she came to Richmond to live on Leigh Street. From January 1, 1864, to June 1865 the home of the Robert E. Lees was a larger house at 707 East Franklin Street, called "The Mess" because it had been occupied by some staff officers.

Always confident of Confederate success, she had watched her family serve and suffer in the war. Of her sons, Custis had been on President Davis's staff; had, as major-general, seen in the last days the field action for which he had longed, and been captured at Sayler's Creek. W. H. F. ("Rooney"), also a major-general, had been wounded at Brandy Station on the march to Gettysburg, taken prisoner and closely confined at Fortress Monroe until February 1864, when he was exchanged, and then been in the thick of things in the Wilderness and before Appomattox. Young Rob had left the University of Virginia to enlist as a private in the Rockbridge Artillery under Stonewall Jackson, and risen to the rank of captain.

Mrs. Lee had been with her daughter Annie when she died at Warren White Sulphur, North Carolina, October 20, 1862. She had been in Richmond near Charlotte, Rooney's high-born wife, when she died in December 1863 while he was a prisoner of war and soon after the death of their young son.

Long a severe sufferer from arthritis, Mrs. Lee was forced to use crutches and a rolling chair. The last days of the Confederacy were, of course, sad and shocking for her. They were the harder to bear because for a short time after the evacuation of Richmond she had to leave her home, which was threatened by fire. Back in the Franklin Street house she devoted her time to knitting and making bandages while she awaited her husband's return from Appomattox. Two weeks after the surrender she wrote this letter to her cousin Mary

Meade. In R. E. Lee *Dr. Freeman quotes from it to show how bravely she rallied from the crushing blow of final defeat.*

Richmond, April 23, 1865

I have just heard, my dear cousin Mary, of an opportunity to Clarke County & write to tell you we are all well as usual, and thro' the mercy of God all spared thro' the terrible ordeal thro' which we have passed. I feel that I could have blessed God if those who were prepared had filled a soldier's grave. I bless Him that they are spared I trust for future usefulness to their poor unhappy country. My little Rob has not yet come in, but we have reason to think he is safe. Tho' it has not pleased Almighty God to crown our exertions with success in the way & manner we expected, yet we must still trust & pray not that *our will* but His may be done in Heaven & in earth. I could not begin to tell you of the startling events that have been crowded into the last few weeks. But I want you all to know that when Gen'l Lee surrendered, he had only 8 thousand 7 hundred muskets; that the enemy by their own account had nearly 80 thousand men well provisioned & equipped, while ours had been out 7 days with only 2 days rations; that they were fighting by day & marching all night without even time to parch their corn, their only food for several days; that even in this exhausted state they drove back hosts of the enemy, but could not follow up their advantage; that had Grant demanded *unconditional* surrender, they had determined to sell their lives as dearly as possible & cut their way thro' his encircling hosts; but the conditions he offered were so honourable, that Gen'l Lee decided it was wrong to sacrifice the lives of these brave men when no object would be gained by it. For my part it will always be a source of pride & consolation to me to know that all mine have perilled their lives, fortune & even fame in so holy a cause. We can hear nothing *certain* from the rest of the army or from our President. May God help and protect them. We can only pray for them. Our plans are all unsettled. Gen'l Lee is very busy settling up his army matters & then we shall *all* probably go to some of those empty places in the vicinity of the White House. Fitzhugh has gone on there to see what we can do; but this place is an utter scene of desolation. So is our whole country & the cruel policy of the enemy has accomplished its work too well. They have achieved by *starvation* what they never could win by their valor; nor have they taken a *single town* in the South, except Vicksburg, that we have not *evacuated*. . . .

Love to all friends. Ever & affectionately yrs,

M. C. LEE

10. ELIZA FRANCES ANDREWS—"AND THIS IS THE END OF THE CONFEDERACY"

Eliza was one of the seven children of Judge Garnett Andrews of Washington, Georgia. In her view the family was not rich, owning only some two hundred slaves. "Our chief extravagance," she says, "was the exercise of unlimited hospitality." Her father bitterly opposed secession, but her brother enlisted in the Confederate Army, and twenty-four-year-old Eliza gave her heart to the Cause.

Near "Haywood," the Andrews house on the north side of the town square, was the old bank building where Jefferson Davis signed his last official paper as President of the Southern Confederacy on May 3. On the same spot today a room is designated: "The Last Cabinet Meeting Chapter of the United Daughters of the Confederacy."

Eliza became a schoolteacher after the war and wrote poems, short stories, three novels and two books on botany. In 1908 she edited and published her old war diary.

April 25, Tuesday. [Washington, Georgia.]—Little Washington is now, perhaps, the most important military post in our poor, doomed Confederacy. The naval and medical departments have been moved here—what there is left of them. Soon all this will give place to Yankee barracks, and our dear old Confederate gray will be seen no more. The men are all talking about going to Mexico and Brazil.

The Irvin Artillery [1] are coming in rapidly; I suppose they will all be here by the end of the week—or what is left of them—but their return is even sadder and amid bitterer tears than their departure, for now "we weep as they that have no hope." Everybody is cast down and humiliated, and we are all waiting in suspense to know what our cruel masters will do with us. . . . Till it comes, "Let us eat, drink and be merry, for tomorrow we die." Only, we have almost nothing to eat, and to drink, and still less to be merry about.

The whole world seems to be moving on Washington now. An average of 2,000 rations are issued daily, and over 15,000 men are said to have passed through already, since it became a military post, though the return of the paroled men has as yet hardly begun. . . .

April 27, Thursday.—The navy department has been ordered away from here—and Washington would seem a very queer location for a navy that had any real existence. Capt. Parker [2] sent Lieut. Peck this morning with a letter to father and seven great boxes full of papers and instruments belonging to the department, which he requested father to take care of. Father had them stored in the cellar, the only place where he could

[1] The first military company organized in Washington. Eliza Andrews said it "contained the flower of the youth of the village."

[2] Captain William Parker had been head of the Naval Academy at Richmond. Before the city was taken over by the Federals he and sixty of the cadets had gone south guarding the government money. They escorted Mrs. Davis from Charlotte to Abbeville, South Carolina; proceeded to Washington, Georgia, and returned to Abbeville, where they stored the treasure in a warehouse before they were disbanded. The boys walked back to Richmond.

find a vacant spot, and so now about all that is left of the Confederate Navy is here in our house, and we laugh and tell father, that he, the staunchest Union man in Georgia, is head of the Confederate Navy.

April 28, Friday.—I was busy all the morning helping to get ready for a supper that father gave to Gen. Elzey [1] and staff. . . . We had a delightful evening, in spite of the clouds gathering about us. . . . We had several sets of the Lancers and Prince Imperial, interspersed with waltzes and galops, and wound up with an old-fashioned Virginia reel, Gen. Elzey and I leading off.

April 29, Saturday.—Visitors all day, in shoals and swarms. Capt. Irwin brought Judge Crump [2] of Richmond to stay at our house. Capt. Irwin seems very fond of him, and says there is no man in Virginia more beloved and respected. He is Assistant Secretary of the Treasury or something of the sort, and is wandering about the country with his poor barren exchequer, trying to protect what is left of it, for the payment of Confederate soldiers. He has in charge, also, the assets of some Richmond banks, of which he is, or was, president, *dum Troja fuit*. He says that in Augusta he met twenty-five of his clerks with ninety-five barrels of paper not worth a pin all put together, which they had brought out of Richmond, while things of real value were left a prey to the enemy.

April 30, Sunday.—When I came in from church in the afternoon, found Burton Harrison, Mr. Davis's

---

[1] Arnold Elzey, of Maryland, made a brigadier on the field of First Manassas, was seriously wounded in the Seven Days' fighting. When partly recovered, he was commissioned major-general and put in command of the Department of Richmond, where he organized the government clerks into a "Local Defense" brigade.

[2] William Wood Crump, a distinguished Virginia jurist.

private secretary, among our guests. He came in with Mrs. Davis, who is being entertained at Dr. Ficklen's. Nobody knows where the President is, but I hope he is far west of this by now. . . . Mr. Harrison probably knows more about his whereabouts than anybody else, but of course we ask no questions. Mrs. Davis herself says that she has no idea where he is, which is the only wise thing for her to say. The poor woman is in a deplorable condition—no home, no money, and her husband a fugitive. She says she sold her plate in Richmond, and in the stampede from that place, the money, all but fifty dollars, was left behind. . . .

May 1, Monday.—Crowds of callers all day . . . Men were coming in all day, with busy faces, to see Mr. Harrison, and one of them brought news of Johnston's surrender, but Mr. Harrison didn't tell anybody about it except father. While we were at dinner, a brother of Mrs. Davis [1] came in and called for Mr. Harrison, and after a hurried interview with him, Mr. Harrison came back into the dining-room and said it had been decided that Mrs. Davis would leave town tomorrow. . . .

May 2, Tuesday.—Mr. Harrison left this morning, with a God-speed from all the family and prayers for the safety of the honored fugitives committed to his charge. . . .

May 3, Wednesday.—About noon the town was thrown into the wildest excitement by the arrival of President Davis. He is traveling with a large escort of cavalry, a very imprudent thing for a man in his position to do, especially now that Johnston has surrendered, and the fact that they are all going in the same direction to their homes is the only thing that keeps them together. He rode into town ahead of his

[1] Jefferson Howell.

escort, and as he was passing by the bank, where the Elzeys board, the general and several other gentlemen were sitting on the front porch, and the instant they recognized him they took off their hats and received him with every mark of respect due the president of a brave people. When he reined in his horse, all the staff who were present advanced to hold the reins and assist him to dismount, while Dr. and Mrs. [M. E.] Robertson hastened to offer the hospitality of their home. About forty of his immediate personal friends and attendants were with him, and they were all half-starved, having tasted nothing for twenty-four hours. Capt. Irwin came running home in great haste to ask mother to send them something to eat, as it was reported the Yankees were approaching the town from two opposite directions closing in upon the President, and it was necessary to hurry him off at once. There was not so much as a crust of bread in our house, everything available having been given to soldiers. There was some bread in the kitchen that had just been baked for a party of soldiers, but they were willing to wait, and I begged some milk from Aunt Sallie, and by adding to these our own dinner as soon as Emily could finish cooking it, we contrived to get together a very respectable lunch. We had just sent it off when the president's escort came in, followed by couriers who brought the comforting assurance that it was a false alarm about the enemy being so near. By this time the president's arrival had become generally known, and people began flocking to see him; but he went to bed almost as soon as he got into the house, and Mrs. Elzey would not let him be waked. . . The party are all worn out and half-dead for sleep. They traveled mostly at night, and have been in the saddle for three nights in succession. Mrs. Elzey says that Mr. Davis does not seem to have been aware of the real danger of his situation until he came to Washington, where some of his friends gave him a serious talk, and advised him to travel with more secrecy and dispatch than he has been using.

Mr. Reagan [1] and Mr. Mallory are also in town, and Gen Toombs [2] has returned, having encountered danger ahead, I fear. Judge Crump is back too, with his Confederate treasury, containing, it is said, three hundred thousand dollars in specie. He is staying at our house, but the treasure is thought to be stored in the vault at the bank. . . .

May 4, Thursday.—I sat under the cedar trees by the street gate nearly all the morning, watching the stream of human life flow by, and keeping guard over the horses of some soldier friends that had left them grazing on the lawn. Father and Cora went to call on the President, and in spite of his prejudice against everybody and everything connected with secession, father says his manner was so calm and dignified that he could not help admiring the man. Crowds of people flocked to see him, and nearly all were melted in tears. Gen Elzey pretended to have dust in his eyes and Mrs. Elzey blubbered outright, exclaiming all the while, in her impulsive way: "Oh, I am such a fool to be crying, but I can't help it!" When she was telling me about it afterwards, she said she could not stay in the room with him yesterday evening, because she couldn't help crying, and she was ashamed for the people who called to see her looking so ugly, with her eyes and nose red. She says that at night, after the crowd left, there was a private meeting in his room, where Reagan and Mallory and other high officials were present, and again early in the morning there were other confabulations before they all scattered and went their ways—and this, I suppose, is the end of the Confederacy. . . .

[1] John H. Reagan, of Texas, postmaster-general.
[2] Robert Toombs, whose home was in Washington, Georgia, after being Secretary of State in the Confederate Provisional Government became a brigadier-general and fought in the Seven Days, at Antietam and in the Atlanta campaign.

BIBLIOGRAPHY

Full bibliographical description and credit are supplied for first listings. Additional selections from the same sources are referred back to the first listing.

The poem "The Confederate Flag" by Mrs. D. Giraud (Louisa Wigfall) Wright, *A Southern Girl in '61: The Wartime Memories of a Confederate Senator's Daughter*. New York: Doubleday, Page & Company; Copyright 1905 by Doubleday & Company, Inc. (By permission of Doubleday & Company, Inc.)

CHAPTER I. HEARTBREAK (May 1863–April 1864)

1. In a Cave at Vicksburg
   Mary Ann Loughborough, *My Cave Life in Vicksburg, with letters of trial and travel*. New York: D. Appleton & Company, 1864.
2. "We Dance at Fort Sumter"
   Diary of Esther Alden. *Our Women in the War*. (*See* II, 12.)
3. Yankees Parade in Natchez
   Mrs. G. Griffin Wilcox, "War Times in Natchez," *Southern Historical Society Papers*, XXX (1902), 135-136.
4. "I Marry My General, the Hero of Gettysburg"
   LaSalle Corbell Pickett, *Pickett and His Men*. Atlanta, Ga.: The Foote & Davies Company, 1899.
5. "Somebody's Darling"
   Marie Ravenel de la Coste, "Somebody's Darling," *The Home Book of Verse*, ed., Burton Egbert Stevenson. New York: Henry Holt and Company, 1912.
6. "Charleston Is in Great Danger"
   Rose O'Neal Greenhow to Jefferson Davis, July 16, 1863; to Alexander Robinson Boteler, July 20, 1863. Jefferson Davis Papers, Manuscript Room, Duke University Library.
7. "An Arrow Struck the Wall Opposite My Window"
   Belle Boyd, *Belle Boyd: In Camp and Prison*. London: Saunders, Otley & Company, 1865.

8. "Many Things Are Becoming Scarce"
Susan Bradford Eppes. *Through Some Eventful Years*.
(*See* I, 2.)

9. Dependent on Our Own Resources
Parthenia Antoinette Hague, *A Blockaded Family: Life in
Southern Alabama during the Civil War*. Boston: Hough-
ton Mifflin Company, 1888.

10. Christmas in Petersburg
Mrs. Roger A. (Sara Rice) Pryor, *Reminiscences of Peace
and War*. New York; the Macmillan Company, 1904. (By
permission of The Macmillan Company.)

11. Smuggling from Memphis
Diary of Belle Edmondson. Southern Historical Collection,
University of North Carolina.

12. "Sister Susan Has Lost Three Sons"
Mary Byson to Margaret Butler, March 21, 1864. Butler
Family Papers, Department of Archives, Louisiana State
University.

13. "Today I Have No Shoes"
Susan Bradford Eppes, *Through Some Eventful Years*.
Macon, Ga.: The J. W. Burke Company, 1926. (By per-
mission of Susan W. Eppes and Alice B. Eppes.)

14. Yankee in Camden, Arkansas
Virginia McCollum Stinson. Mrs. M. A. Elliott, ed., *The
Garden of Memory: Stories of the Civil War*. Camden,
Ark.: H. L. Grinstead Chapter, U. D. C., [n. d.].

15. "They Left Us Alone with Our Dead"
Varina Howell Davis, *Jefferson Davis: A Memoir by His
Wife*. New York: The Belford Company, 1890.

CHAPTER II. BLOWS OF THE HAMMER
(May–October 1864)

1. Special Agent
Loreta Janeta Velazquez, *The Woman in Battle: A Narra-
tive of the Exploits, Adventures and Travels of Madame
Loreta Janeta Velazquez, Otherwise Known as Lieutenant
Harry T. Buford, Confederate States Army*, ed., C. J.
Worthington. Hartford, Conn.: T. Belknap, 1876.

2. "How Alone General Lee Seems!"
Sarah Alexander Lawton to her sister, May 9, 1864.
Marion Alexander Boggs, ed., *The Alexander Letters,
1787–1900*. Savannah, Ga.: privately printed for G. F.
Baldwin, 1910. (By permission of A. Leopold Alexander.)

3. "General Stuart Died Last Night"
[Judith Brockenbrough McGuire], *Diary of a Southern*

Refugee during the War, by a Lady of Virginia. New York: E. J. Hale & Son, 1867.

4. Hunter Burns the V. M. I.
   Cornelia Peake McDonald, *A Diary with Reminiscences of the War and Refugee Life in the Shenandoah Valley, 1860–1865,* ed., Hunter McDonald. Nashville, Tenn.: Cullom & Ghertner, 1934. (By permission of Hunter McDonald.)

5. "You Burned My Home"
   Henrietta Bedinger Lee to General David Hunter, July 20, 1864. *Southern Historical Society Papers,* VIII (1880), 215-216.

6. "I Am an Exile"
   Issa Desha Breckinridge to her husband, July 30, 1864. Breckinridge Papers, Manuscript Division, Library of Congress.

7. In Besieged Petersburg
   Mrs. Roger A. (Sara Rice) Pryor, *Reminiscences.* (See I, 10.)

8. "I Am for a Tidal Wave of Peace"
   Agnes to Sara Rice Pryor, August 26, 1864. *Reminiscences.* (See I, 10.)

9. Our Exchange Prisoners
   Phoebe Yates Pember, *A Southern Woman's Story.* New York: G. W. Carleton & Company, 1879.

10. Chasing My Hospital
    Kate Cumming, *A Journal of Hospital Life in the Confederate Army of Tennessee from the Battle of Shiloh to the End of the War. . . .* Louisville, Ky.: John P. Marton & Company, 1866.

11. The Battle for Atlanta
    Mary Ann Harris Gay, *Life in Dixie during the War.* Atlanta, Ga.: Charles P. Byrd, 1897.

12. "They Took Possession of Atlanta Quietly"
    Diary of Mary Rawson. "The Margaret Mitchell Memorial Library," Atlanta Historical Society, Atlanta, Ga.

13. "A Better Son Never Lived"
    Mrs. Henrietta Morgan to her daughter-in-law, October 1, 1864. John Hunt Morgan Papers, Southern Historical Collection, University of North Carolina.

CHAPTER III. WINTER OF DESPERATION
(November 1864–March 1865)

1. "Lead, Blood and Tears"
   Mary Ann Harris Gay, *Life in Dixie.* (See II, 11.)

2. **"Things Is Worse and Worse"**
   A soldier's wife to her husband, December 17, 1864.
   Pickett and His Men. (*See* I, 4.)
3. **Hood Is Defeated at Nashville**
   Rebeccah C. Ridley, "Behind the Lines in Middle Ten-
   nessee, 1863–1865: The Journal of Bettie Ridley Black-
   more," ed., Sarah Ridley Trimble, *Tennessee Historical
   Quarterly,* XII (March 1953). (By permission of *Ten-
   nessee Historical Quarterly.*)
4. **Running the Blockade**
   Journal of Mary Ellen Arnold. Arnold-Appleton Papers,
   Southern Historical Collection, University of North Caro-
   lina.
5. **Fort Fisher Is Bombarded**
   Mrs. William Lamb, "The Heroine of Confederate Point:
   An Interesting Contemporaneous Account of the Heroic
   Defense of Fort Fisher, December 24th and 25th, 1864,
   by the Wife of the Commandant, Colonel William Lamb,"
   Southern Historical Society Papers, XX (1892), 301-306.
6. **"I Thought of the Gayety of Paris"**
   [Judith Brockenbrough McGuire], *Diary of a Southern
   Refugee.* (*See* II, 3.)
7. **The Treasury Note Department Leaves Columbia**
   Mrs. Malvina Gist Waring (Malvina Black Gist), "A Con-
   federate Girl's Diary," *South Carolina Women in the
   Confederacy,* I, ed., Mrs. Thomas Taylor and others.
   Columbia, S. C.: The State Company, 1903.
8. **"Poor Old Columbia!"**
   Journal of Emma Florence LeConte, December 31, 1864,
   to August 6, 1865. Southern Historical Collection, Uni-
   versity of North Carolina.
9. **"The Enemy Comes to Our Plantation"**
   Diary of Charlotte St. Julien Ravenel. Susan R. Jervey
   and Charlotte St. Julien Ravenel, *Two Diaries from Middle
   St. John's, Berkeley, South Carolina.* Charleston, S. C.:
   St. John's Hunting Club, 1921. (By permission St. John's
   Hunting Club.)

CHAPTER IV. OUR CONFEDERACY IS GONE
WITH A CRASH (March–May 1864)

1. **"We May Have To Fly from Richmond"**
   Mrs. Malvina Gist Waring (Malvina Black Gist), "A Con-
   federate Girl's Diary." (*See* III, 7.)
2. **"The Sound of Cannon Is Ever in Our Ears"**
   [Judith Brockenbrough McGuire], *Diary of a Southern
   Refugee.* (*See* II, 3.)

3. "They Marched into Mobile to the Tune of 'Yankee Doodle'"
   Journal of Mary D. Waring, July 26, 1863, to April 16, 1865. Manuscript Room, Alabama State Department of Archives and History.
4. "With Hearts Bowed Down by Despair We Left Richmond"
   Varina Howell Davis, *Jefferson Davis*. (*See* I, 15.)
5. "The Women of the South Still Fought Their Battle"
   Phoebe Yates Pember, *A Southern Woman's Story*. (*See* II. 9.)
6. "Like a Vivid, Horrible Dream"
   [Judith Brockenbrough McGuire], *Diary of a Southern Refugee*. (*See* II, 3.)
7. President Davis in Danville
   Mrs. W. T. Sutherlin. J. William Jones, *The Davis Memorial Volume: Or Our Dead President, Jefferson Davis, and the World's Tribute to His Memory*. Richmond, Va.: B. F. Johnson & Company, 1889.
8. "General Lee Has Returned"
   [Judith Brockenbrough McGuire], *Diary of a Southern Refugee*. (*See* II, 3.)
9. "Our Poor Unhappy Country"
   Mary Custis Lee to Miss Mary Mead, April 23, 1865. *Mrs. Robert E. Lee*. Boston: Ginn & Company, 1939. (By permission of J. Lewis Scoggs.)
10. "And This Is the End of the Confederacy"
    Eliza Frances Andrews, *The War-Time Journal of a Georgia Girl, 1864–1865*. New York: D. Appleton & Company, 1908.

REBEL ROSE

Life of Rose O'Neal Greenhow,
Confederate Spy

Ishbel Ross

Famous Washington hostess, friend of senators and presidents, adept at political intrigue and often involved in scandal, Rose became one of the most celebrated spies in U.S. history.

Even after her capture by the famous detective Allen Pinkerton, she operated one of the most successful espionage systems of the Civil War — one that was largely responsible for the Southern victory at Manassas.

$4.95

Prices subject to change.

MOCKINGBIRD BOOKS

Available at your local bookstore or mail the coupon below.

MOCKINGBIRD BOOKS
P.O. Box 71088, Marietta, GA 30068

Please send me the following book:

QUANTITY	NO.	TITLE	AMOUNT
_____	6026	Rebel Rose, $4.95	_____
Mailing and handling			1.50
Please enclose check of money order.		**TOTAL**	_____

We are not responsible for orders containing cash.
(PLEASE PRINT CLEARLY)

NAME _____

ADDRESS _____

CITY _____ STATE _____ ZIP _____

LOOK FOR MOCKINGBIRD BOOKS

Paperback books of special interest to Southern readers.

SEND FOR YOUR FREE MOCKINGBIRD CATALOG TODAY!

Our complete listing includes important Southern regional authors, Civil War memoirs, and natural history, all available to you in inexpensive paperback editions.

Just send us a post card with the information below or use this handy coupon:

If you would like to order our complete listing of Southern regional paperbacks for an interested friend or relative, just include their name and address along with your own.